Join the Recommended Country Inns® Travelers' Club and save!

The Recommended Country Inns® guides are the preeminent regional guidebooks to the finest country inns in the United States. Authors personally visit and recommend each establishment listed in the guides, and no fees are solicited or accepted for inclusion in the books.

Now the Recommended Country Inns® guides offer a special new way for purchasers to enjoy extra savings through the new Recommended Country Inns® Travelers' Club. For example, members can enjoy savings such as:

> 10% discount each night; or
> 25% discount each night; or
> Stay 2 nights, get the third night free.

All establishments in the guide have been invited to participate **on a voluntary basis.** No fees are charged to the establishments for offering Recommended Country Inns® Travelers' Club discounts, nor are Recommended Country Inns® series authors influenced to list inns because innkeepers have participated in the Recommended Country Inns® Travelers' Club program.

How to Save: Read the listing for each inn in this guide to see if it offers special savings to Recommended Country Inns® Travelers' Club members. For participating establishments, the information appears at the end of the inn's listing.

How to Join: If you wish to become a Recommended Country Inns® Travelers' Club member, simply fill out the form on the next page, and send it, **along with your receipt for purchase of the guide,** to: Recommended Country Inns® Travelers' Club
c/o The Globe Pequot Press
P.O. Box 833
Old Saybrook, CT 06475

Upon receipt, we will send you a membership card. Simply mention ~~~~~~~~~~~~~~ your reservation, and show the card when you check in to participating establishments. All offers from participating establishments are subject to availability.

Sign up today and you can start enjoying savings right away as a Recommended Country Inns® Travelers' Club member!

(Offers from inns expire December 31, 1996)

Recommended Country Inns® Travelers' Club
Membership Form

Name_____Phone No. (____)_____

Address_____City_____State_____Zip_____

Age: under 18_____; 18–35_____; 36–50_____; over 50_____

Nights stayed at an inn per year: 0–3_____; 4–6_____; 7–10_____; more than 10_____

I usually visit inns: alone_____; with spouse or friend_____; with family_____

Annual Household Income: under $20,000_____; $20,000–$35,000_____;
   $35,000–$50,000_____; $50,000–$75,000_____; $75,000–$100,000_____;
   over $100,000_____

Credit cards you own: Mastercard___; Amex___; Visa___; Discover___; Other_____

Sex: Male_____; Female_____   Marital Status: Married_____; Single_____

Book purchased at: Store name_____; City_____; State_____

Send completed form, along with receipt for purchase of the guide, to:
   RECOMMENDED COUNTRY INNS® TRAVELERS' CLUB
   The Globe Pequot Press
   P.O. Box 833
   Old Saybrook, CT 06475

RO

Recommended
Romantic Inns™
OF AMERICA

Second Edition

by
Julianne Belote ❦ Brenda Boelts Chapin
Doris Kennedy ❦ Eleanor S. Morris ❦ Sara Pitzer
Bob Puhala ❦ Elizabeth Squier
(the Authors of the Recommended Country Inns® Series)

A Voyager Book

The Globe Pequot Press

Old Saybrook, Connecticut

Text design: Saralyn D'Amato-Twomey

Recommended Romantic Inns is a trademark of The Globe Pequot Press, Inc.

ISBN 1-56440-515-X
ISSN 1078-554X

Manufactured in the United States of America
Second Edition/First Printing

Contents

Indexes

Romantic Inn-Sights

When the mind and body have been kept too long to the tasks and worries of the workplace and, yes, even to those of the old homestead, the spirit rebels and begs for attention. "Ah, but for a little romance," your inner voice may sigh. This book is for you.

Describe romance in any terms you like, and you're likely to find an inn in these pages to satisfy your yearnings. Take your partner's hand and prepare to soak up delight after delicious delight at one of these most soul-soothing hostelries.

Researched and selected by seven incurable romantics, the inns profiled here define romance. If you are looking for starlight and moonglow, soft rain and sea breezes, shimmering sunsets and breathtaking vistas, Mother Nature will provide them. If you need candlelight, bubble baths, champagne, porch swings, fabulous food, breakfast in bed, carriage rides, secluded picnics, and turret bedchambers, the inns will provide them. And if you need whispered promises, urgent kisses, and passion of any sort these inns inspire you to kindle, *you* will provide them. True romance, after all, is what you bring with you.

Among these romantic establishments are inns at the seashore and inns in the mountains; inns miles (but not too many miles) from nowhere and inns close to hubs of culture and entertainment; inns with room for scores of travelers and inns with room for just a few (or even only two). The authors have chosen island inns, city inns, inns that provide gourmet meals and inns that will guide you to fine restaurants. Many of the inns are in historic structures; some are new or nearly new; but all share the ambience that harkens back to quieter times.

As in other volumes of the *Recommended Country Inns®* series, every inn in this book has been personally visited. Their inclusion depends on meeting the highest standards of atmosphere, service, comfort, hospitality, history, and location: the elements that make inn travel unique. Where but at an inn can you relax near a crackling fire, sipping wine or feeding each other strawberries? Where else can you stroll through glorious gardens to secluded benches and arbors specially placed so that none but the roses will hear your murmurs?

These innkeepers have endeavored to ensure your pleasure, delight your senses, renew your spirit, and relight your passion. Our authors have endeavored to share their experience that, for any excuse at all, you can rendezvous most romantically at each and every one of these memorable inns.

About This Inn Guide

This inn guide contains descriptions of 140 inns in seven regions of the United States. These inns were selected by the authors of The Globe Pequot Press's seven regional *Recommended Country Inns®* guides as the most romantic inns in their regions. *All inns were personally visited by the authors. There is no charge of any kind for an inn to be included in this or any other Globe Pequot Press inn guide.*

The guide is arranged geographically by region, beginning along the Atlantic Ocean. These regions, in order, are: New England; Mid-Atlantic and Chesapeake Region; the South; the Midwest; the Southwest; Rocky Mountain Region; and the West Coast. Within each region, the states are listed alphabetically; within each state, the towns are arranged alphabetically.

Preceding each region's listings is a regional map and a numbered legend of the twenty romantic inns found in that region. The map is marked with corresponding numbers to show where the inns are located.

Indexes: At the back of the book are various special-category indexes to help you find inns located on a lake or at the seashore, inns with golf or tennis, inns with skiing, inns with swimming pools, and more. There is also an alphabetical index of all the inns in this book.

Rates: The guidebook quotes current low and high rates to give you an indication of the price ranges you can expect. They are more than likely to change slightly with time. Be sure to call ahead and inquire about the rates as well as the taxes and service charges. The following abbreviations are used throughout the book to let you know exactly what, if any, meals are included in the room price.

EP: European Plan. Room without meals.
EPB: Room with full breakfast. (No abbreviation is used when continental breakfast is included.)
MAP: Modified American Plan. Room with breakfast and dinner.
AP: American Plan. Room with breakfast, lunch, and dinner.

Credit cards: MasterCard and Visa are accepted unless the description says "No credit cards." Many inns also accept additional credit cards.

Reservations and deposits: These are so often required that they are not mentioned in any description. Assume that you'll generally have to pay a deposit to reserve a room, using a personal check or a credit card. Be sure to inquire about refund policies.

Pets: No pets are allowed unless otherwise stated in the description. Always let innkeepers know in advance if you are planning to bring a pet.

Wheelchair access: Some descriptions mention wheelchair access, but other inns may be feasible for the handicapped. Therefore, if you're interested in an inn, call to check if there is a room suitable for a handicapped person.

Air conditioning: The description will indicate if an inn has rooms with air conditioning. Keep in mind, however, that there are areas of the country where air conditioning is totally unnecessary. For example, in the Rocky Mountain region, where the inn is at a high elevation (stated in the description), you will be comfortable without air conditioning.

Television: Some inns offer televisions and VCRs in guest rooms; the room description will mention if the rooms are so equipped. Sometimes there's a television or VCR in a common room. *Note:* Most innkeepers say there is so much to do at the inn or in the area that guests generally don't watch television. In addition, most inns inspire true romantics to engage in pleasures the television can't enhance.

Telephone: Assuming that when you yearn for romance you want to get away from it all, the descriptions generally do not state if you will find a telephone in your room.

Smoking: More than 60 percent of these inns forbid or restrict smoking. See the *Rooms* entry of each profile for specific information.

BYOB: It is often acceptable to bring your own bottle, especially if an inn has no bar service. If you see no mention of BYOB or a bar in the description, you may want to check in advance.

Meals: Most of the inns profiled offer dinner as well as breakfast. Those that do not are more than happy to make reservations for you at fine, nearby restaurants. Some inns also offer brunches, lunches, hors d'oeuvres, or afternoon tea. The authors often indicate some favorite foods they enjoyed at an inn, but you should not expect the menu to remain the same forever. Menus usually change seasonally or monthly. The description of the inn's food should give you a general idea of the meals served; with notice, innkeepers and chefs are happy to fill special dietary requests or create celebration cakes or the like.

Recommended Country Inns® Travel Club: Please observe the discount, free night's stay, or other value offered by inns welcoming club members. Note that all discounts listed refer to room rates only, not to meals, and that a number of offers are subject to availability.

A final word: The authors have convinced the editors that these innkeepers are themselves the soul of romance. Drink deeply of their sweet ministerings and renew the promises romance makes so easy to whisper.

New England

by Elizabeth Squier

New England is a very special place, and you the visitor are in for a special treat whatever season you decide to come. Spring is so romantic; the trees bud and flowers poke up from sometimes-lingering snow. The birds do their mating dances; beautiful swans sit on their nests. Oh, yes—romance is all around. Country inns are a special part of the romance of New England—after all, this is the region where they started.

For this book I have selected some of the most romantic country inns I have visited. Each has been chosen for one romantic reason or another—a quiet corner, wonderful dinners, breakfast in bed, a walk in the snow. Just remember they are off the beaten track, and romance is everywhere. Winter brings its own magic—the snow, the glow of a fire. I know of nothing more romantic than sitting by a fire, a glass of wine and someone very special by your side.

Many of the inns have common areas with magazines and newspapers for guests to read—even whole libraries to browse in. There are puzzles to put together, games to play, televisions, and VCRs for movies. Special touches in the rooms are also important criteria for romance—fluffy pillows, good mattresses, extra blankets, good lighting, and chairs for reading. For bed readers like me, good bed lamps are a must.

In the fall, when the leaves are turning glorious colors, what a romantic feeling it is to turn up the driveway of a beautiful inn, meet a welcoming innkeeper, relax near a crackling fire, and enjoy a lovely, romantic interlude.

I can remember a few occasions when my husband and I were caught in one of these lovely inns either by rain or snow. We sat by the fire, played some gin rummy, and sipped some fine concoction to warm the tummy. Oh, what romantic times we had.

Well, by now you know it—I am a romantic, and I love my inns and their innkeepers. All inns in their own way are romantic. Come on up to New England and enjoy.

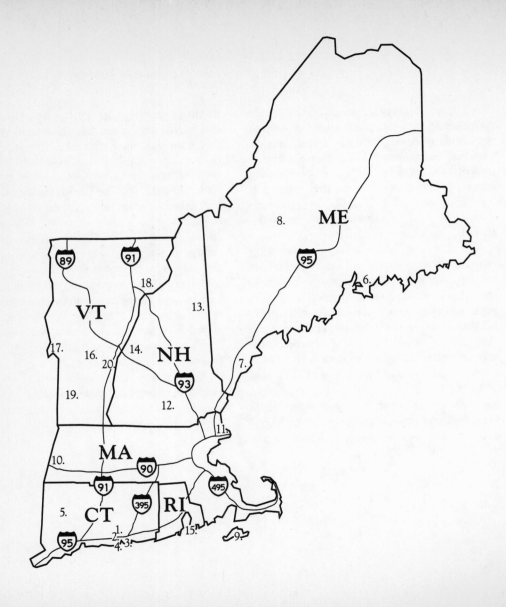

New England

Numbers on map refer to towns numbered below.

Olive Metcalf

The Inn at Chester
CHESTER CONNECTICUT 06412

John D. Parmelee, the original owner of this inn built from 1776 to 1778, would not know the place today, but he'd probably enjoy it. The old house now serves as a private dining room and has a private suite. An L-shaped bar now graces the tavern, called Dunks Landing (after the boat landing of the same name in the yesteryear shipbuilding heyday of the town of Chester on the Connecticut River). The tavern serves light dinners and daily specials, plus lunch. Try the spare ribs grilled with an oriental barbecue sauce, chicken wings cajun-style, or crabcakes and more, while you listen to live music and enjoy your favorite cocktail.

There is much to do in the inn. Downstairs

is the Billiard Room, where you can play billiards, backgammon, or cards. The library is filled with books—a nice place to have nearby. There is an exercise room with weights, stationary bikes, a treadmill, and a Nordic ski machine. Get a massage here or use the sauna. On the grounds are tennis, boccie, and croquet courts, and bicycles for your riding pleasure.

Each of the inn's rooms is individually appointed with Eldred Wheeler reproductions. They really are lovely and include telephone, television, and air conditioning.

The chef of the inn's Post and Beam restaurant is very talented. Try Mediterranean fish soup, warm duck salad, or entrees such as fillet of beef, pork loin, lamb stew (so nice to have this on the menu), and lots of other wonderful dishes. The breast of duck sautéed in port wine with peaches, blueberries, and nutty wild rice sounds scrumptious. This is a lovely inn in a beautiful part of Connecticut. Schedar is the inn cat—do ask about her beginnings. And ask Deborah about her seafaring days.

How to get there: Take exit 6 off Route 9 and turn west on Route 148. Go 3²⁄₁₀ miles to the inn. By private plane, fly to the Chester airport.

Innkeeper: Deborah Lieberman Moore
Address/Telephone: 318 West Main Street, (203) 526–9541
Rooms: 42, plus 2 suites; all with private bath and air conditioning, some specially equipped for handicapped.
Rates: $95 to $175, double occupancy; $205 to $425, suites; continental breakfast.
Open: All year.
Facilities and activities: Lunch, dinner, Sunday brunch. Bar and tavern, elevator, sauna, exercise room, tennis court, conference room, gift shop.
Recommended Country Inns® Travel Club Benefit: 10% discount, Monday–Thursday.

Copper Beech Inn
IVORYTON, TOWN OF ESSEX, CONNECTICUT 06442

One of the most beautiful copper beech trees in Connecticut shades the lawn of this lovely old inn and is the reason for the inn's name.

The grounds are beautiful. Eldon, who really is a gardener, has done wonders with the property. There is an authentic English garden, many bulbs are in bloom at different times of the year, and everything is just breathtaking.

Sally is an interior designer, and her expertise really shows in this inn. There is a lovely parlor on the first floor with bookcases and a table for playing cards or writing or whatever. Very warm and comfortable.

Accommodations at the Copper Beech are wonderful. There are four rooms in the inn itself,

and they have unbelievable old-fashioned bathrooms. The towels are soft and fluffy. Nine more guest rooms are in the carriage house, and each one has a Jacuzzi tub, so wonderful after a day of exploring the lovely towns of Essex, Mystic, and other area attractions. The carriage house has an elegant country atmosphere. The halls have very nice early nineteenth-century botanical prints. In fact, there is nineteenth-century art all over the inn and a wonderful collection of fine oriental porcelain.

The four dining rooms have comfortable Chippendale and Queen Anne chairs. The Garden Porch, which is a favorite place for me, features white wicker and nice Audubon prints on the walls. The spacious tables are set far apart for gracious dining. Fresh flowers are everywhere and the waiters are friendly and courteous.

The hors d'oeuvres menu is a beauty. One hors d'oeuvre is made of layers of delicate puff pastry, with smoked salmon and mousse of smoked salmon, garnished with crème fraîche, diced onions, and capers. Another is a salad of chilled poached lobster and fresh orange with an orange-truffle vinaigrette. The lobster bisque is always spectacular, and there are about eight more appetizers to choose from. Good fresh fish is used for entrees. The lobster is always easy to eat; no struggling with it here. My companion and I ordered different veal dishes. The veal was so tender, we didn't need to use a knife. Beef

Wellington and roast rack of lamb are always winners here, and so are the fresh sweetbreads and a very different breast of chicken—a little French and a little oriental. Desserts are super. I love chocolate and raspberries, so I had some in the form of a cake and mousse and berries. No matter what you order, it is good at the Copper Beech and always exquisitely presented.

The Victorian conservatory is a wonderful addition to this fine inn. It's so nice for an aperitif before dinner or coffee and cognac after.

How to get there: The inn is located 1 mile west of Connecticut Route 9, from exit 3 or 4. Follow the signs to Ivoryton. The inn is on Ivoryton's Main Street, on the left side.

Innkeepers: Eldon and Sally Senner
Address/Telephone: 46 Main Street; (203) 767–0330
Rooms: 4 in inn, 9 in carriage house; all with private bath, carriage house rooms with whirlpool tub, deck, and TV.
Rates: $120 to $160, double occupancy, continental breakfast.
Open: All year.
Facilities and activities: Restaurant closed on Mondays; Tuesdays in winter; Christmas Eve, Christmas Day, and New Year's Day. Dinner, full license. Greenhouse cocktail lounge open Saturdays. Victorian-style conservatory.
Recommended Country Inns® Travel Club Benefit: Stay two nights, get third night free, Monday–Thursday, except holidays.

Bee and Thistle Inn
OLD LYME, CONNECTICUT 06371

This lovely old inn, built in 1756, sits on five and one-half acres bordering the Lieutenant River in historic Old Lyme, Connecticut. During summer the abundant flower gardens keep the inn filled to overflowing with color.

The guest rooms are all tastefully decorated. Your bed, maybe a four-poster or canopy, is covered with a lovely old quilt or afghan. The bath towels are big and thirsty. How I love them. The cottage is air-conditioned and has a reading room, bedroom with queen-sized bed, kitchen, bath, and a large TV room. A deck goes around the outside. There is also a fireplace and a private dock on the river.

There are six fireplaces in the inn. The one in the parlor is most inviting—a nice place for a cocktail or just good conversation. On weekends there is music by A Wrinkle in Time, a wonderful husband-and-wife duo who make magic with their music. There is also a harpist on Saturday nights.

The innkeepers are very romance-minded, and they will help in any way they can—even as far as proposing. Ask them for details; it's pretty funny.

Be sure to say hello to Callebaut (Bo), the Nelsons' large chocolate Lab, and to Jack, a real inn dog.

Breakfast in bed is an especially nice feature of the inn. Freshly squeezed orange juice is a refreshing way to start any day. Muffins are made fresh each day, buttery crepes are folded with strawberry or raspberry preserves, and there's much more. Lunch is interesting and inventive. Try the wild mushroom lasagne, Maryland-style crabcakes, or the Bee and Thistle shepherd's pie. Sunday brunch is really gourmet. Fresh rainbow trout, chicken hash, three different omelets—I could eat the menu. And, of course, dinners here are magnificent. Candlelit dining rooms, a good selection of appetizers and soups, and entrees such as spiced breast of chicken, pork medallions, shrimp, scallops, veal, and rack of lamb. The list goes on and on. Desserts are wonderful. The menu changes seasonally, each time bringing new delights.

Afternoon tea is served from November 1 to May 1 on Monday, Wednesday, and Thursday from 3:30 to 5:00 P.M. The tea service is beautiful; coffee and aperitifs are also available.

This is a fine inn in a most interesting part of New England. You are in the heart of art, antiques, gourmet restaurants, and endless activities. Plan to spend a few days when you come.

How to get there: Traveling north on I–95, take exit 70 immediately on the east side of the Baldwin Bridge. At the bottom of the ramp, turn left. Take the first right at the traffic light, and turn left at the end of the road. The inn is the third house on your left. Traveling south on I–95, take exit 70; turn right at the bottom of the ramp. The inn is the third house on your left.

Innkeepers: Bob and Penny Nelson, Jeff and Lori Nelson
Address/Telephone: 100 Lyme Street; (203) 434–1667 or (800) 622–4946, fax (203) 434–3402
Rooms: 11, plus 1 cottage; 10 with private bath, all with telephone.
Rates: $69 to $125, double occupancy; $195, cottage; EP.
Open: All year except Christmas Eve, Christmas Day, and first two weeks of January.
Facilities and activities: Breakfast; lunch and dinner every day except Tuesday; Sunday brunch; afternoon tea, November 1 to May 1. Bar, lounge, library.

Olive Metcalf

Saybrook Point Inn & Spa
OLD SAYBROOK, CONNECTICUT 06475

"Experience the magic at Saybrook Point Inn & Spa." These are the inn's words, and they're so true. The panoramic views of the Connecticut River and Long Island Sound are magnificent. From the moment you walk into the lobby, the Italian marble floors, beautiful furniture, and glorious fabrics let you know this is a special inn. Even the carpet is hand loomed.

All the guest rooms and suites have a water view, and most have a balcony. They are lavishly decorated with eighteenth-century–style furniture, and Italian marble is used in the bathroom with whirlpool bath. Also in the rooms are a miniature wet bar and refrigerator; an unbelievable telephone that turns on lights; double,

queen-, or king-sized bed; and hair dryer.

This is a full spa, with indoor and outdoor pools, steamroom, sauna, and whirlpool. The licensed staff will pamper you with a therapeutic massage, European facial, manicure, pedicure, even a quality makeup application. There's also an exercise room with life bikes.

Breakfast, lunch, and dinner are served in an exquisite room that overlooks the inn's marina, the river, and the Long Island Sound. There was a full moon the evening I dined here. What a beautiful sight to enhance the memorable food. Such appetizers as smoked Norwegian salmon, escargots, smoked pheasant, and Beluga caviar are an elegant way to begin your dinner. Pastas are cannelloni, linguine, or wild mushroom. I had one of the best racks of lamb I have ever had. There is always a fresh seafood special. My friend had shrimp Provençale—shrimp sautéed with garlic, shallots, and scallions. A flower may be a garnish on your plate; you can eat it.

Do try to save room for dessert. I had chocolate–chocolate chip cake, which was dark and beautiful and delicious. The service is also superb.

Sunday brunch is a winner. Too much to list, but believe me, you will not go away hungry.

How to get there: From I–95 northbound take exit 67 (southbound, take Exit 68) and follow Route 154 and signs to Saybrook Point.

Innkeeper: Stephen Tagliatela; John Lombardo, general manager

Address/Telephone: 2 Bridge Street; (203) 395–2000, or (800) 243–0212 (outside Connecticut), fax (203) 388+1504

Rooms: 63, including 6 suites; all with private bath, phone, TV, air conditioning, and refrigerator, 40 with working fireplace.

Rates: $135 to $275, double occupancy; $275 to $495, suites; EP. Package plans available.

Open: All year.

Facilities and activities: Breakfast, lunch, dinner, Sunday brunch. Banquet and meeting facilities; health club with whirlpool, sauna, and steam; spa; indoor and outdoor pools; marina with 120 slips and floating docks. Nearby: charter boats, theater.

The Mayflower Inn
WASHINGTON, CONNECTICUT 06793

The Mayflower Inn is glorious. The entrance hall is huge and well appointed with antiques, Persian rugs, and many works of art. Much of it has been collected by the Mnuchins over the years during their travels. There is a cherry-paneled library off this, and the other side has a large gameroom full of beautiful things.

The Shop at Mayflower, watched over by Jeffrey, has unusual vintage jewelry, cashmere gloves, sweaters, and silks; it is just grand.

There are rooms in three buildings: the Mayflower, the Standish, and the Speedwell. Facilities are sumptuous and include feather beds and down comforters and pillows. Quality linens are on the beds, which are either queens, kings,

or a pair of twins. Some rooms have a balcony, and others have a fireplace. There is also nightly turndown service.

You can dine in one of three dining rooms or, if the weather is nice, outside on the dining terrace that overlooks the grounds and woods. The English pub-style lounge, which has a piano, leads out to the porch, where there is wicker furniture in the summer. It is called the "drinking porch."

The tea house is an executive retreat; what a wonderful place for conferences. The spa, with a very strong emphasis on massage, is an added plus.

Dining here is grand. I had a nice thick veal chop and salad. The inn has special Mayflower mashed potatoes, and boy, are they good. The menu changes not only seasonally, but frequently. Foods from the local farms are used. There is not enough room to elaborate on breakfast, or the luncheon specials, or even dinner. But wow, save room for the desserts.

Everyone who works here has a smile, and they are more than willing to make your stay a pleasant one.

Orchids are everywhere, the *New York Times*

is brought to your door, and a minibar is in your room. One night was not enough for this inn creeper.

How to get there: From Hartford, take I–84 west to exit 15, Southbury. Follow Route 6 north through Southbury to Woodbury. It is exactly 5 miles from I–84 to "Canfield Corners" (an 1890s building on your right). Go left here on Route 47 to Washington. It is 8²⁄₁₀ miles to the inn.

Innkeepers: John Trevenen; Adriana and Robert Mnuchin, owners
Address/Telephone: 118 Woodbury Road (mailing address: P.O. Box 1288); (203) 868–9466, fax (203) 868–1497
Rooms: 18, plus 7 suites; all with private bath, some with balcony, some with fireplace.
Rates: $225 to $350, double occupancy; $395 to $495, suites; EP.
Open: All year.
Facilities and activities: Breakfast, lunch, dinner. Bar and lounge, gift shop, spa, heated pool, tennis.

Olive Metcalf

The Pentagöet Inn
CASTINE, MAINE 04421

The Pentagöet is a lovely inn located on the unspoiled coast of beautiful Penobscot Bay. Built in 1894, this Victorian inn offers the traveler warmth and a very friendly atmosphere.

Part of the inn is Ten Perkins Street, the building next door, which is more than 200 years old. The suite is here. My husband and I stayed in it, and it's a gem. It has a working fireplace, and wood is supplied so that you can light yourself a fire some cold evening. It's a very romantic spot.

All the rest of the rooms in both buildings are lovely, too. Some have little alcoves with views of the town and harbor. Some are small and have odd shapes, but this goes well with a coun-

try inn. Seven rooms have a queen-sized bed.

There is a library to the right as you come in the door of the main inn. Lots of books, a piano, soft stereo music, and very restful couches give this room the perfect atmosphere. The sitting room is to the left with a wood-burning stove and a beautiful picture window.

The wraparound porch is a delight. Good food is served in the dining room. Breakfast when we were here included Maine strawberries, which arrived early in the morning, freshly picked at a local farm. Homemade granola, sourdough blueberry pancakes, homemade jellies, and lots more add up to a good breakfast. All baking is done right here. Good dinner appetizers include shrimp piccata—prepared with little Maine shrimp—lobster crepes, and Maine crabmeat crepes. Pork tenderloin, peppered ribeye steak, and lobster thermidor are some of the entrees. I had lobster pie, a lazy and delicious way to have lobster.

The Maine Maritime Academy is located here, and its training ship, *State of Maine*, is docked at the town wharf. The local professional theater group, Cold Comfort Productions, performs four nights a week.

The innkeepers and Bilbo Baggins, the inn cat, will really make your stay here a pleasant one. There is also Tara, a very nice German shepherd.

How to get there: Take I–95 to Augusta, take Route 3 East to coast. Connect with Route 1 at Belfast, and follow Route 1 north to Bucksport. Two miles beyond turn right onto Route 175. Take Route 175 to Route 166, which takes you into Castine.

Innkeepers: Virginia and Lindsey Miller
Address/Telephone: P.O. Box 4; (207) 326–8616 or (800) 845–1701
Rooms: 15, plus 1 suite; all with private bath, suite with fireplace. No smoking inn.
Rates: $159 to $179, double occupancy, MAP.
Open: May through October.
Facilities and activities: Bar, extensive wine list. Nearby: fishing, sailing, golf.

White Barn Inn
KENNEBUNKPORT, MAINE 04046

A pre–Civil War farmhouse and its signature white barn have been transformed into this lovely inn, which is just a short walk from the beach and the charming village of Kennebunkport with its colorful shops, galleries, and boutiques. When you consider the inn's exquisite food and its warmth and graciousness, it comes as no surprise that it is the only Maine member inn of *Relais et Châteaux* and one of just twenty in the United States.

A feeling of hospitality is evident throughout the inn. When you enter your room, you find a basket of fruit, flowers, luxurious toiletries, and a robe for you to wear. At night your bed is turned down and a pillow treat is left.

The rooms in the inn itself are attractively decorated with antiques, armoires, and brass and iron beds in a variety of sizes. The Gate House's rooms are large, with cathedral ceilings, ceiling fans, dressing areas, queen-sized beds, and wing chairs. May's Annex has six suites with king-sized four-poster beds and large sitting areas with fireplaces. There are oversized marble baths with whirlpool baths and separate showers. The towels are large and lush.

The sunroom is the boardroom, seating up to fourteen people; it's a perfect, sunny spot for small meetings, retreats, and reunions. The breakfast room is large and cheerfully decorated with flower arrangements. The main dining room is the barn; a lovely lounge and piano bar are here, too. Candlelight, linen, and soft music are nice touches. The menu changes weekly.

When I think about the food, I want to go back for more. The restaurant has received five diamonds and an AAA listing; these are prestigious awards and well deserved. The menu changes weekly in order to offer the freshest and finest of ingredients. I know the greens are fresh—I watched them being picked. Soups are amazing: A light cream soup of potato, leek, and watercress is scented with thyme; lobster minestrone comes with black beans, roasted tomatoes, olive-oil croutons, and a bacon *pistou*.

The appetizer of homemade ravioli is glorious. Dinner choices the week I was here included pan-seared striped bass with sautéed eggplant, Niçoise olives, and basil oil in a roasted tomato broth. The veal rib chop came grilled with glazed baby turnips, Swiss chard, garlic-roasted Parisienne potatoes, and a herb sauce. You can guess there are lots of seafood offerings from this Maine inn—lobster, halibut, and salmon were also on the menu.

No matter what size your party—two or eight—when your dinner is ready, that number of waiters arrives to stand behind each diner's chair and on cue serves everyone simultaneously. What a sight.

The little bar is copper, with eight upholstered chairs. The piano bar has a huge flower arrangement in its center.

After dinner, go relax in the living room with a glass of port or brandy, a book from the inn's well-filled bookshelves, or one of the many current magazines. Or you could be ambitious and go for a ride along the beach on one of the inn's bicycles. Just go and enjoy.

How to get there: From the Maine Turnpike, take exit 3 to Kennebunk. Follow Route 35 south 6 miles to Kennebunkport, then continue through the fourth traffic light onto Beach Street. The inn is in ¼ mile on the right.

Innkeepers: Laurie J. Bongiorno and Laurie Cameron
Address/Telephone: Beach Street (mailing address: P.O. Box 560-C); (207) 967–2321
Rooms: 18, plus 7 suites; all with private bath, some with phone, TV, and Jacuzzi, 11 with fireplace.
Rates: $120 to $270, double occupancy, continental breakfast and tea. Packages available.
Open: All year.
Facilities and activities: Dinner, full license. Meeting room, bicycles. Nearby: beach, shops, galleries, golf, tennis.

The Inn on Winter's Hill
KINGFIELD, MAINE 04947

The Inn on Winter's Hill, located in the midst of western Maine's Bigelow, Sugarloaf, and Saddleback mountains, sits on top of a six-acre hill on the edge of town. This Neo-Georgian manor house was designed by the Stanley (steam car) brothers and built at the turn of the century for Amos Greene Winter as a present for his wife, Julia. It is listed on the National Register of Historic Places. Today it is owned by a brother and sister who are doing a great job as innkeepers, following a longtime tradition of casual elegance and warm hospitality.

Accommodations are varied and range from the turn-of-the-century luxury rooms in the inn to the modern rooms in the restored barn. Every one is very comfortable, with nice bathrooms, wonderful views, cable television, and telephone.

Julia's Restaurant is elegant and the food served here is excellent. The night we were here, I had crackers and garlic cheese spread and pineapple wrapped in bacon for appetizers. My garden salad with house dressing was followed by a light sorbet and then Sole Baskets, which were superb. The other entrees were Drunken Duck, chicken Cordon Bleu, and beef Wellington. Salmon in phyllo—Atlantic salmon fillet baked in phyllo with a parmesan-cheese cream sauce—is superb; I had this on my last trip. Desserts are grand. Oh, it's all so good, it's hard to choose.

In the lounge area is an old piano, which came by oxcart from Boston for Julia Winter. It took two and a half months to arrive.

Spring, summer, fall, or winter, there is so much to do up here. Winter brings cross-country skiing from the door and ice skating on the lighted outdoor rink. And remember, downhill skiing at Sugarloaf is minutes away. Hunting, fishing, canoeing, and hiking along the Appalachian Trail welcome outdoors people in the other seasons.

How to get there: Kingfield is halfway between Boston and Quebec City, and the Great Lakes area and the Maritimes. Take the Maine Turnpike to the Belgrade Lakes exit in Augusta. Follow Highway 27 through Farmington to Kingfield. The inn is on a small hill near the center of town.

Innkeepers: Richard and Diane Winnick and Carolyn Rainaud
Address/Telephone: RR 1, Box 1272; (207) 265–5421, (800) 233–9687
Rooms: 20, in 2 buildings; all with private bath, phone, and cable TV, 1 specially equipped for handicapped.
Rates: $75 to $150, double occupancy, EP. Golf and fly-fishing packages available.
Open: All year.
Facilities and activities: Full breakfast, dinner for public daily, by reservation. Wheelchair access to dining room. Bar, lounge, meeting and banquet facilities, hot tub, swimming pool, croquet court, tennis, cross-country skiing, ice skating. Nearby: downhill skiing, hunting, fishing, hiking, golf, canoeing, Stanley Steamer Museum, dog-sled rides, white-water rafting.

Olive Metcalf

The Charlotte Inn
EDGARTOWN, MASSACHUSETTS 02539

The start of your vacation is a forty-five-minute ferry ride to Martha's Vineyard. It's wise to make early reservations for your automobile on the ferry. There also are cabs if you prefer not to take your car.

When you open the door to the inn, you are in the Edgartown Art Gallery, with interesting artifacts and paintings, both watercolor and oil. This is a well-appointed gallery featuring such artists as Ray Ellis, who has a fine talent in both media. The inn also has an unusual gift shop, now located next to the Garden House.

Four of us had dinner in the inn's lovely French restaurant named L'Etoile. The food was exquisite. Capon breast stuffed with duxelles, spinach, and sun-dried tomatoes with coriander mayonnaise was the best I have had. I tasted everyone's food—nice occupation I have. Rack of lamb, served rare, with red wine and rosemary sauce and accompanied by potato and yam gratin was excellent. They also have a special or two, but then everything is so special, the word does not fit. At brunch, the cold cucumber soup was served with chives and followed by entrees like blueberry soufflé pancakes with crème fraîche. For breakfast I had a strawberry crepe that I can still remember vividly. Freshly squeezed juices and fruit muffins. . . Heaven!

The rooms are authentic. There are Early American four-poster beds and fireplaces. The carriage house is sumptuous. The second-floor suite with fireplace I could live in. Paula has a touch with rooms—comfortable furniture, down pillows, down comforters, and all the amenities. As an example, the shower curtains are of eyelet and so pretty. As a finishing touch, there are plenty of large towels.

Across the street is the Garden House, and it is Edgartown at its best. The living room is unique and beautifully furnished, and its fireplace is always set for you. The rooms over here are just so handsome. The Coach House is magnificent, furnished with fine old English antiques, a marble fireplace, and a pair of exquisite chaise longues in the bedroom. It is air conditioned.

Paula, by the way, has green hands, and all about are gardens that just outdo one another.

Gery and Paula are special innkeepers, but they do need the help of Andrew and Morgan, the dogs, and Oscar and Princess, the cats.

How to get there: Reservations are a must if you take your car on the ferry from Woods Hole, Massachusetts. Forty-five minutes later you are in Vineyard Haven. After a fifteen-minute ride, you are in Edgartown, and on South Summer Street is the inn.

Innkeepers: Gery and Paula Conover
Address/Telephone: South Summer Street; (508) 627–4751
Rooms: 21, plus 3 suites; all with private bath, some with fireplace, air conditioning, and phone.
Rates: In-season, $195 to $295; interim-season, $125 to $205; off-season, $95 to $175; suites, $195 to $550; double occupancy, continental breakfast.
Open: All year.
Facilities and activities: In-season, dinner daily. Off-season, dinner on weekends. Sunday brunch year-round. Reservations a must. Gift shop and gallery. Nearby: sailing, swimming, fishing, golf, tennis.

olive Metcalf

$\mathcal{W}$heatleigh
LENOX, MASSACHUSETTS 01240

In the heart of the beautiful Berkshires, overlooking a lake, amid lawns and gardens on twenty-two self-contained acres stands the estate of Wheatleigh, former home of the Countess de Heredia. The centerpiece of this property is an elegant private palace fashioned after an Italian palazzo. The cream-colored manse re-creates the architecture of sixteenth-century Florence. You must read the brochure of Wheatleigh, for it says it all so well.

Patios, pergolas, porticos, and terraces surround this lovely old mansion. The carvings over the fireplaces, cupids entwined in garlands, are exquisite. In charming contrast, the inn also has the largest collection of contemporary ceramics in the New England area. There are many lovely porcelain pieces on the walls. In the dining room are tile paintings weighing more than 500 pounds. They are Doultons from 1830; this was before it became Royal Doulton. They are just beautiful.

The grill room, which is open in-season, provides an à la carte menu of light fare prepared to the same high standards of the dining room. Its casual ambience features an elegant black-and-white color scheme—the plates are beautiful.

There is a service bar in a lovely lounge, and boy, you sure can relax in the furniture in here. It has a wonderful fireplace, and the views from here are glorious. And imagine a great hall with a grand staircase right out of a castle in Europe. There are also exquisite stained-glass windows in pale pastels, plus gorgeous, comfortable furniture. From the great hall you can hear the tinkle of the fountain out in the garden.

The whole inn was done over very recently and, wow, the rooms are smashing. Do you long for your own balcony overlooking a lovely lake? No problem. Reserve one here.

At the entrance to the dining room, the homemade desserts are beautifully displayed along with French champagne in six sizes from a jeroboam to a small bottle for one. This is very nice indeed. I chose grilled quail on young lettuce leaves and raspberries for a dinner appetizer; it was superb. Tartare of fresh tuna was so beautifully presented, just like a Japanese picture, and delicious. I also had chilled fresh pea soup with

curry and sorrel, followed by monkfish coated with pistachios, sautéed, with red wine sauce. Homemade sorbets are very good, but then, so is everything here.

Susan's description of the inn is "elegance without arrogance," and Lin's is "the ultimate urban amenity." Mine is "a perfect country inn."

How to get there: From Stockbridge at the Red Lion Inn where Route 7 turns right, go straight on Prospect Hill Road, bearing left. Go past the Stockbridge Bowl and up a hill to Wheatleigh.

From the Massachusetts Turnpike, take exit 2, and follow signs to Lenox. In the center of Lenox, take Route 183, pass the main gate of Tanglewood, and then take the first left on West Hawthorne. Go 1 mile to Wheatleigh.

Innkeepers: Susan and Linfield Simon
Address/Telephone: West Hawthorne; (413) 637–0610, fax (413) 637–4507
Rooms: 17; all with private bath, air conditioning, and phone, 9 with working fireplace.
Rates: $145 to $525, double occupancy, EP.
Open: All year.
Facilities and activities: Lunch for houseguests, dinner, Sunday brunch, in season. Grill room, lounge. Swimming, tennis, cross-country skiing.

Yankee Clipper Inn
ROCKPORT, MASSACHUSETTS 01966

When you are lucky enough to be here and see a sunset, you will be overwhelmed. It's a golden sea and sky, with the town of Rockport in the distance. No camera could truly capture this scene. Wait a while longer, and the moonlight on the sea is an awesome sight.

Three buildings make up the Yankee Clipper. The inn is an oceanfront mansion. Here the rooms have antique furniture, oriental rugs, and some canopied beds. Some rooms have porches. You're sure to enjoy the television lounge with cable television and a really big screen. All meals are served in this building.

The Quarterdeck has large picture windows providing a panoramic view of the ocean.

Upholstered chairs are placed in front of the windows. Sit back and relax; it's almost like being on a ship that does not move. All of the rooms in this building are beautifully furnished. Some of the rooms in the Bullfinch House have water views. If you stay here you are on the EPB plan; the other buildings are MAP.

There is a function room, with a wonderful water view and just lovely for small weddings or executive meetings.

The Glass Veranda dining room has marvelous views that are matched by the marvelous food. David Pierson is a chef with imagination. I started my dinner with a taste of one appetizer—lobster polenta, which was a baked blend of cornmeal and native lobster, served with Boursin cheese sauce—and the soup of the day—cold zucchini soup.

I went on to the seafood au gratin, which was shrimp, scallops, and haddock, baked in cream and herbs, and topped with cheddar cheese and bread crumbs. Vegetarian Wellington was new to me; a medley of fresh vegetables was baked in puff pastry with Boursin cheese. Delicious.

To work off some of the calories, you might want to swim in the heated saltwater pool at the inn. In the area there are whale-watching trips, fishing, and in the town of Rockport, fantastic shopping. It really is fun to walk around here.

How to get there: Take Route 128 north and east to Cape Ann. Route 128 ends at traffic lights. Turn left onto Route 127. Drive 3 miles to where Route 127 turns left into Pigeon Cove. Continue on Route 127 for 1⅓ miles to Yankee Clipper in Pigeon Cove.

Innkeepers: Bob and Barbara Wemyss Ellis

Address/Telephone: 96 Granite Street; (508) 546–3407 or (800) 545–3699

Rooms: 27, including 6 suites, in 3 buildings; all with private bath, air conditioning, and phone.

Rates: $98 to $198, double occupancy, EPB; $50 more for MAP. $209-299 $179

Open: February 15 to December 20.

Facilities and activities: Dinner. Small function room, heated saltwater pool.
   Nearby: fishing, boating, shopping, whale watching.

Recommended Country Inns® Travel Club Benefit: 10% discount, Sunday–Thursday, except holiday Sundays, exclusive of other special offers and travel agent bookings.

Olive Metcalf

The John Hancock Inn
HANCOCK, NEW HAMPSHIRE 03449

Operated as an inn since 1789, the John Hancock has recently changed hands. Old friends and good innkeepers, Joe and Linda are now in charge.

This is a nice old inn. Its name stems from the fact that John Hancock, the founding father, once owned most of the land that comprises the present town of Hancock. Set among twisting hills with a weathered clapboard facade, graceful white pillars, and a warm red door, the inn represents all that is good about old inns.

The dining rooms are lovely, and the food is superb. They have been awarded the best of the best award: four diamonds, designating this to be one of the top 100 restaurants in the country in the category of American food. Appetizers like cranberry shrub, Maryland crab cake, baked Brie are followed by good soups and an excellent house salad. Their famous Shaker cranberry pot roast is worth the trip alone, but perhaps you'd like to try the roasted maple duck, rainbow lake trout, or summer garden linguine.

At the end of the day, you will retire to the comfort of a four-poster bed, where the sound of the Paul Revere bell from a nearby steeple will gently lull you to sleep. This is a town that hasn't changed much in the past two centuries.

Carefully preserved is The Mural Room, believed to date back to the early years of the inn. The recently remodeled Carriage Lounge is a comfortable and very unusual common room and bar.

Swim in summer in Norway Pond, within walking distance of the inn. Climb mountains, or just sit and listen to the church chimes during foliage time. Alpine and cross-country skiing are nearby in winter. Or browse in the antiques shops on a cool spring morn.

The inn dog is Duffy, a springer spaniel.

How to get there: From Boston take Route 128, then Route 3 to 101 west. Hancock is located just off Route 202, 9 miles above Peterborough.

Innkeepers: Joe and Linda Johnston
Address/Telephone: Main Street; (603) 525–3318, (800) 525–1789 (outside New Hampshire), fax (603) 525–9301
Rooms: 11; all with private bath, air conditioning, and phone. No smoking inn.
Rates: $88 to $108, double occupancy, EPB.
Open: All year.
Facilities and activities: Dinner, lounge. Wheelchair ramp into the inn. Parking. Nearby: swimming, hiking, antiquing, summer theater, skiing, tennis.

Olive Metcalf

The Inn at Thorn Hill
JACKSON, NEW HAMPSHIRE 03846

Over the Honeymoon Bridge to The Inn at Thorn Hill you go, and when you get there you will find a Victorian beauty. Mountains are everywhere you look from this inn. Relax on the porch in a New England rocking chair and enjoy the view. Even on a bad day it is spectacular.

I loved the Victorian parlor, with its baby grand piano, and the spacious drawing room with its wood stove and unbelievable view. A pair of Victorian mannequins in their finery stand at the windows next to the lovely old Victrola. There are board games, cards, and books for you to enjoy. A cozy pub with a fireplace and five bar stools has lots of cheer.

Elegant country dining by candlelight is what you get, and the food is good. The menu is revised seasonally to offer variety and popular seasonal dishes. A seafood sausage of scallops, shrimp, and lobster served with lemon caper butter is an example of their good appetizers. The soups and salads are interesting. And the entrees are grand. Lobster Pie Thorn Hill, served with brandy Newburg sauce in a puff pastry shell. Crisp roast duckling, served with Cointreau sauce and sautéed orange slices. Lamb chops stuffed with tomato, feta cheese, and fresh mint. The list goes on. The desserts that follow are excellent. There are more than 100 different wines. There is an impressive list.

There is a Victorian flair to all the inn rooms. A variety of beds is available—canopies, singles, doubles, kings, and queens—and all rooms have wonderful views of the mountains. The carriage house next door has a 20-by-40-foot great room with a fireplace and seven guest rooms, so bring several couples. This is the place to be. The cottages are very nice and just great for those who want more privacy.

There is much to do here. The inn has its own swimming pool; hiking and downhill skiing are close at hand; and cross-country skiing begins at the doorstep and joins the 146-kilometer Jackson touring network.

No wonder the inn was one of ten winners of Uncle Ben's Best Country Inn awards.

How to get there: Go north from Portsmouth, New Hampshire, on the Spaulding Turnpike (Route 16) all the way to Jackson, which is just above North Conway. At Jackson is a covered bridge on your right. Take the bridge, and two roads up from the bridge on the right is Thorn Hill Road, which you take up the hill. The inn is on your right.

Innkeepers: Jim and Ibby Cooper
Address/Telephone: Thorn Hill Road; (603) 383–4242 or (800) 289–8990, fax (603) 383–8062
Rooms: 19, in 2 buildings, plus 3 cottage suites, all with private bath. No smoking inn.
Rates: $70 to $111, per person, double occupancy, MAP.
Open: All year.
Facilities and activities: Bar, swimming pool, hot tub, cross-country skiing. Nearby: downhill skiing, golf club, tennis, horseback riding, canoeing, ice skating, sleigh rides.

Home Hill Inn

PLAINFIELD, NEW HAMPSHIRE 03781

Roger's brochure said Home Hill Country Inn and French Restaurant, and we could hardly wait to get there.

Roger was born in Brittany in northwest France, and he speaks with a pleasant accent. He has an authentic French restaurant here. The food presentation is picture perfect, and the taste is elegant. No gravies, only sauces, and no flour, cornstarch, or fillers are allowed. Roger believes in innovative French cooking.

The menu changes every day. You might try the cream of onion soup, then veal slices, very thin and young with French mushrooms. You may have the salad before, with, or after dinner, and the house dressing is gorgeous.

Roger joined us at dinner and had duck prepared with white plums. I tasted it; it was very moist and delicious. Another dish served occasionally is veal with fresh wild mushrooms. Grilled New England sea scallops with red-pepper coulis sounds great. Desserts, as would be expected, are superb. The wine list features both French and California wines.

In the kitchen is a lovely, long pine table where breakfast is served. What a homey spot at which to enjoy the continental breakfast of juice, croissants, butter, jams, and coffee.

The rooms are charming. The cottage is large enough for eight persons. There are French and American antiques, reproductions, and comfort.

The lounge-library is lovely; in fact, you will find it hard to find any fault with this inn.

The carriage house, also on the property, has three bedrooms, each with a bath. This is a nice addition to the inn. We stayed in one of these rooms—a wonderfully romantic spot.

Roger's Great Dane is Bacchus. The inn is on twenty-five acres, only 500 yards from the Connecticut River. There are a swimming pool (a bar is out here), tennis courts, and cross-country skiing. Any season, any reason, head for Home Hill.

How to get there: Take I–89 to exit 20. Follow Route 12A south 3 miles to River Road and turn right. In 3½ miles you'll find the inn on the left.

Innkeeper: Roger Nicolas

Address/Telephone: River Road; (603) 675–6165

Rooms: 6, plus 3 suites; all with private bath.

Rates: $95 to $150, double occupancy, continental breakfast. Fall season and holidays slightly higher.

Open: All year except Sundays and Mondays, two weeks in March, and two weeks in November.

Facilities and activities: Dinner, bar, lounge. Swimming pool, tennis court, cross-country skiing, fishing in Connecticut River, walking trails.

Recommended Country Inns® Travel Club Benefit: 10% discount, Monday–Thursday, except holidays and September 25–October 15.

Olive Metcalf

The Inn at Castle Hill
NEWPORT, RHODE ISLAND 02840

Newport is a fabulous place to visit any time of the year. And to be able to go to Newport and stay at The Inn at Castle Hill is a rare treat. I have always loved the warm atmosphere of this inn. It was built as a private home in 1874 and has been little changed over the years. Thirty-two acres of shoreline right on the entrance of Narragansett Bay offer a natural setting for almost anything a person could desire. The views from any place in or about the inn are breathtakingly beautiful. The Atlantic Ocean and the bay are at your feet. The lighthouse at Castle Hill is the official finish line for the Annapolis to Newport yacht race.

As for things to do, there is the Tennis Hall of Fame, and Newport is famous for its great "cottages" lining the waterfront.

The inn has four dining rooms. The small one, with only six tables, each set with different serving plates, is very special. Another is a light and airy oval room, which, like the others, looks over the water. The chef is very good, and the food he creates is delicious. The menu changes seasonally. Veal, beef, lamb, fowl, and seafood are prepared many ways and are beautifully served. Every day there are three homemade soups, together with an endless variety of appetizers. On my most recent trip to the inn, I had good and garlicky escargots, asparagus soup, fresh Dover sole, and an excellent Linzer torte.

The Tavern is a different room, with a beauty of a bar and a view unmatched, if you love the sea. There are Chinese teak and marble tables in the living areas, and the banister on the staircase is its own delight.

Almost all the rooms are quite large and beautifully furnished. The paneling is magnificent, as are the oriental rugs that have been left here.

Innkeeper McEnroe has refurbished the entire inn with wallpapers that are color coordinated with spreads and drapes, plus thick towels. Here the view outside is not enough for our innkeeper. He cares about the interior look, too.

The 10-mile ocean drive is among the most strikingly beautiful areas in New England. And do remember that Sunday brunch is very active with jazz.

How to get there: From the north take Route 138 into Newport, and follow Thames Street about 4½ miles to Ocean Drive. Look for the inn's sign on your right. From the west come across the Newport Bridge and take the scenic Newport exit that goes into Thames Street.

Innkeeper: Paul McEnroe; general manager, Jens Thillemann
Address/Telephone: Ocean Drive; (401) 849–3800
Rooms: 10; 7 with private bath. One chalet with 5 rooms and 3 baths.
Rates: Depending on the season, rates range from a low of $50 to a high of $230, double occupancy, continental breakfast.
Open: All year.
Facilities and activities: Restaurant closed from November 1 through March. Lunch daily May through October. Dinner and Sunday brunch April through late October. Bar, entertainment, live jazz on Sunday afternoons, private ocean beach.

Olive Metcalf

Twin Farms
BARNARD, VERMONT 05031

Twin Farms is a 235-acre hideaway estate that was owned by novelist Sinclair Lewis and given to his wife, Dorothy Thompson, as a wedding present. During the 1930s and '40s, they came here to rest and entertain many literary figures of the time.

You arrive at the entry gate and dial a number indicating who you are. Then you enter an unbelievably unique property. Drive down the lane and along a circular drive to the main house.

The game room, with a beautiful fireplace, has many games and Stave wood puzzles. Off this is the Washington Suite, where we stayed. It has beautiful quilts and down-filled beds, two televisions, a CD player, and a bathroom with a large skirted antique tub and a huge shower. The sitting room has a bay window with a nice view, good couches, and a beautiful fireplace. There's a fireplace in the bedroom, too.

Dorothy's Room, on the second floor, is where she preferred to read and write. Red's Room, the original master suite, is glorious, with a view of Mount Ascutney. Red was Sinclair's nickname.

The guest room's walls and curtains are covered in a green-and-ivory French linen that tells a story. It's just beautiful.

The cottages have fireplaces, sumptuous baths, very private screened porches, and lots of comfort.

A covered bridge takes you to the pub. Here are a self-service bar, pool table, fireplace, and television. Below this is a fully equipped fitness center. In-room massages are available. Up the road is a Japanese Furo. There are separate tubs for men and women, separated by fragrant pine walls, and one larger one for both men and women.

The main dining room is rustic; however, you may dine wherever you choose. We were in the original dining room, and both the food and service are incredible. Cocktails are at 7:00 P.M. There are two bars for you to help yourself from, anytime day or night. Lunch may take any form, and you may have it anywhere. Tea is glorious.

There is much to do here, whatever the season. Tennis and croquet; a lake for swimming, canoeing, or fishing; walking; biking. You can use the inn's mountain bikes. The inn also has its own ski slopes, ski trails, snowshoes, toboggans, and ice skating.

This is an experience few may be able to afford, but what a wonderful trip. This inn was definately made for romance. Say hello to Maple, the golden inn dog.

How to get there: Take I–91 north to I–89 north. Take the first exit off I–89 (exit 1). Turn left onto Route 4 to Woodstock, then Route 12 to Barnard. At the general store, go right and follow this road for about 1½ miles. As the road changes from blacktop to dirt, you will see two stone pillars and a wrought-iron gate on your right, marking the driveway entrance.

Innkeepers: Shaun and Beverly Matthews; Thurston Twigg-Smith, owner
Address/Telephone: Barnard; (802) 234–9999 or (800) 894–6327, fax (802) 234–9990
Rooms: 4 suites, 3 cottages, 1 lodge; all with private bath, phone, TV, minirefrigerator, and CD player.
Rates: $700 to $1500, double occupancy, all inclusive.
Open: All year except April.
Facilities and activities: Full license, spa, all winter sports, mountain bikes, tennis, croquet, swimming, canoeing, fitness center.

Olive Metcalf

Vermont Marble Inn
FAIR HAVEN, VERMONT 05743

The inn was built of locally quarried golden marble by descendants of Ethan Allen's family in the 1860s. The original carriage house and well house are still here, too. The fireplaces in the inn are marble. The ceilings are 13 feet high, and the carved moldings are elaborate. Crystal chandeliers are suspended from rosette medallions. The Victorian parlors are beautifully furnished. The library, which has a fireplace, has a chess set ready to play and a television available for watching. From one end of this Victorian beauty to the other, the inn is gorgeous, and there are three stories of it.

In 1926 an Art Deco wing was added. You really must see it to believe it. A two-faced Raggedy Ann doll, who is fifty or sixty years old, sleeps up here. There is a beauty of a bathroom on the third floor.

The rest of the rooms are named for English authors. There is a 120-year-old French brass bed in Lord Byron's room. The rooms reflect the style of the persons for whom they are named. Believe me, they are sumptuous. The beds are turned down at night, and a sweet is left for you.

A hundred-year-old stone wall separates the woods from the meadow. You can hike to the banks of the Castleton River from here.

The dining rooms are charming. The formal one has the original ceiling of papier-mâché and plaster. Tables are set with pink-and-white linens. The food is outstanding. Just consider: wine-poached shrimp with a spicy cocktail sauce; loin lamb chop grilled with garlic and served with onion–bell pepper salsa; braised duck with port and raspberry sauce; and roast quail. These are only a few of the possibilities. Desserts are made by Bea, the dessert chef, who is great.

If you want, you can dine in privacy in the front parlor, with candlelight and roses.

Shirley is the breakfast chef. Breakfast is served on the porch, which has lots of windows overlooking the grounds. Freshly squeezed orange juice is always a joy. However, it is only one of the courses of a five-course breakfast served with candlelight—what a treat. The inn has four stars from Mobil and four diamonds from AAA.

How to get there: Take Route 4 from Rutland and watch for signs to Fair Haven. The inn is on the green.

Innkeepers: Shirley Stein; Bea and Richard Taube
Address/Telephone: Fair Haven Green (mailing address: 12 West Park Place); (802) 265–8383 or (800) 535–2814
Rooms: 12; all with private bath, 8 with fireplace.
Rates: $145 to $210, double occupancy, MAP.
Open: All year except two weeks in April and November.
Facilities and activities: Full liquor license. Wheelchair access to dining room. Nearby: skiing.
Recommended Country Inns® Travel Club Benefit: 10% discount, January–April, except holidays or special event weekends.

Rabbit Hill Inn
LOWER WATERFORD, VERMONT 05848

In 1795 Rabbit Hill became an inn. It has had a few owners over the years; however, this pair of innkeepers has really done justice to this lovely old inn.

Each of the inn's rooms is done according to a theme. Some are the Doll Chamber, the Toy Chamber, and Carolyn's Room (which has a blue-and-white canopy bed). One has a cranky rabbit sitting on a bed. I have never seen so many stuffed rabbits, dolls, and such, all so tastefully arranged. I was in Victoria's Chamber, which has a king-sized bed and wonderful Victorian touches.

The Magees have come up with a beauty of an idea. Each room has a cassette player and a tape that explains what you would have seen from your window more than a century ago. The hats that Maureen has had made are worth the trip alone. A diary is in each room for people to write in during their stay. They are fun to read. The suites are in the tavern building. One of the suites has wheelchair access, a special bathroom equipped for the handicapped, and features designed for blind or deaf guests.

The porch on the second floor faces the Presidential Range. It's a special place to just sit and rock with Jake, the inn dog, or Zeke, the cat.

The Snooty Fox Pub, modeled after the eighteenth-century Irish pubs, has an old crane in the fireplace for doing hearth cooking. The doors of the two intimate dining rooms remain closed until 6:00 P.M. They are then opened to reveal highly polished 1850s Windsor chairs and pine tables set with silver and lit by candlelight.

It takes two hours to dine here; it is all done right. The menu changes seasonally, and no processed foods are used in any of the meals. Try the pork and venison pâté or the smoked salmon and seafood sausage to start. Then sample the Vermont turkey and okra chili, the grilled twelve-spice duck breast, rack of lamb, swordfish, vegetarian plate, or beef tenderloin. Be sure to savor the homemade sauces, mustards, and salsas prepared from the vegetables, herbs, and edible flowers from the inn's garden. Save room for dessert. Whiskey toddy cake sounds divine. So does white chocolate tart. These are only a sam-pling of what you might find at this AAA four-diamond restaurant.

In the evening while you're dining, your bed is turned down, your radio is turned on to soft music, your candle is lit, and a fabric heart is placed on your pillow. You are invited to use it as your do-not-disturb sign and then to take it home with you. Now if this touch isn't romantic, I do not know what is.

The inn is glorious. So is the whole area. You will not be disappointed with this one.

How to get there: Take Route 2 east from St. Johnsbury and turn right onto Route 18. Or coming from Route 5, take Route 135 east to Lower Waterford.

Innkeepers: John and Maureen Magee
Address/Telephone: Route 18, Box 55; (802) 748–5168 or (800) 76–BUNNY (800–762–8669), fax (802) 748–8342
Rooms: 15, plus 5 suites; all with private bath, radio, and cassette player, 1 specially equipped for handicapped. No smoking inn.
Rates: $159 to $239, double occupancy, MAP. EPB rates available.
Open: All year except April and first two weeks in November.
Facilities and activities: Bar, library, wheelchair access to dining rooms, snowshoeing, tobogganing, cross-country skiing, trout fishing, lawn games. Nearby: ice skating, golf.
Recommended Country Inns® Travel Club Benefit: 20% discount, Sunday–Thursday, January–March, excluding holiday periods.

The Village Country Inn

MANCHESTER VILLAGE, VERMONT 05254

Manchester's favorite front porch beckons you as you arrive at the Village Country Inn, located in the heart of town. The porch is 100 feet long, with wicker furniture and rockers covered with rose chintz. It's full of pink flowers all summer long. It's the icing on this beautiful inn.

This is a French country inn done in shades of mauve, celery, and ecru, and stunning inside and out. Anne was a professional interior decorator, and the inn reflects her expertise. Mauve is a color I adore. The boutique is The French Rabbit, with well-dressed rabbits to greet you. Anne has wonderful taste, and the boutique is full of very nice things.

Tavern in the Green, the bar and lounge,

has an upright piano and nice people who play and sing. One night when I was here, a playwright was in this room with a marvelous selection of music and songs. What an unexpected treat. A door from here leads out to the swimming pool and gardens. During the winter the large patio is flooded for ice skating. The inn has a large collection of skates for guests to use, and twinkling lights are hung in the trees all around the patio. In the summertime breakfast and dinner may be served out here.

In the living room is a large fieldstone fireplace dating back to 1889 and comfortable couches and chairs around it. Tables are provided for all sorts of games.

The rooms are magnificent and each one is different. They are done in ice cream colors. Lots of canopied beds, lace, plush carpets, down pillows, and nice things on dressers and tables give the rooms an elegant atmosphere. Good towels are such an important feature to inn guests and, needless to say, they are here.

Dining is a joy in the lovely dining room. The bishop-sleeve lace curtains and trellis alcoves create a cozy and romantic atmosphere for the glorious food. Chilled tomato bisque with dill is excellent. Salads aren't run of the mill, and entrees are creative. Grilled loin of lamb with rosemary and juniper sauce, and medallions of veal with wild mushrooms, shallots, and Madeira in a natural veal sauce are just two of the selections. Vermont lamb chops with black currant cassis and almonds are a house favorite. I chose crème brûlée for dessert. It was grand. Freshly made bread pudding with apples and hazelnuts captivated my dinner companion. Very good indeed. Breakfast is a full one, with many choices.

The Village Carriage Company comes to the inn with a horse and carriage and coachmen decked out in top hats and tails. The inn offers package plans for using the carriage, such as a champagne picnic in the carriage. Other special packages abound, including the French Rabbit Affair. As you can imagine, Christmas is really special.

How to get there: Coming north on historic Route 7A, you will find the inn on your left in Manchester Village.

Innkeepers: Jay and Anne Degen
Address/Telephone: Route 7A (mailing address: P.O. Box 408, Manchester); (802) 362–1792 or (800) 370–0300
Rooms: 30 rooms and suites; all with private bath and phone, some with TV. No smoking in rooms.
Rates: $150 to $210, per room, double occupancy, MAP. Special packages available.
Open: All year.
Facilities and activities: Bar-lounge, boutique, swimming pool, tennis, ice skating. Nearby: golf, skiing, shopping.

The Inn at Weathersfield
WEATHERSFIELD, VERMONT 05151

This beautiful old inn was built circa 1795 and has a wonderful history. Prior to the Civil War, it was an important stop on the Underground Railroad, sheltering slaves en route to Canada. The inn is set well back from the road on twenty-one acres of property. Your rest is assured.

Everything that Mary Louise and Ron do to improve this lovely inn is done with class and lots of care. In the reconstructed barn attached to the inn are five beamed-ceiling guest rooms with sensational old bathtubs. These are real honest-to-goodness Victorian bathrooms. There are twelve fireplaces in the inn, and each of these rooms has one. Two of the suites have a bedroom

and sitting room—the innkeepers say these are ideal for honeymooners. All the rooms are beautiful with fresh flowers, fresh fruit, canopied beds, and feather pillows.

Over the years Ron has built an extensive and well-balanced wine cellar. The tavern is modeled after eighteenth-century Massachusetts taverns. The nonsmoking greenhouse–dining room is a handsome complement to the other rooms. Stencils copied from those used in the early 1800s decorate many of the rooms, as do many of Mary Louise's beautiful antique quilts.

Excellent food is served here. Game consommé with chanterelle and leek and roasted quail with Tokay grapes and chèvre might begin your meal. Six or more entrees such as rack of Vermont lamb or the inn's own farm-raised pheasant with roasted corn, red peppers, and spring onion are offered each night. The menu changes daily, taking advantage of what is in season. They grow their own herbs in a special space in the garden. Be sure to save room for desserts, as they are glorious. Mary Louise and her culinary staff are an extraordinary team. A wassail cup is served from a cauldron in the keeping room fireplace. High tea, served each afternoon, is special.

Daughter Heather and husband, Jack, are potters. Their fine work is used in the inn and is sold in the inn's gift shop.

The horse named Dick will take you on a winter sleigh ride or for a summer ride on old country roads in an 1890 restored carriage. All of this and a beautiful country inn and, of course, a nice inn dog named Oreo Cookie, and Wednesday and Friday, the cats.

How to get there: Take I–91 North to exit 7 (Springfield, VT). Take Route 11 to Springfield, and then take Route 106 in town to the inn on your left, set well back from the road.

Innkeepers: Mary Louise and Ron Thorburn
Address/Telephone: Route 106, Box 165; (802) 263–9217 or (800) 477–4828, fax (802) 263–9219
Rooms: 9, plus 3 suites; all with private bath, 8 with fireplace.
Rates: $87.50 to $103 per person, double occupancy, MAP and afternoon tea.
Open: All year.
Facilities and activities: Tavern, recreation room with aerobics equipment, tennis, sauna, pool table, TV and VCR with movies, large library, gift shop. Outside amphitheater, gardens and recreation area suitable for weddings or small conference groups, horse box stalls for rent, horse-drawn sleigh and carriage rides.
Recommended Country Inns® Travel Club Benefit: 25% discount, Sunday–Thursday, excluding month of October, Christmas week, and holidays. Call at last minute for availability during restricted times.

Mid-Atlantic & Chesapeake Region

by Brenda Boelts Chapin

Are you one of those who would sooner travel without your map than without your gold-rimmed wine glasses boxed in velvet? Is your romantic streak searching for a poetic place to fulfill your fantasies?

M. F. K. Fisher once referred to food as love. At country inns we experience multiple layers of love. The savory foods of the Mid-Atlantic—Chesapeake Bay crab, mountain trout, farm-raised lamb, and seasonal vegetables and fruits—are a memorable part of any journey. There are inns to suit every romantic mood and taste. From the Hunt Country of Virginia to the sandy Atlantic shores, from the New York Finger Lakes to Maryland's Eastern Shore, I've selected Victorian inns, mountain lodges, and inns of avante-garde architecture. Some are located in small towns, some in woodland settings, and others in rolling countryside. If you're like us, you enjoy sharing this diversity of style and take pleasure in experiencing the regional terrains, histories, and people that leave you emblazoned with the unity of having succumbed to romantic travels together.

I envy you. You are about to explore the places we've enjoyed. To select only twenty romantic Mid-Atlantic inns for this inn guide out of the more than 200 inns we've seen every other year posed a delicious dilemna—one that required great restraint—which is something you can leave behind when you depart. Indulge yourselves to the loving extremes.

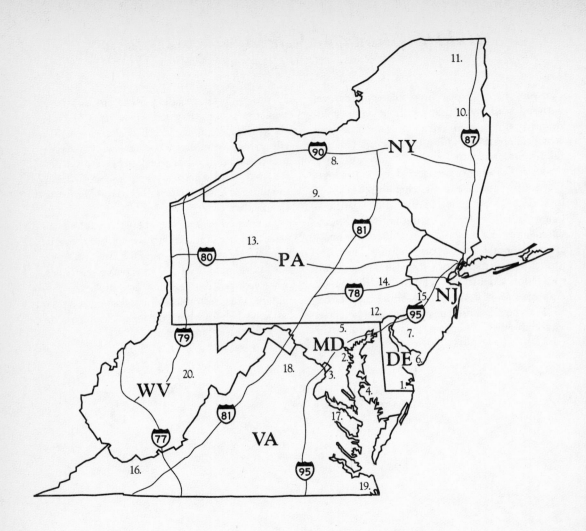

Mid-Atlantic & Chesapeake Region
Numbers on map refer to towns numbered below.

olive Metcalf

The Corner Cupboard Inn
REHOBOTH BEACH, DELAWARE 19971

The summer lighting filters through the tall, old shade trees onto the inn's cozy patios and creates a mood of total leisure. You chat with your companion after a day at the beach.

Around dinnertime on a summer Saturday night, your waiter opens a fine wine, the one you brought in a little brown bag. The ceiling fans turn. Dinner begins: crab imperial with just a touch of green pepper, or beautifully fried soft-shell crab, homemade bread, and more. After dinner, you saunter down the street for a moonlit stroll along the ocean.

This inn is in a lovely residential neighborhood located on the Atlantic seashore. You find comfortable parlors and sun porches. I like the

former attic room with an appealing private patio nestled in the treetops. "Eastwind" is a small cottage with a private brick patio. Each room is different. You feel as if you've stepped into a simpler past.

The rooms change according to the season. During summer, the inn is floored with grass mats; these are exchanged for oriental carpets in winter. In the inn, some rooms have antiques and wooden or iron beds. Two queen-sized beds are available.

Elizabeth's decorating is a tasteful homey blend of family heirloom and eclectic furnishings. The antique corner cupboard is in the living room. The long porch room, called the hat room for all the straw hats on the wall, is paneled and breezy in summer. A good selection of magazines and newspapers lines the parlor tables.

In the winter, couples return from a brisk walk on the beach and meet around the fireplace, sipping brandies and discussing sweet nothings. Here, the cares of the world are washed away, and love takes its leisurely role.

How to get there: From Route 1, exit into Rehoboth, cross canal bridge, take first left onto Columbia Avenue, and continue to Second Street, turn right. Go 1 block to Park and turn left; inn is located in the middle of Park.

Innkeeper: Elizabeth G. Hooper

Address/Telephone: 50 Park Avenue; (302) 227–8553

Rooms: 18; all with private bath, some with air conditioning. Pets allowed, charge.

Rates: Memorial Day weekend to mid-September: $140 to $225, double occupancy, MAP. Rest of year: $75 to $125, double occupancy, EPB.

Open: All year. Sometimes closes November through February 1.

Facilities and activities: Reservations for breakfast and dinner a must. Dinner price range: from $12.50. BYOB. Nearby: beach, tennis, bicycling, golf, historic town of Lewes (15 minutes away).

Olive Metcalf

Mr. Mole
BALTIMORE, MARYLAND 21217

Why would someone name a lovely urban inn after a mole? One guest named the inn "Monsieur Molet"—implying that grace and style marked Paul and Collin's bed and breakfast. Of course, many of you have known Mr. Mole from the children's book *Wind in the Willows*. On a childish whim, you might steal away here together.

Located in a nineteenth-century brick townhouse in Baltimore, the inn has 14-foot ceilings in three contiguous parlors painted a brilliant yellow that complements the innkeepers' collections: Collin's porcelains and Paul's ecclesiastical antiques and small boxes. An appreciation for the comforts of lovers, a well-set tea, a delicious hot breakfast, and a knack for

story telling characterize the innkeepers.

Breakfast is served buffet style at the hour you choose the night before. You'll find yourself gathering up rich Amish cake made with walnuts and apples, fresh breads, perhaps a fragrant country cheese, and juices and meats. Then you select a small table for two and compose your itinerary for the day.

"Couples," admits Paul, "seem to prefer this time for privacy. Most don't really wake up until after they've had their morning coffee and tea. Of course, spontaneous friendships occasionally form around afternoon tea, and sometimes we hear total strangers making dinner plans together."

Each bedroom has a romantic personality.

The innkeepers obviously had fun developing themes with treasures collected in Amsterdam, Brussels, London, and local markets. Hand-painted wooden fish hang above the fireplace in the Explorers Room, history books and English porcelains are in the London Suite, and stuffed moles of various sizes and descriptions in the Mr. Mole Suite. In the Garden Room, a sunporch is filled with seasonal flowers and white wicker furniture. You and your lover can choose according to your fantasies.

Located 5 blocks from Baltimore's light rail, the inn is convenient for touring in this easy-to-negotiate city. Should you wish to sequester yourself for the weekend, you might amble over to the coffee shop on the next block and enjoy the urban mix that characterizes the neighborhood.

We love to walk the bountiful stalls of Baltimore's famed Lexington Market, where some family-owned businesses are a century old, catch a matinee at the Mechanic Theater, and still have time for a sumptuous Italian meal in Little Italy. The next morning we dawdle over breakfast until the nearby antiques shops open.

Where else but at Mr. Mole would you have eighteenth-century antiques and a rubber ducky propped on the rim of the bathtub? Mr. Mole made them do it. Mr. Mole makes them do it all. He's the alter ego of the place. Like him, the innkeepers had fun collecting all their treasures. The result is an indulgent inn that leaves you to dream together, while being cared for in all the right ways.

How to get there: From I–95, take exit 53 to I–395. Exit onto Martin Luther King, Jr., Boulevard, bearing right, and continue 2 miles. Turn left on Eutaw Street, go 6/10 mile, turn right at fourth stop light, on McMechen Street. Go 1 block to stop sign at Bolton Street. Inn is diagonally across intersection.

Innkeepers: Paul Bragaw and Collin Clark
Address/Telephone: 1601 Bolton Street; (410) 728–1179, fax: (410) 728–3379
Rooms: 5; all with private bath, air conditioning, and phone.
Rates: $90 to $145, double occupancy, EPB and afternoon tea. Enclosed parking. No smoking inn.
Open: All year.
Facilities and activities: Nearby: Mechanic Theater, Myerhoff Symphony Hall, Lyric Opera House, Antique Row, Walters Art Gallery, Lexington Market, Orioles Park at Camden Yards, Babe Ruth Birthplace, Inner Harbor: Science Museum, National Aquarium.

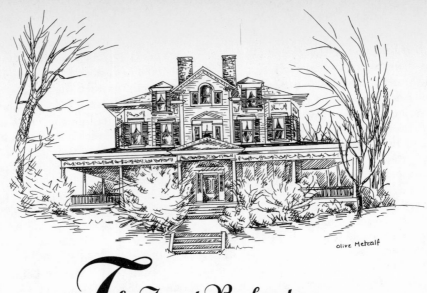

Olive Metcalf

The Inn at Buckeystown
BUCKEYSTOWN, MARYLAND 21717

Enter an old-fashioned setting so romantic that it emits aromatic scents and tender feelings from the moment you step inside. Dan Pelz's general good-naturedness influences the ambience while his cuisine influences the palate; both inspire a beautiful tranquil interlude.

It's customary to glance at the menu on top of the hall bureau. Dinner begins at 7:30 P.M. with Dan's award-winning soups. Among his eighty-seven soup creations is the famed Jack O'Lantern Soup, a creamy pumpkin soup. You will be seated around central dining tables unless you request a table for two. Such a communal gathering enhances your occasion.

Here's the weekly scenario: Saturday, expect to find a savory steak or beef dish; Monday, it's either pork or poultry; Tuesday means lamb or veal; Wednesday, it's a perfectly baked duck prepared in German style; Thursday is for beef, as in London broil; and Friday, it's fresh fish. It's fowl every Sunday, early and by reservation. Each night of the week a multicourse dinner appears upon antique china around candlelit oak tables. Dinner is a single entree served at one shared seating, and it's a bundle of entertainment.

Buckeystown is a nationally registered historic village on the Monocacy River. In the spring pink and purple azaleas, lilacs, and forsythia accent the lawn. The dreamy eighteen-room inn is an Italianate Victorian with two parlors and a wraparound front porch; the wood-work is chestnut and oak, and the floors are heart-of-pine. Sitting on a bureau in your room is Dan and Chase's guide, "'Inn' Joying." It directs you to the best in Civil War sites, antiquing, golf, walking and cycling tours, orchards, and luncheon restaurants.

The inn is filled with collections that reflect Dan and Chase's appreciation for art. The parlors are softly lit with Art Nouveau and Tiffany lamps. There are Phoenix glass and Van Brugal pottery to admire along with Dan's clown collection, which grows as a result of guests' thoughtfulness and generosity. Chase, who has a fine arts degree, works in oils; when a spare moment appears, he retreats to his studio and paints. It's his green thumb that's nurtured the gardens and makes the orchids flourish throughout the inn.

The romantic rooms are furnished with antiques, and the antique beds have been rebuilt to accept larger mattresses. You find everything from cozy pillows, dolls, Indian paintings, and finely carved jade to handmade quilts and rockers. The honeymoon suite, St. John's Cottage (formerly a chapel), is a gentle walk down the hill. Outside the door is a hot tub graced by wisteria. The loft bedroom, which overlooks the parlor and fireplace, makes you feel sybaritic.

The inn pets include Briard, the French sheepdog, and his dear friend Mr. Stubbs, the Scotty dog.

This inn weaves a rich tapestry of friendship, food, and wine. The only choice you have is the choice to come and for lovers, that's the best one of all.

How to get there: From I–270 north of Washington, D.C., exit Route 85 South to Buckeystown. The inn is on the left in town.

Innkeepers: Chase Barnett, Rebecca Shipman-Smith; Dan Pelz, innkeeper/chef
Address/Telephone: Main Street (General Delivery, Buckeystown); (301) 874–5755 or (800) 272–1190
Rooms: 7, plus 2 cottages, 1 suite; all with private bath, 2 with fireplace. No smoking inn.
Rates: $209 to $230 per couple per weekend (gratuity and tax included), MAP; $167 to $188 per couple midweek, MAP; cottage $230. Rates slightly higher on holidays. Checks preferred. Two-night minimum some weekends.
Open: All year.
Facilities and activities: Dinner, public invited by reservation: $30 weeknights, $36 weekends. (Prices include wine.) Two acres of land with pre–Civil War graveyard.
Nearby: shops, antiquing, canoeing, bicycling, Antietam Battlefield, Harper's Ferry.
Recommended Country Inns® Travel Club Benefit: Stay two nights, get third night free, subject to availability.

Olive Metcalf

Victoriana Inn
ST. MICHAELS, MARYLAND 21663

While we sat in the white summer chairs along the canal and exchanged intermittent thoughts, a robin trilled in flight and mute swans paddled up the creek. It's only fair to expect a small waterfront inn to have a peaceful panorama, and Victoriana Inn looks out to the village harbor. From the porch a wide lawn stretches to the canal. Across the footbridge are the comings and goings of people, boats, and animals— enough to entertain you between sips of lemonade and a good read. In your lawn chair you're near the fish pond filled with koi carp and chirping distance from the purple martin house. For privacy there's a white picket fence surrounding the spacious lawn. One block from here is the St.

Michael's Maritime Museum, filled with boats and Bay lore. You might express a great sigh of relief at being here together.

Janet sailed into St. Michaels several years ago and was smitten with the Chesapeake Bay village. She returned and found a house on the harbor in the very heart of town. "This is it," she says. "This is where I'll stay." You'll be happy if you two also decide to stay.

The inn is named for Janet's golden retriever, Victoriana, whose regal poses and mellow ways make her a charmer.

Arriving in the wintertime, you might have a seat in a windowed alcove of the living room. With the fire warmly crackling away, you can have a glass of sherry, play a game of dominoes, or plan your future. An exquisite antique grape-and-pear chandelier casts a soft light over the scene.

This is a good base for bicyclers, who can follow these flat Eastern Shore roads on a marked trail. Janet provides bicycle storage for those who bring their bikes. She will also set you in the right direction for sailing or boarding a wide range of boats.

The rooms are named for islands of the Chesapeake Bay. You sleep soundly, as if the two of you are island-bound for the night. The antiques are of a fine quality, the towels are carefully folded and fill a basket, and the spreads are thick and comfy. These are beautiful lodgings with hardwood floors and handsome armoires.

In the morning flowers adorned the coffee cake. Everyone was seated throughout the parlor; we were before the fireplace, using small trays.

Soon Janet brought in hot, delicious French toast and syrup. In the summer you can have breakfast on the veranda and watch the ducks swim along the canal or the boats depart for a day on the water.

The second week in December, Santa Claus comes to town. He rides down to the dock in a horse-drawn carriage, and all around him the boats are decorated with lights and holiday trim. There are special services at the churches, and the shops are filled with gifts and goodies. "The town," explains Janet with a contented smile, "looks like a Christmas card." It makes a romantic interlude all the sweeter.

How to get there: From Main Street in St. Michaels, turn north on Cherry Street (toward the water), go to the Victorian fence, and turn right into the parking lot of the inn.

Innkeeper: Janet Bernstein
Address/Telephone: 205 Cherry Street; (410) 745–3368
Rooms: 5; 2 with private bath, 3 with lavatory, 2 with fireplace, and all with air conditioning. No smoking in bedrooms.
Rates: $95 to $135, double occupancy, EPB.
Open: All year.
Facilities and activities: Guest refrigerator. Nearby: restaurants, St. Michaels Maritime Museum, sailing, bicycling (storage provided at inn), annual Waterfowl Festival, Christmas walk second weekend of December.

Antrim 1844
TANEYTOWN, MARYLAND 21787

The frosty light of the full moon emerged from the clouds and reflected off the snow as we drove; the farms and fields of rural Carroll County seemed to await passage to warmer days. We, however, found immediate warmth in the elegant Antrim 1844, named by its original builder for Antrim County, Ireland. Richard and Dort added the year it was built to its name.

Today the inn's twenty-three acres surrounding the brick plantation house have given the innkeepers the space to add an outdoor swimming pool, tennis court, croquet lawn, and chipping green. When they purchased the derelict property, it lacked even electricity, and the neglected smokehouse, now a restaurant,

was in marked disrepair.

The three-story building spans a hillside on the edge of a very small town. It's a large, sumptuous inn filled with antiques that knowledgeable collectors appreciate. After viewing the exquisite bedrooms, elegant mirrored parlor, cozy tavern, and the romantic dining areas, many a bride and groom choose this as their wedding site.

A wedding reception filled two of the parlors that night, but we felt we had the place to ourselves. At 7:30 P.M. Stuart, the maître d', seated us before a blazing fire in the smokehouse for dinner.

We began with a mushroom tartlet, and then had a fine salad of seasonal greens with Montrachet cheese, roasted peppers, and raspberry vinaigrette. I chose a salmon with an excellent barbecue sauce and a crème brûlée for dessert that came in a heart-shaped terrine with a crusty top, burnished as it should be.

For breakfast Richard might prepare Belgian waffles along with bacon and scrambled eggs. The sun blasts into the 14-foot dining rooms through great, lusciously curtained windows. On a winter's day the marble fireplace will be glowing. I think I've never seen an inn with so many fireplaces.

In the evening, when you go up to your room, chocolates and cordials are served upon a butler's tray. On the same tray, coffee, a muffin, and the newspaper arrive in the morning, so you can emerge from your room slowly. By 9 A.M. you're in shape to meet others at the formal breakfast table, though leaving your stately room may prove difficult. You might have slept in a nineteenth-century rosewood half-tester from New Orleans or the 1790s canopied bed with its lace and ruffles, or

the 1820 Honduras mahogany canopy with its 150-pound posts. The third-floor rooms have double Jacuzzis. Other choices include the remodeled barn overlooking the creek with its skylights and decks and the Ice House English cottage with a view of the pool and formal gardens.

Climb the ladder in the third-story hallway and take a look at the expansive view of peaceful, rolling countryside. Make a vow to your future together.

How to get there: From Baltimore Beltway 695, take exit 19 or 795 north. Exit Route 140 West to Taneytown. In town, turn left on Trevanian Road and go 150 feet to inn on right. From Frederick, take 194 North to Taneytown. Turn right at light on Route 140, proceed ½ mile, turn right at fork onto Trevanian Road. Go 150 feet, inn on right. Signs indicate where to park.

Innkeepers: Richard and Dort Mollett

Address/Telephone: 30 Trevanian Road; (410) 756–6812 or (800) 858–1844

Rooms: 9 in main house, 4 in adjacent cottages and barn; all with private bath, 6 with Jacuzzi, 9 with fireplace. No smoking, except in tavern.

Rates: $150 (any room) Sunday through Thursday; $175 to $300 weekends; double occupancy, EPB and morning and evening refreshments. Special packages available on holidays. Two-night minimum if stay includes Saturday night.

Open: All year.

Facilities and activities: Tavern, 23 acres, swimming pool, tennis court, croquet lawn, golf-chipping green, formal gardens. Dinner by reservation, Wednesday through Sunday (fixed price $50, higher on holidays). Nearby: 12 miles to Gettysburg. Golf courses: Wakefield Valley, Carroll Valley, Bear Creek.

Olive Metcalf

Alexander's Inn
CAPE MAY, NEW JERSEY 08204

Romance, elegant cuisine, sumptuous bedrooms, an elegant flower-filled parlor, a wide wraparound porch filled with inviting furniture—the epitome of twentieth-century Victorian comfort—these are your surroundings at Alexander's Inn.

When you meet Larry, you may find yourself trying to place his resonant voice. He hosts a weekly two-hour New Jersey radio show called "On the Soap Box," during which he interviews a wide range of people, including politicians. "I've always had an interest in politics," he admits, "and this gives me a chance to debate the lawmakers and bring out issues they might not otherwise hear."

If you've come to escape the news, however, Larry and Diane astutely provide inviting private guests' spaces, such as the Victorian parlor and the wide, wraparound, wicker-filled porch for doing nothing more than lounging away a summer afternoon in preparation for a dining extravaganza.

Be inquisitive. Larry and Diane are well-informed Victorian preservationists who harmonize authenticity with loving comfort. Every turn reveals a discovery. Come to dinner at Alexander's and you discover the fine touches. The silver wine carafes, the finger bowls floating with rose petals, the crystal, the china—but more than the accoutrements, it's the dining that sends you into un-Victorian excesses.

You might begin with the sausage-nut strudel—layers of pastry encasing sausage, cream cheese, almonds, walnuts, pecans, and herbs. And for an entree, perhaps grilled mako shark with a stuffing-filled pocket surrounded with a sauce, or classic filet mignon *à la bourguignonne*, grilled and served on Holland rusk with pâté and sauced with a heavenly dark burgundy wine sauce. You may go into ecstasy over desserts. The crème brûlée is a glimpse of heaven. It's almost torture to decide. If you've never had homemade white-licorice ice cream (created by Diane so it wouldn't stain the teeth), this is the moment.

Don't be surprised if a diner at the next table is proposing marriage. The dining inspires such occasions.

Afterward you may want to walk 2 blocks down to the beach on a moonlit night, return and have a cordial on the porch, and finally retire satiated to one of the lavish rooms. One has French wallpaper and an ornate Victorian antique bedroom suite; across the bed is a gray-satin spread trimmed in frilly lace. It's a dream of a room.

In the morning, breakfast is brought to your room. A tray is filled with a delicate carafe of hot coffee, fresh croissants, and a large bowl of fruit. A single long-stemmed red rose lies across the white linen.

The Queen herself would approve.

How to get there: From the ferry, take Route 9, then 109 to Cape May. Continue on Lafayette Street, turn left on Franklin Street, and turn right on Washington Street to the inn on the right. (Garden State Parkway leads into Lafayette Street.)

Innkeepers: Larry and Diane Muentz

Address/Telephone: 653 Washington Street; (609) 884–2555

Rooms: 6; all with private bath and air conditioning.

Rates: May to mid-June: Sunday–Thursday $100, 2-night weekend $275. Mid-June to October: Sunday–Thursday $100, 3-night weekend $395. Mid-October to May: Sunday–Thursday $100, 2-night weekend $295. Holiday weekends may require longer stay. EPB and afternoon tea; beach passes and parking included. Request Christmas packages.

Open: All year.

Facilities and activities: Dinner. Nearby: beach (2 blocks away), Victorian House Tours, Victorian Week in October, Christmas Celebration, Emlen Physick Estate, carriage and trolley rides, bicycling, boating, summer band concerts.

Recommended Country Inns® Travel Club Benefit: 10% discount, Monday–Thursday, October 20–November 15 and January 2–May 15, excluding holidays and special events, subject to availability.

olive Metcalf

Cabbage Rose Inn
FLEMINGTON, NEW JERSEY 08822

The fire was going in our room—Lavender & Lace—and now as we relaxed, we studied the photographs and prints—all of women—that accented the walls and dresser. We savored the time together at the day's end.

Later, as we visited with Pam and Al before the fire, we listened to stories about Al's childhood on the Maine seacoast, Pam's love of the theater, and how they first met in the corporate world of AT&T. We were reminded of the effort that went into their renovation and how, after they finished, they were married in the inn parlor before they embarked on their new innkeeping career together. This was a romantic beginning for a dreamy little inn.

As we sat beside the fire, Al, with a sweep of his hand, referred to the town of Flemington, outside the front door. Sixty percent of the village is on the National Register of Historic Places. Many couples overlook the historic sites because the surrounding area is so rich with biking, hiking, and touring opportunities. The neighboring towns of New Hope (Pennsylvania), Lambertville, and the wonderful Delaware riverside villages also beckon. Al gave expert directions for rambling country drives and scenic out-of-the-way places. Within a block of the inn are Flemington's village-style shopping outlets, including those that trace back to the glass-making industry that began at the turn of the century. You can also walk up the street and visit the courthouse where the famed Lindbergh kidnapping trial was held.

For dinner we went off to an old stone inn, where we dined on excellent salmon and beef fillet adjacent to a fireplace in a most lovely setting. Dinner here is included in a romantic package that also includes champagne and roses and is provided, on request, by the Cabbage Rose.

Next morning, we were intrigued that there were midweek independent business travelers at breakfast, each enjoying the inn as much as any love-struck couple (well, almost!). The conversation at breakfast left people full and happy, as did the delicious oatmeal and compote, appetizing muffins, fresh juices, and coffee.

When Pam was a little girl, her Aunt Rose would gather her onto her lap and commence telling stories by pointing to a favorite charcoal drawing that hung on the parlor wall. It was Aunt Rose, too, who took her to auctions and antiquing and taught her to appreciate fine things. As you sign the guest book, you'll see the mysterious drawing, with its enticing woodland path that sparked many a happy afternoon.

Upon departure, we couldn't resist a box of handmade chocolates, which Pam sells at the inn. We departed with ornately designed milk chocolates—and romantic memories that are as palpable as any quality antique or oil painting.

How to get there: From I–78, take exit 17 to 31 south to Flemington. From I–287, take exit 10 (on left) to 202 south to Flemington. Turn right at Flemington sign (opposite Grand Union), turn right again on Main Street, and continue to inn. Park in rear.

Innkeepers: Pam Venosa and Al Scott
Address/Telephone: 162 Main Street; (908) 788–0247
Rooms: 5; all with private bath and air conditioning, 1 with fireplace, 4 with ceiling fan. No smoking inn.
Rates: $85 to $110, double occupancy, EPB.
Open: All year.
Facilities and activities: Parking. Nearby: walking distance to outlet malls and downtown; Lambertville, New Hope, hiking, biking, village touring, and golf course.

Olive Metcalf

Morgan-Samuels B & B Inn
CANANDAIGUA, NEW YORK 14424

Were I marking the changing of the seasons, this is where I'd come. In the first bloom of spring, I'd walk between the silver maples that line the lane; as the leaves hinted harvest colors, I'd visit the fall wineries and select jams and grape pies from the roadside stands; following a snowfall, I'd call for a winter's date on the horse-drawn sleigh; and when the first blush of summer heralds its becalming force, I'd canoe the lake to out-of-the-way places. Whatever the season this refined setting with its placid rural surroundings offers elegant seclusion. A day spent luxuriating in this country house inn is a day complete in itself.

Julie's artistic background has gracefully influenced each room; five have their own fire-places and one an antique French parlor stove. The suite is a dream; its two-room bath has a shower, a tub, and a Jacuzzi lit by a window that overlooks the fields. Each piece of furniture opposite the fireplace is inlaid with wood and overlaid with finely carved details.

Julie recommends romantic pleasures. She gives thought to where you might go that would particularly suit your taste. She suggested a canoe ride for the two of us or a summer afternoon lunch in the Sonnenberg Gardens, with its sixty acres of plants, or maybe we just wanted to lounge beside the rose garden while listening to the fountain trickle and savoring our favorite tea.

John is the chef. Early every morning he and

son Jonathan, who's still in preschool, depart together for the market to purchase the fresh fruits and oranges for juice. If an omelet has crossed his mind on the drive, he selects the six cheeses and green and red peppers that compose this delicious masterpiece. If a meat is called for, his own selection of savory garden herbs is admixed with the sausage that awaits frying.

Some mornings they call upon the nearby monastery for freshly baked whole-grain breads or flours for the fruit or nut pancakes. While all this is occurring, we are sleeping soundly.

The inn is named for Judson Morgan, an actor, and Howard Samuels, who invented the plastic bag. Each owned the mansion at one time. Yes, I should have asked more about the architecture and furnishings. I saw and marveled at the hand-hewn beam in the 1810 section and the stone and brick work and wondered who these early craftsmen were. The impressive array of antiques and oil paintings could have prompted innumerable questions as well. But one falls under a spell here, and lingers on the patio under the

trees or in the breakfast room beside the fire. One sits to breakfast, where the delicious pancakes or fabulous omelets emerge hot from the kitchen.

One steps out the mansion door not expecting to find a black Oriental chicken who busses the ground for seeds while a peacock turns his head sharply and then leisurely fans his massive tail feathers in a paced walk. One hears the rustle of leaves and sees cows peering from behind a stone fence. Or one returns to the library, hears the sound of the fire crackling and smiles at the beauty of a moment shared with your spouse— whether you've been married for many decades or merely a day.

The location is rural, yet five minutes from Lake Canandaigua and the eponymous town— an ideal setting with articulate hosts.

How to get there: From I–90 East take exit 43 and turn right onto Route 21. Proceed to Route 488 and turn left. Turn right at the first stop sign onto Smith Road and proceed ¾ mile to inn on the right.

Innkeepers: John and Julie Sullivan
Address/Telephone: 2920 Smith Road; (716) 394–9232
Rooms: 6; all with private bath and air conditioning, 5 with fireplace, 1 with parlor
    stove, 2 with Jacuzzi. No smoking inn.
Rates: $99 to $195, double occupancy, EPB.
Open: All year.
Facilities and activities: Dinner for 8 or more by reservation (approximately $50 each),
    BYOB, forty-six acres. Nearby: horse-drawn sleigh rides during winter, Canandaigua
    Lake, Sonnenberg Gardens, wineries.

Olive Metcalf

Rosewood Inn
CORNING, NEW YORK 14830

It was a serendipitous meeting among couples gathered about the blazing fire, with the scent of hot chocolate chip cookies filling the air. We bounced ideas and experiences around like we were old chums. We touched on everything from the artists who have made Corning and its glass world famous to how each of us had met our companion. The camaraderie we were experiencing made the Rosewood Inn seem like a modern-day salon. It made our time together alone all the richer for this shared experience.

Stewart encouraged us all toward the tea and reminded everyone that another batch of cookies was in the oven, while Suzanne alternately nudged the conversation or sat back and listened.

"What hippopotamus?" she once teased when a guest asked about the abundance of hippos. We had seen purple, blue, pink, and a couple of slate gray ones around the inn. Eventually the hippo story came, as did so many others. A lovely Englishman, a glassmaker, came to visit. When he departed, he left the Stewarts with an exquisite piece of art glass for the mantel. He wanted a legacy for the glassmakers he admired, whom he knew would eventually stay here.

This little glassmaking mecca has a population of only 13,000, yet Corning's international fame draws the finest artists, who either live here or come for lectures. The Corning Glass Museum is renowned not only for its depth, but for its breadth—26,000 objects on display span the history of glass since 1500 B.C. Less known, say Stewart and Suzanne, is the Rockwell Museum, with its collection of American Western Art and 2,000 pieces of Steuben glass.

The shop-filled streets and easy drive to the nearby Finger Lake vineyards also explain why this is the third most popular place to visit in New York State. It's the combination of small town, city museums, great restaurants, and an inn that you'd return to regardless of location. The Rosewood is located in a quiet neighborhood that's within walking distance of the heart of town.

Stewart is a chef by avocation; he prepares fresh fruits, lovely omelets, heavenly French toast, homemade breads, and fresh juices. Suzanne, meanwhile, sets an elaborate centerpiece for the breakfast meal, and everyone's place has a nameplate for social ease.

While the inn's exterior is English Tudor, the interior is furnished with antiques and decorated with romantic Victorian collectibles. Choose from Eastlake or queen-sized canopy beds in rooms that are named for renowned personages, such as Mark Twain, Frederick Carder Steuben, or Lewis Carroll.

The mix of romantic pleasures that compose Corning and The Rosewood is in your best interest. The inn is addictive, but this addiction is a happy, healthy one that your physician would recommend. You might even meet her here with her lover.

How to get there: From Route 17 in town, turn south on Chemung Street, go 1 block, turn right on First Street, proceed to 134 on south side of street.

Innkeepers: Stewart and Suzanne Sanders
Address/Telephone: 134 E. First Street; (607) 962–3253
Rooms: 7, plus 2 suites; all with private bath and air conditioning. No smoking inn.
Rates: $70 to $115, double occupancy, EPB and afternoon tea.
Open: All year.
Facilities and activities: Nearby: Corning Glass Museum, Rockwell Museum of Western Art, glass shops, National Soaring Museum, Watkins Glen International Race Track, Finger Lakes wineries, golf.

Olive Metcalf

The Lamplight Inn
LAKE LUZERNE, NEW YORK 12846

We came on a clear winter afternoon and soon scurried up the street to the frozen lake, where we cross-country skied until sundown. Then we returned to relax by the fire and visit over cups of hot tea in the great room. It was a magic time of serenity. Gene and Linda are naturals at making people happy.

Their inn story began when they, like lovers will, followed their intuition. They were on vacation together in Lake Luzerne and saw a derelict mansion on a hill that would make a great inn. Impulsively, they acted on their romantic streaks and bought it. Two years later, their dream became a beautiful reality. They also had vital talents to back that challenging deci-

sion. Gene knows construction, Linda is a textile designer, and together they make a dynamic team.

The inn looks as a dream inn should. The great room is 20 by 44 feet, trimmed warmly in chestnut, and arranged with several seating areas, a waiting chess game, and the crackling fireplace. In an oak chest is Linda's collection of Madame Alexander dolls and her small turtle collection. It's a place you want to linger. Notice the Christmas cards she designed; she's a talented artist. The furniture vies for your attention; each piece suggests it's more comfortable than the next. They recognized snuggling as essential in their inn.

The Lamplight has a terrific location. Gene and Linda's inn is near the oldest rodeo in the United States, Lake George, Saratoga Springs and its sights, horse racing, white-water rafting, snowmobiling, and bicycling, and it's within walking distance of the town lake. Scenic touring is a breeze. You'll never need to search for activities. The inn is a short drive away from two fine restaurants. Request the inn newsletter for special romantic events.

Each bedroom has its own personality. Our mountain view room looked brand new; Gene finished it in 1986. That's how clean the inn is. The sheets and towels are color coordinated, and during winter flannel sheets cover new mattresses. You tuck yourselves in beneath thick, fluffy comforters. Five of the rooms have gas fireplaces; each has an individual heat thermostat, and one

has a large skylight. The teddy bears across the pillow are moved to the far corner facing the wall.

Gourmet breakfasts are served in the sunroom. There are hot fruit compotes, homemade granola (deliciously made by Linda), huge chocolate chip muffins or sour cream coffee cake, stacks of hot French toast or waffles, or even a four-egg omelet (expertly made by Gene). Your taste buds memorize a meal this fine in this sunfilled setting. You look conspiratorily toward your companion, praising the weekend together.

How to get there: From the south, I–87 North, take exit 24 (Albany); then proceed on Northway to Exit 21. Go left onto 9N; the inn is 10 miles on the right in Lake Luzerne.

Innkeepers: Gene and Linda Merlino

Address/Telephone: 2129 Lake Avenue (mailing address: P.O. Box 70); (518) 696–5294 or (800) 262–4668

Rooms: 10; all with private bath and air conditioning, 5 with gas fireplace.

Rates: $85 to $150 (seasonal), double occupancy, EPB. Two-night minimum in busy season. Weekend packages available.

Open: All year.

Facilities and activities: Service bar. Nearby: restaurants, Lake Luzerne, white-water rafting, cycling, horseback riding, cross-country skiing, snowmobiling, professional rodeo summer Friday nights, Lake George (10 miles), Saratoga Springs (18 miles).

Olive Metcalf

The Interlaken Inn and Restaurant
LAKE PLACID, NEW YORK 12946

The Olympics forever changed Lake Placid. At times it looks European, other times American, but what distinguishes it are three things: the endless sporting competitions; the people who converge here and their love of skiing, hiking, and sports; and the ski jump complex on its eastern horizon.

At the end of an athletic day, however, one likes to retreat to a romantic little village inn. The Interlaken Inn is located outside the fray, 2 blocks from Mirror Lake and the village center, on a residential street. Carol and Roy Johnson and clan were scattered about the inn preparing dinner with their guests in mind.

We'd arrived just in time for afternoon tea.

It was while munching on Key lime tarts and lovely petits fours that we discovered Carol (the master chef) and Roy (an architect) came east from California to establish their Adirondacks inn. "You need an architectural background," Roy explained, "to restore and repair a 1906 country inn." Combining their talents—Carol's art degree and Roy's building experience—they also build and paint bird houses, jelly cabinets, Christmas decorations, and other craft works for their inn gift shop.

Dinner happened like this: Around 6:00 P.M. guests began arriving in the parlor for a drink. My traveling companion headed for the pub, where he immediately found Roy and Carol's golf-ball collection and discovered that they shared his love of golf.

Soon we were seated in the posh dining room and reading the dinner menu: "Mushroom strudel, salad with Caesar dressing, scallops in puff pastry, filet mignon with mustard cognac cream sauce, poached salmon with fresh dill sauce, chicken Normandy with a sauce of Granny Smith apples and calvados." Happily, decisions were concluded and gastronomic directions taken. Finally the evening tapered; coffee came with individual chocolate pots and Chantilly cream; couples moved to the living room or small bar; some lingered; some went for an evening walk down to the lake.

Upstairs, the pretty rooms are softly furnished, some with lace curtains and thick carpeting; you'll find several antiques from the Johnsons' California home.

On each bedroom door hangs a straw hat garlanded with flowers. There's also one on the front door near the doll carriage filled with antique dolls. The hats are Carol's touch. She's reminding us we're on a romantic holiday, and that's, indeed, the mood that Interlaken induces.

How to get there: From the intersection of Main Street and Saranac Avenue, continue north (a left turn from Saranac, a right hand turn from Main) on Main Street along the lake. The second street on the left is Interlaken. Climb the steep hill and you'll see the inn on the left. (*Note:* There may be no street sign for Interlaken Avenue.)

Innkeepers: Roy and Carol Johnson

Address/Telephone: 15 Interlaken Avenue; (518) 523–3180

Rooms: 12, including 1 suite; all with private bath.

Rates: $110 to $180, double occupancy, MAP and afternoon tea. Plus 22 percent gratuity and state tax. EPB rate available Tuesday and Wednesday, $60 to $120. Two-night minimum on weekends.

Open: All year.

Facilities and activities: Dinner Thursday through Monday. Public invited by reservation ($30). Pub, parlor with television, gift shop. Nearby: lake and shops of Lake Placid, hiking, downhill and cross-country skiing, horseback riding, Olympic sites, year-round sporting events, golf.

Recommended Country Inns® Travel Club Benefit: Stay two nights, get third night free, Monday–Thursday, subject to availability.

The Inn at Twin Linden
CHURCHTOWN, PENNSYLVANIA 17555

Our physical state of arrival—hot and exhausted—improved so swiftly that we wondered, did the outside world exist any longer? If it did, we'd forgotten, having stepped into the small world of the stone mansion inn. Bob had smiled in his direct, relaxed manner and led us up the stairs to our quarters. Along the way we admired his photographs of Italy, Ireland, Maine, and the farmlands surrounding Twin Linden. Sweet indulgence—the tenor of our visit—focused on the palate and the garden and matters of the heart. We could have been on a ship in the sea, contentedly marooned with a chef and photographer at the helm.

The inn is in Philadelphia's bread basket,

Lancaster County, where the rich farmland produces strawberries the size of a fist; vegetables are consumed within hours of picking; and choice meat, fowl, and fish can be had from a number of local purveyors. It's also convenient to Temple University, where Bob teaches photography.

Our suite was a study in light and grace with a comfortable sitting area; the Palladian window overlooked fields, a distant farm, and a low mountain range beyond. I concluded that winter here must be as cheering as the warm months. I envisioned myself perusing a book of photography, chardonnay in hand and woolen lap afghan in place, while toasting in front of our room's wood-burning stove and occasionally gazing outside at Mother Nature's frost finery.

Many of the rooms have handmade four-poster beds, which were delivered upon a horse-drawn sleigh. The walls are ivory with Colonial-green woodwork. Donna has added Laura Ashley quilts and handmade afghans, warm touches that beckon.

After a soak in the Jacuzzi in our room, we went to tea, which was served in the large foyer, where a three-tiered tray held luscious cookies and sweets. Some couples settled in the parlor, others at nearby tables, or on the patio, which overlooks the linden trees and garden—a small, spectacular affair of benches and bushes, flowers, and orna-mentals. Nearby are more benches for observing the fields beyond. We would come here later after dinner with our cordials to watch the soft summer breeze sway the corn and wish for a falling star.

Dinner was served in the Hunt Country Restaurant, where travelers in search of innova-tive, vibrant tastes savor Donna's creations. (The menu changes weekly.) It was elaborate. We began with summer asparagus tips with lemon and herbs in pastry, followed by Belgian endive with tortellini, pesto, and red peppers. For an entree I was presented the scrumptious grilled jumbo shrimp, served with fresh-roasted red pep-per coulis. My companion chose the jumbo sea scallops with a heavenly champagne and tar-ragon sauce, baked under a flaky, light pastry lid. For dessert the freshest of strawberries arrived with rich whipped cream.

We learned Donna was invited to cook at the prestigious James Beard House Restaurant in New York City, an engagement offered only to outstanding American chefs. Breakfast began with fruits, fresh-squeezed juice, and pastries; then came an elaborate cheese omelet.

This is a place for a coupling of minds and taste buds..

How to get there: From the Pennsylvania Turn-pike, take exit 22 (Morgantown) to Route 23 (less than 1/10 mile) and proceed west 4 miles into Churchtown. Inn is on the left, in the center of village.

Innkeepers: Bob and Donna Leahy
Address/Telephone: 2092 Main Street; (215) 445–7619
Rooms: 6; all with private bath.
Rates: $85 to $125, double occupancy; $200, suite; EPB.
Open: All year.
Facilities and activities: Dinner served Friday and Saturday ($16 to $22) by reservation. BYOB. Garden and gift shop. Nearby: The People's Place and Old Country Store in Intercourse, Railroad Museum in Strasbourg, country quilt shops, factory outlets, Artworks Complex, farmers' markets.

olive Metcalf

Gateway Lodge
COOKSBURG, PENNSYLVANIA 16217

The place captures you, instilling a sense of safety and comfort, and leaves you with recurring fantasies of being back in the lodge living room before the fire.

The lodge sits like an immense hillside sentinel near the gateway to 6,422-acre Cook Forest State Park, where hemlocks and white pines have grown steadily taller for the past two or three centuries. Reflecting the surrounding forest, massive logs shape the lodge's walls. The ceilings are of pine and hemlock, the walls of wormy chestnut; the flooring is oak. The mood is one of romantic warmth.

Anne Marie, a young woman on the staff with a pleasant demeanor, showed us the inn on

the way to our room. She paused before the smallest tavern with cozy dark woods and petite tables. Then we advanced to the game room, where afternoon tea would be served.

Next we entered the living room; a fire crackled in the stone fireplace while guests reposed in the warmth. A mother and daughter were letting their hair dry naturally after a swim in the inviting indoor pool. (Both the pool and sauna are heated with a wood-burning stove, which Joe built.)

Linda and Joe happened upon the lodge more than fifteen years ago and were so smitten they drove up and knocked on the front door. Built for vacation travelers in the 1930s, it was then a private home. The owners sold them the lodge several years later; they have kept it an intimate size.

At teatime, Linda pauses to visit and introduce everyone before the wood-burning stove, just as she did ten years ago, when I first ventured here. Then you help yourself to tea and delectable sweet bars and cookies. The place (or is it Linda?) seems to dissolve tension. The staff deserves special mention—each member is as soft-spoken, personable, and helpful as the next.

When we went to dinner in the dining room, the lanterns around the wooden tables were lit. We accidentally learned they are booked for New Year's Eve through the year 2002. "But we do nothing for New Year's; it's like every other night here, quiet, the fire blazing, dinner and wine by soft light in the woods," commented Joe. "That's why we love it," my companion responded, "because it's a time for peace and renewal. But you don't really need an official holiday to come for that."

We began dinner with a large, fresh salad laced with a delicious dressing. I chose a baked flounder amply stuffed with a spinach, crabmeat, and feta cheese filling. For dessert the Chocolate Lover's Delight was enormous and sinfully delicious.

At bedtime you climb the stairs (a slight creak here or there), insert the key, open the plain wooden door, and there it is: tiny, cozy, as snug as the handmade quilt on the bed and the print curtains on the latched windows. You undress and crawl into bed.

How to get there: From I–89, take Route 36 North. The inn is on the right just before the park. Fly-in, Clarion County Airport.

Innkeepers: Linda and Joseph Burney
Address/Telephone: Route 36 (mailing address: P.O. Box 125); (814) 744–8017; Pennsylvania only (800) 843–6862
Rooms: 22, plus 8 cabins; 11 with private bath.
Rates: Private bath: $100 to $120, double occupancy, EPB; $170 per couple, MAP. Shared bath: $90 to $110, double occupancy, EPB; $160 per couple, MAP. Cabins: $100 to $130, double occupancy, EP.
Open: All year except Thanksgiving and Christmas.
Facilities and activities: Dinner daily except Monday, reservations required; tea served daily. Tavern, indoor swimming pool for lodge guests (not cabin residents), gift shop. Nearby: theater, cross-country skiing, fishing, hunting, golfing, bicycling, canoeing and tubing on Clarion River, horseback riding, carriage and sleigh rides, 6,422-acre Cook State Park.

olive Metcalf

*G*lasbern

FOGELSVILLE, PENNSYLVANIA 18051-9743

Had we passed by chance, we'd have stopped and driven down the cobblestone lane, intent on discovering what purpose this visually compelling structure held for lovers on a happenstance excursion.

Beth Granger gave the inn its name, Glasbern, meaning "glass barn." It's a Pennsylvania-German barn architecturally transformed in 1985 by the Grangers to create a unique contemporary inn amid the serenity of a stream, a pond, and the romantic green hills of the countryside.

You enter the Great Room, the heart of the inn. Intact are the original haymow ladders. The beams in the vaulted ceiling are exposed, and the stone walls were cut open with a diamond-edged saw to let in the sunlight. The lighting reminded me of a cathedral designed by Le Corbusier I once visited in France. The Great Room is an elegant setting within a former hand-hewn "bank" barn.

The inn is a good place to commune together with nature. On a clear fall day, you can board a hot-air balloon that departs from the inn. Walk the inn's country paths. Travel to the nearby antiquing markets or the sights of Historic Bethlehem. Then return, this time perhaps on a winter's eve after a day of skiing, and ease into the whirlpool with the warmth of the nearby fireplace for total bliss. You may never leave the place.

The carriage-house suites have fireplaces

framed either in stone or barn-wood siding. In the corner suites, two-person whirlpools are surrounded by windows opening out to the countryside. The rooms are a blend of today's comforts, good lighting, and quality-built furnishings tastefully selected by Beth.

By evening guests gather in the Great Room, where you must reserve in advance, since the chef has a following. First you have a drink around the great stone fireplace. Once you're seated hot fresh breads are served with crispy salads. You might have ordered a New York strip brushed with olive oil and rosemary, then broiled; perhaps you selected a range chicken or Dover sole sautéed with country-style vegetables, tomatoes, herbs, and a reduced sweet cream and served with lemon angel-hair pasta. Later comes a light cheesecake soufflé coated with raspberry sauce. Some guests enjoy a liqueur upon returning to the stone fireplace or go for a walk under the stars around the pond.

Breakfast is served, in leisurely style, in the sunroom. That morning we ate whole-wheat pecan pancakes coated with maple syrup and thick slices of bacon. We felt recharged. And we noticed others looked that way, too. Was it the fresh air, the country walks, the fine meal, the whirlpool, and the fireplace? Or had someone anointed us with newfound energy and affection during the night?

How to get there: From I–78, take Route 100 North short distance to Tilghman Street and turn left. Go ⅓ mile and turn right on North Church Street; go ⁷⁄₁₀ mile and turn right on Pack House Road. The inn is ⁸⁄₁₀ mile on the right.

Innkeepers: Al and Beth Granger

Address/Telephone: 2141 Pack House Road, R.D. 1; (610) 285–4723

Rooms: 10, plus 13 suites; all with private bath, air conditioning, TV, VCR, and phone, 10 with fireplace, and 16 with whirlpool bath.

Rates: $100 to $115, double occupancy; $115 to $230, suite; EPB. Two-night minimum on certain weekends.

Open: All year.

Facilities and activities: Dinner nightly ($21 to $25 for entrees), service bar. Outdoor swimming pool, pond, hot-air balloon rides, 16 acres farmland. Nearby: Hawk Mountain Sanctuary, antiquing in Kutztown and Adamstown, ski Blue and Doe mountains, visit wineries, and tour Historic Bethlehem.

Olive Metcalf

The Whitehall Inn
NEW HOPE, PENNSYLVANIA 18938

Chocolate, you say; that and your lover are your not-so-secret addictions? There's no better place to indulge both at once.

Suella does for chocolate what Beethoven and others have done for music. Every April she and Mike host the chamber group from the Philadelphia Orchestra, who perform during Chocolate Lover's Getaway. She teases the appreciative nuances and lifts the spirits of gourmandizers through the palate. Every delicious morsel (even the tea) is chocolate. While those scents and sounds linger in your recent memory, the following morning consists of an entire chocolate breakfast.

"We are told by musicians," said Mike, "that the acoustics of our living room are like the small European chamber halls." I imagined the sounds: the harpist who plays on New Year's Eve and the Rondeau Players with their baroque music rippling through the inn in May.

While some come for the gala events of Candlelight Champagne New Year's Evening Concert, the Baroque Tea Concert, or Picnic Weekends, others prefer the quiet times. They enjoy the inviting waters of the swimming pool, seek a game of tennis, have a look at the thoroughbred horses, and are seen heading out the lane toward the country roads. You can also follow "inn-side" tips to mansions, art galleries, covered bridges, and antiques shops. You might get hooked by the puzzle that covers the table on the front porch. Or linger beside the fire in the great room, which is lined with bookshelves and musical instruments.

Rarely, I feel, should one arrive precisely on time—but never, ever arrive at Whitehall late. Tea is served at 4:00 P.M., and a relaxed 3:30 P.M. arrival is suitable. Later, you'll congratulate yourself.

Breakfast is served at 9:00 A.M. It begins with a secret blend of coffee and freshly squeezed orange juice. Two baskets soon appear: In the first is an artistic prizewinning ribbon cinnamon bread; another bears an immaculately light sourdough biscuit. Now taste the baked pear stuffed with golden raisins, walnuts, and lemon rind and coated with caramel sauce. You think you'll never eat another bite, but at the appearance of a gravity-defying soufflé with aromatic Buck's County sausage, your appetite sharpens anew. Handmade Whitehall chocolates are the vivacious finale. You feel like applauding.

The sunny rooms are attractively furnished with antiques and are expertly wallpapered.

Everywhere you turn are thoughtful details to captivate the heart. Robes, a bottle of good local wine, and other amenities contribute to the quality of the experience.

King Ferdinand of Spain so coveted chocolate when it first came to Europe that he kept it a secret by ordering to death anyone who let its existence become public knowledge. The king would rejoice here. Mike and Suella would treat him as they do everyone every day of the week—as gastronomic royalty.

How to get there: From New York City, take New Jersey Turnpike south to exit 10, Route 287 North for 15 miles to U.S. 22 West and U.S. 202 South. Take U.S. 202 South to Delaware River Bridge. Continue on U.S. 202 South toward Doylestown for 4⁶⁄₁₀ miles to Lahaska. Turn left on Street Road (past Jenny's Restaurant). Go to the third intersection and turn right on Stoney Hill. Turn left on Pineville Road. The inn is on the right, 500 yards.

Innkeepers: Mike and Suella Wass
Address/Telephone: Pineville Road (mailing address: R.D. 2, Box 250); (215) 598–7945
Rooms: 6; 4 with private bath, all with air conditioning, most with fireplace. No smoking inn.
Rates: $130 to $180, double occupancy, EPB and afternoon tea. Two-night minimum on weekends, 3-night minimum on holiday weekends.
Open: All year.
Facilities and activities: Swimming pool, tennis court. Nearby: restaurants, walking or biking country roads, James A. Michener Arts Center, art galleries of New Hope, Mercer Mansion in Doylestown, antiquing, historic sites.

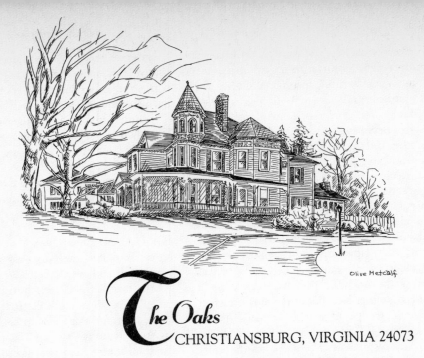

Olive Metcalf

The Oaks
CHRISTIANSBURG, VIRGINIA 24073

Propose your amorous purpose, then pack the Baccarat champagne flutes and flee.

The Oaks is named for seven ancient oak trees. Margaret and Tom have received a grant to preserve the trees with the help of experts from the America the Beautiful program. The oldest, a white oak, is estimated to be around four hundred years old and has the girth to match. Couples young and old have made this place their rapturous destination.

Exteriorwise, the inn is a Queen Anne Victorian, now painted buttercup yellow, which was designed by a New York architect in 1889 for Major W. L. Pierce and his wife and seven children. The original beauty of gleaming hardwood floors, stained glass, and trim is intact.

The bedrooms are oases of loving comfort. You might retreat fervently up to the third floor and select Lulu's Lair, painted in red and cream, or gallantly choose Lady Melodie's Turret, a skylit room with a king-sized canopy bed, gas fireplace, and sunset view. The inn has inviting common areas (which perhaps explains why the inn ended up in a PBS television special). On the wraparound porch are rocking chairs; the backyard patio has an enchanting garden and fish pond; there's a second-story sundeck; and indoors a sunroom with a fireplace, well stocked with books, games, and movies. The two of you will find your niche.

When at last you do depart from your charmed oasis for lunch or dinner, Margaret and Tom help you make a wise choice. They might suggest a romantic mountain vineyard where the vintner is also a French chef and the wine and dining are conducive to your mood.

One guest once asked, "Margaret, what's your philosophy of art?" It's more a response to beauty than a particular philosophy. Together the Rays select what inherently pleases them. As a result, there's a Joe King above the fireplace that's an evocative painting of the painter's wife; there are photographs by Darvish, and sculptures, and prints. "The human spirit needs the sensitivities of the arts," Margaret once said. And the affection of another soul mate.

Breakfast is served in a style conducive to conversation. The place mats are handmade lace, the china (inherited from Tom's grandmother) is Dresden, the coffeepot is an unusual heirloom, a silver-over-porcelain piece. You might receive a dish of curried eggs laced with shiitake mushrooms and wine sauce or a broccoli-lemon quiche and apricot and pumpkin tea bread or Southern buttermilk biscuits. Meats, if you wish, range from ginger-braised chicken to herbed sausages. One tends to linger over breakfast, because these are among the moments you'll recapture together.

How to get there: From I–81 take exit 114 to Roanoke Street, proceed 3 miles to East Main and turn right, go 1 mile to fork in road, and bear right on Park to The Oaks parking.

Innkeepers: Margaret and Tom Ray
Address/Telephone: 311 East Main Street; (703) 381–1500
Rooms: 6, plus 1 cottage; all with private bath, 1 with Jacuzzi and telephone.
Rate: $95 to $120, double occupancy, EPB. Add 5 percent for credit card use.
Open: All year.
Facilities and activities: Parlor, patio, hot tub. Nearby: 24 miles to Blue Ridge Parkway; Transportation Museum in Roanoke, antiquing, outlet shopping, Long Way Home Outdoor Drama.

The Bailiwick Inn
FAIRFAX, VIRGINIA 22030

We binged on pleasure. But who wouldn't?

In retrospect it was to be expected—a historical restoration of this caliber that caters to sweethearts with bewitching rooms and Virginia dining.

When we arrived, Ray opened the historic Federal brick building's large front door, painted in faux bois, and led us through the parlor, where the lush raspberry colors and Duncan Phyfe and Sheraton furnishings merged in the posh Colonial setting. We liked the way he laughed, slightly embarrassed at his and Anne's portraits above the fireplaces in the double parlors. These were gifts from the interior decorators, which were painted in the tradition of itinerant Colonial portrait painters, who prepared several canvases but left blank spaces for the heads. They'd travel to plantations, where they'd fill in the owners' faces.

Ray chatted his way through the dining room. He has an infectious smile and rosy cheeks: a bona fide innkeeper.

Dinner began with a chilled peanut soup and an appetizer of artichokes in beer batter with sweet mustard sauce. After a salad with mustard-honey dressing, we continued with seared tenderloin steak with smoked duck and Madeira wine sauce and roast pheasant with a cherry sauce. Every taste was informed by the finest of Vigonier wines.

Selecting a room for the night hadn't been easy; we liked them all. The Thomas Jefferson Room, with its private fireplace, has a desk chair similar to the one Jefferson used at Monticello. A huge, satiny mound of feather comforter tops each bed along with a bounty of pillows. The Lord Fairfax Room is furnished in English pieces styled after the Fairfax family castle in Leeds, with the family coat of arms on the wall. In the George Washington Room, you find a plethora of green, his favorite color, as well as a four-poster bed and darkly stained woods.

The dining room overlooks a small, bricked patio, where grapevines and espallier-twilled shrubs grow during summer. The building is a brick structure dating to 1830. The first skirmish of the Civil War occurred on Main Street on June 1, 1861, says a plaque outside.

For breakfast you are seated privately at a table overlooking the courtyard. Using a historical recipe modified for contemporary palates, Ray might prepare Robert E. Lee Eggs—an English muffin served with poached eggs laced with mushroom sauce along with Virginia ham. Or perhaps it will be a sausage-and-egg casserole or a crabmeat omelet.

We traveled here from an impressive distance—all of 17 miles—to reach the inn for a birthday celebration of my companion. Regardless of how far guests travel, they feel like they have arrived in another world, and a civilized one at that. They can't resist the lure of splendid cuisine and the knowledge that they will be pampered in such elegant surroundings.

The inn is only 17 miles from Washington, D.C., and its multitude of museums, gardens, and music. It is also within short walking distance of Fairfax's shops and restaurants and is positioned nicely between city and country.

How to get there: From I–66, take Route 123 East toward George Mason University. It's 1½ miles to the inn, which is opposite the old courthouse. Off-street parking behind the inn.

Innkeepers: Anne and Ray Smith

Address/Telephone: 4023 Chain Bridge Road; (703) 691–2266 or (800) 366–7666

Rooms: 14, including 1 suite; all with private bath and air conditioning, 4 with fireplace, 2 with whirlpool bath. Wheelchair access. No smoking inn.

Rates: $130 to $180, double occupancy; $275, suite; EPB and afternoon tea.

Open: All year.

Facilities and activities: Serve dinner nightly, except Monday and Tuesday, by reservation. Nearby: restaurants (within walking distance), Washington, D.C. (17 miles), Manassas Civil War Park, George Mason University, Mount Vernon, swimming, golf, tennis, historic sites.

Recommended Country Inns® Travel Club Benefit: 25% discount, subject to availability.

Olive Metcalf

Brookside Bed and Breakfast
MILLWOOD, VIRGINIA 22646

We found this Virginia landscape particularly endearing. The rush of millrace water sounds across the shamrock green lawn, shaded by trees in the inn's parklike setting. From its source—Burwell Spout Run—the water ripples to the eighteenth-century Burwell Mill. The inn is situated on a rise overlooking the mill. You motor across the stream to reach the inn, and as you traverse the slate steps, you pass the remains of an archeological dig where Civil War pottery chards, buckles, and other pieces appear whenever earth is moved.

Brookside Inn, which dates from 1780, is one of the most romantic Colonial restorations I've ever seen. The Konkels' liberal historical interpretation includes authentic antiques and contemporary conveniences—quality mattresses are mounded with featherbeds. There's a fireplace in every room—parlor, dining room, and bedrooms. The beds have canopies, and there is a custom-made queen-sized cabinet bed, adapted to today's size preferences. The walls are bone white, and the floors are stained a deep sienna. A short distance from the inn is a private cottage with a fireplace and small kitchen. Spending a week together here is my idea of heaven.

Down a path you find the innkeepers' antiques shop, one of several in Millwood, a wisp of a Shenandoah village. In addition to the shops, this hamlet has one country store, a few residences, and the historic Burwell-Morgan Mill, which is open May through October, Wednesday through Saturday. Built in 1782, the gristmill was fully operational until 1953. Now members of the Clarke County Historical Association give tours and grind flour and grains for sale.

We arrived on a beautiful spring day and had already toured the antiques shops and walked the nearby Virginia State Arboretum. We also visited Sky Meadows State Park. Carol was right when she noted that there are too many things to do in this rich countryside. The inn is also a convenient base for horseback riding, winery tours, and going to country places for dinner.

We didn't have time to visit Long Branch Mansion or the Trappist monastery, Holy Cross Abbey, where you can attend vespers and purchase breads and fruitcakes. The annual quilt fair in nearby Berryville would also have to await a future trip. Matters of the heart came first.

Breakfast is served on small wooden tables; in the center of the room is a chandelier filled with white candles. Gary is the inn's chef. His specialties include a fruit-preserve-filled French bread that arrives hot and delicious on a flower-garnished plate. The silver napkin rings are placed in a wall basket after breakfast. Then everyone busily packs, and you understand why Carol says her guests rarely take time to visit in the parlor. The rooms with their fireplaces are each an invitation to dalliance.

How to get there: From Washington, D.C., take I–6 West to exit 23: Route 17 North. Continue 60 miles to blinking light at Route 50. Turn left, and after you cross the Shenandoah River, take second right on Route 723. Go 1¼ miles to Millwood and when you see the mill, turn left into parking lot, cross stream, and park.

Innkeepers: Carol and Gary Konkel
Address/Telephone: Route 723; (703) 837–1780
Rooms: 4, plus 1 cottage; all with private bath, fireplace, and air conditioning.
Rates: $95 to $140, double occupancy, EPB.
Open: All year.
Facilities and activities: Nearby: antiques shopping, horseback riding, bicycling, hiking on Appalachian trail, fox hunting, wineries, Holy Cross Abbey, Virginia State Arboretum, Long Branch mansion, annual quilt show (in Berryville).

The Page House Inn
NORFOLK, VIRGINIA 23507

"Champagne tastes and jogging shoes," my lover said as Stephanie, wearing an attractive warm-up suit, swung open a highly polished oak door to an elegant foyer. We beheld other guests in the formal dining room; they were laughing, sipping cappuccino, and savoring the cookies. We couldn't believe our good fortune at finding The Page House in Ghent—Norfolk's prestigious historic neighborhood. It is within walking distance of the Chrysler Museum, the opera, and the Hague, a tranquil canal where boats lie at anchor year-round.

We'd come back to the neighborhood where we lived the first year of our marriage. This was an anniversary excursion.

Stephanie introduced us to a pair of small black-and-white boxers named Charlie and Tootsie, who went off to their private lodging while we followed her up the wide oak stairway. She presented to us a "definitive" honeymoon suite. We admired the boldly printed wallpaper and window furnishings and the canopied bed with its antique handmade spread and coverlets. We had hardly caught our collective breath when Stephanie opened the door to the commodious sitting room with love seat and bay windows. Here, as in the other rooms of the inn, were lovely antiques.

Returning down the stairs, Stephanie pointed to a basket full of goodies for guests, should momentary hunger strike at any time of the day. A collection of games, books, and magazines were organized beside a rocking chair.

We walked the old, familiar streets; had lunch in a former church that had become a restaurant; booked a seat at the Opera House, which is a five-minute stroll from the inn; and explored our old favorite places.

Stephanie named the inn for Herman L. Page, the mover who first laid out and developed the Ghent area in the late 1800s. But Stephanie is a mover and shaker in her own right. She had to break through the town's codes, prohibiting a historical bed and breakfast, to create her first-class, award-winning restoration. With Ezio, her Italian woodworking husband, she renovated the Georgian Revival mansion.

Next morning, we rose early for a breakfast of perfectly textured scones and fruit jams, home-made granolas, and bagels, served in the dining room. Just as we finished, a honeymoon couple descended. We wished them a happy marriage, knowing they'd chosen wisely to begin their life and the first age—for love has ages—by lodging here.

How to get there: From I–63 East or West take exit for I–264 (toward downtown Norfolk) and follow signs (staying in left lane) to Waterside Drive. Continue on Waterside Drive, which curves and becomes Boush Street. Turn left on Olney Street (after Grace Street). Turn left on Mowbray Arch, go 1 block to Fairfax Avenue, and turn right. Inn is on the left; park behind.

Innkeeper: Stephanie DeBelardino
Address/Telephone: 323 Fairfax Avenue; (804) 625–5033
Rooms: 4, plus 3 suites; all with private bath, 2 with fireplace, 1 with whirlpool bath.
Rates: $75 to $120, double occupancy; $135 to $195, suite; continental breakfast and afternoon refreshments.
Open: All year.
Facilities and activities: Smoking allowed only on porches. Nearby: Chrysler Museum; Virginia Opera, Symphony, and Stage Company; Naval Base Tour; Hampton Roads Naval Museum; Mariner's Museum; Harbor and Sailing Tours; Virginia Beach.
Recommended Country Inns® Travel Club Benefit: 10 discount, two night minimum, subject to availability.

Olive Metcalf

Cheat Mountain Club
DURBIN, WEST VIRGINIA 26264

We care not the season when we come here, since the inherent beauty of Appalachian pine forest, river, and mountain sunsets dons each seasonal mantle as smoothly as a queen her cape and crown.

Our first impression is no less vivid for the lapse of time. We arrived on a hot summer's day amid the lustrous green space and tall trees that surround the inn, then heard the Shavers Fork River tumbling coolly over rocks. We had lunch on the patio, lazing in deep wooden chairs and eating hearty sandwiches, pasta salad, and large chocolate brownies. We had come for a nature lover's holiday in a mountain lodge.

If you come in spring, summer, or fall, the hiking and mountain biking is endless: The inn's acreage is contiguous with the 900,000-acre Monongahela National Forest. On a recent visit, though, we'd come to witness the wintery scape. Within minutes of arrival we were clipped into skis and moving upriver. Along the trail the rhododendron stood as tall as 15 feet. Once, while we rested, we listened to cracking river ice and heard a woodpecker hammering; we watched as wood flecks fell from his 60-foot-high perch. We rested at times and absorbed the beauty and peace and time alone together in the woods.

Back at the lodge, a fire was burning in the great room's stone fireplace, and several guests were visiting. The lodge was built of spruce and pine one hundred years ago by a German fish biologist. It's located at 3,600 feet, where the climate is reminiscent of Canada. The rooms have pine walls and maple furnishings; they are quite comfortable. Most share the large, clean, health-club-style men's and women's bathrooms. Request the room with the queen-sized bed.

In summer you might take the canoes on the Shavers Fork for a lazy afternoon, go for a walk hand-in-hand along the river to the old fort embankments, or take a fly-fishing lesson together. Jack is a licensed hunting and fishing guide, and fishing is his passion.

At dinner time we joined other couples, which led to stories of how we'd met and married. Upon white linen table cloths were arrayed delicious foods, such as the chicken with marsala-wine sauce that came with fresh vegetables and breads—which fragrantly scented the inn while baking. Near the honor bar Libbo

stocked fresh fruits, cookies, and granolas for between-meal snacks. For lovers who are planning to spend the day in the woods, she packs scrumptious lunches. The single-entree dining means the freshest of everything is expertly prepared. In the summer they often grill steaks and chicken, and occasionally ribs outdoors. Breakfast specialties include buckwheat pancakes and a wonderful sausage grilled on a large coal- and wood-burning stove.

The naturalist John Burroughs once gathered Thomas Edison, Henry Ford, and Harvey Firestone for a caravan trip here back in 1918. They called themselves the vagabonds, but they missed the point.

How to get there: From the intersection of Route 250 and Route 92 near Monterrey, proceed 12½ miles north on Route 250 to the inn sign on the left. The inn is about 2 miles from the first sign.

Innkeepers: Jack Jackson and Libbo Talbott
Address/Telephone: Route 250 (mailing address: P. O. Box 28); (304) 456–4627
Rooms: 8, including 1 suite; 1 with private bath, all with sink.
Rates: $79 to $109, per person, double occupancy, AP. No credit cards; checks accepted.
Open: All year.
Facilities and activities: Public is served by reservation (lunch, $7 to $10; dinner, $18 to $20). 180 acres; located on Shavers Fork River. Service bar. Mountain bikes, cross-country skis, canoes, Funyaks, and fishing equipment available; badminton, hiking trails, and cross-country trails, birding.

The South

by Sara Pitzer

What's more romantic—a starry evening watching boats on the Mississippi River or a night in an elegant suite in Georgia with real gold fixtures in the bath? You can't really answer for anyone but yourselves because places aren't romantic—people are. It's what you bring to an inn that makes it romantic: your personal taste, your ideas of pleasure. A romantic getaway is to share the pleasures you enjoy most with someone special in a way that lets you be together at your best.

My parents took a two-week camping-canoe trip down the Delaware River on their honeymoon. It was, they've always assured me, truly romantic. (And that's before insect repellent was invented!) My own memorable romantic time was a vacation my husband and I took years ago, staying in an inexpensive room with shared bath, getting dressed to the nines, and eating outrageously expensive dinners in a gourmet restaurant every night. At the end of each meal, we'd sip our liqueurs and sigh with pleasure.

If romance means being in special places, you almost can't go wrong in good Southern inns. Each one offers pleasures you just don't find everywhere. To choose well, all you need do is reflect on what appeals to you. Seclusion? How about Little St. Simons Island? Opulence? Maybe the Gastonian. Casual accommodations on top of a mountain from where you see no other man-made structures? Hickory Nut Gap Inn. Gourmet food, lots of privacy, museum-quality art and antiques, city pleasures, unspoiled nature—you can find it all in Southern inns.

Each of the twenty inns I've described differs conspicuously from the others. I've explained what's special about each place. Those that sound like they'd make *you* feel good will make you feel romantic, too. I promise.

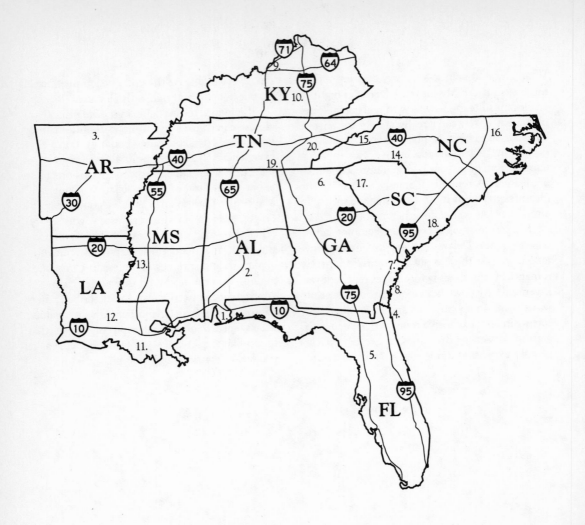

The South

Numbers on map refer to towns numbered below.

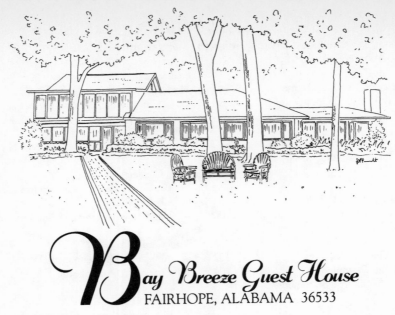

Bay Breeze Guest House
FAIRHOPE, ALABAMA 36533

Here is a place romantically secluded yet close to everything you could want for fun.

The inn sits on a three-acre site right on the shores of Mobile Bay. The grounds are filled with mature shrubs and trees that give you a feeling of being in the woods. The stucco building was built in the 1930s and has been variously remodeled and enlarged over the years to accommodate the family's changing needs. It works beautifully as an inn.

The entire downstairs—a sitting room with fireplace, glassed-porch bay room, living room, and kitchen—is devoted to guests. (The Joneses have private quarters upstairs.) Most of the furnishings in the main house are family heirlooms going back as far as five generations. The mix of wicker, stained glass, and hooked and oriental rugs produces a romantic feel no designer could duplicate. "And everything has a story," Becky says.

For perfect privacy, try one of the cottage suites. They have pickled white-pine walls, old brick floors, vaulted ceilings, and lots of generously sized windows. One of these cottages is well equipped for the handicapped, with wide spaces to accommodate a wheelchair, grab bars in the proper places in the bathrooms, and flexible shower wands. The cottages are decorated with just the right combination of antiques, oriental rugs, new sofas, and good beds. You feel comfortable but not overwhelmed with stuff. Becky has been careful to keep the suites light and spacious. Staying in one of these is a lot like playing house—but without the responsibility, because Becky takes care of everything.

As a hostess, she knows how to find out what you like and provides it without apparent effort: a special jelly, a particular bread or coffee or drink. And if you come back again, she'll remember what you liked and have it ready for you.

How to get there: From I–10 take U.S. Highway 98 toward Fairhope and exit right onto Scenic/Alternate Highway 98 at the WELCOME TO FAIRHOPE sign. At the third traffic light, turn right onto Magnolia Avenue. Go 4 blocks and turn left on South Mobile Street at the municipal pier. Bay Breeze Guest House is about a mile farther, on the right.

Innkeepers: Bill and Becky Jones
Address/Telephone: 742 South Mobile Street (mailing address: P.O. Box 526); (205) 928–8976
Rooms: 2 in main house, plus 2 cottage suites; all with private bath and TV, cottage suites with phone, small kitchen, and wheelchair access. Third room available in main house for large parties. No smoking inn.
Rates: $85, single or double; $95, suites; EPB in main house, continental breakfast in suites.
Open: All year.
Facilities and activities: Private pier, decks, and beach on Mobile Bay. Nearby: walking distance to downtown historic Fairhope, restaurants, and shops.

Red Bluff Cottage
MONTGOMERY, ALABAMA 36101

You enjoy a wonderfully romantic sense of privacy at Red Bluff Cottage without giving up the opportunity to spend time with other guests when you feel like it. The guest rooms are all on the ground floor, with the kitchen, dining room, living room, den, and music room on the second floor, which makes the guest rooms quiet and the public rooms exceptionally light and airy, looking out over the yard and gardens.

The flower gardens are an important part of Red Bluff Cottage; guest rooms are filled with fresh flowers, and seasonal blooms adorn the breakfast table. Anne has been a passionate gardener for years, an especially rewarding activity in Montgomery's climate where it's moist and

warm most of the year. When I visited, her border, full of intertwined patches of pink, white, yellow, and blue, looked like Monet's garden.

The Waldos' personal passions influence the look of the rooms inside the inn as well. In the music room, a harpsichord, a piano, and a recorder testify to the talent in the family—no guarantee that you'll hear a little concert during your stay, but it does happen.

In the guest rooms, you see furniture that's been in the family for years: the bed Anne slept in as a child, an antique sleigh bed that was her great-great-grandmother's, a spread crocheted by Mark's grandmother, and an old leather trunk from his great-aunt in Wisconsin, which contained invitations to firemen's balls dated 1850.

But artifacts of family past don't mean much unless you enjoy the present family. I enjoyed these people and the sense of old-fashioned love they communicate tremendously. Mark was the rector of an Episcopal parish in Montgomery for almost thirty years. During these years, the Waldos raised six children, all of whom keep in touch regularly. They have funny tales of those tumultuous times.

After Mark's retirement, the Waldos became innkeepers because they wanted to keep new people coming into their lives. Where better to discover romance than under the roof of people who love flowers and books and music and can raise six kids and still be enthusiastic about taking in more of the human race?

How to get there: Take exit 172 off I–65. Go toward downtown (east) on Herron Street 1 block. Turn left on Hanrick Street. Parking is on the right off Hanrick by the inn's rear entrance.

Innkeepers: Anne and Mark Waldo
Address/Telephone: 551 Clay Street (mailing address: P.O. Box 1026); (205) 264–0056
Rooms: 4, plus 1 children's room; all but children's room with private bath, television on
request. No smoking inn.
Rates: $55 to $65, double, EPB. No credit cards.
Open: All year.
Facilities and activities: Guest refrigerator and coffee maker, children's fenced-in play yard,
gazebo. Nearby: restaurants, Alabama State Capitol, historic sites, Jasmine Hill
Gardens, Montgomery Museum of Fine Arts, Alabama Shakespeare Festival
Theatre.
Recommended Country Inns® Travel Club Benefit: Stay two nights, get third night free,
subject to availability.

Dairy Hollow House: Century Inn and Restaurant
EUREKA SPRINGS, ARKANSAS 72632

We use the word "unique" sparingly, because so few things really are. But Dairy Hollow House *is* a uniquely romantic experience and has been since the moment Crescent and Ned (who've maintained an obvious longtime romance of their own) set their hands to creating this inn.

Dairy Hollow House started as a restored Ozark farmhouse painted a creamy peach and trimmed in deep teal. It has grown to include a second building that is now the main house, where three suites, the restaurant, and a central, front-desk check-in area are housed.

We slept in the Iris Room, which got its name from the predominant color of its decor.

The blue quilts on the beds are handmade. The window blinds are woven in shades of blue from fabrics Crescent chose to coordinate with the quilt.

Every room and suite has a fireplace trimmed in local "Eureka limestone." The recently renovated Main House is decorated as the original Farmhouse is, with antiques, fresh flowers, and eye-catching colors, including a turquoise that sounds unlikely until you see how well it works.

You haven't had the full Dairy Hollow experience unless you have dinner in the restaurant. The food is fresh and regional, but regional with a contemporary twist. Crescent and Ned call it Nouveau 'Zarks. They received an Inn of Distinction award from Uncle Ben's Rice for being named a Top Ten Country Inn three years running.

So many people asked for Crescent's unusual recipes that she and a cooking colleague wrote the *Dairy Hollow House Cookbook*, with more than four hundred recipes and a lot of commentary about Eureka Springs. And the *Dairy Hollow House Soup and Bread Cookbook* has come out. What better way to bring back some romantic moments later than by re-creating some of the Dairy Hollow House specialties at home?

How to get there: Starting from the historic downtown area of Eureka Springs, take the old historic loop (old 62B, Spring Street) past the post office and all the other houses. Go just over 1 mile to where Spring Street curves sharply toward the original inn. The main house, where guests check in, is at the intersection of Spring Street and Dairy Hollow Road.

Innkeepers: Crescent Dragonwagon and Ned Shank
Address/Telephone: 515 Spring Street; (501) 253–7444 or (800) 562–8650
Rooms: 3 in the Farmhouse, 3 suites in the Main House; all with private bath, 2 with Jacuzzi.
Rates: $125 to $175, double, EPB (breakfast delivered to rooms in a basket). Two-day minimum stay on weekends.
Open: All year.
Facilities and activities: Dinner at the Restaurant at Dairy Hollow (five nights a week in season; weekends only off-season) for guests and public. Reservations preferred, one seating nightly at 7:00 P.M., brown bagging permitted. Wheelchair access to restaurant. Fireplaces, 700-gallon outdoor hot tub. Nearby: restaurants; within walking distance of most Eureka Springs tourist attractions and historic sites.

The 1735 House
AMELIA ISLAND, FLORIDA 32034

So you'd like to sail away to a desert isle but you can't quite pull it off. Here's something almost as good. The 1735 House is a Cape Cod–style inn directly facing the ocean, furnished with antiques, wicker, and neat old trunks.

Maybe there will be no room at the inn, and you'll stay instead in the lighthouse. Its walls are covered with navigation maps. As you enter, you can either step down into a shower-and-bath area or take the spiral stairs up to the kitchen. A galley table and director's chairs make a good spot for playing cards, chatting, or ocean gazing, as well as eating. The stairs keep spiraling up to a bedroom with another bath, and finally up to an enclosed observation deck, which is the ultimate spot for romantic ocean gazing for two.

Wherever you stay, in the evening all you have to do is tell the staff what time you want breakfast and they'll deliver it right to your room in a wicker basket, along with a morning paper.

The physical setup is uncommon, but the staff have the true inn spirit. They'll give you ice, towels for the beach, bags for your shell collection or wet bathing suit, and just about anything else you need. All you have to do is ask.

The staff are full of helpful recommendations about good eating places, of which there are many on Amelia Island, too. The Down Under Seafood Restaurant, under the Shave bridge on A1A, is in keeping with the nautical mood of the inn and the lighthouse. The seafood is all fresh from the Intracoastal Waterway. There's a boat ramp with a dock, and the atmosphere is correspondingly quaint. You can enjoy cocktails and dinner.

If staying at The 1735 House gets you in the mood for more inns, you're welcome to browse through a large, well-used collection of books about inns in the office.

How to get there: Amelia Island is near the Florida/Georgia border. Take the Yulee exit from I–95 onto Route A1A and follow the signs toward Fernandina Beach. The inn is on A1A.

Innkeepers: Gary and Emily Grable

Address/Telephone: 584 South Fletcher; (904) 261–5878 or (800) 872–8531

Rooms: 5 suites, plus 1 suite in lighthouse; all with private bath and TV.

Rates: $75 to $125, double, continental breakfast.

Open: All year.

Facilities and activities: Cooking and laundry facilities, beachfront. Nearby: restaurants, downtown historic Fernandina Beach shopping and sightseeing, boating from the marina.

$\mathcal{C}$halet Suzanne
LAKE WALES, FLORIDA 33859

Chalet Suzanne epitomizes the fairy-tale version of romance.

Everyone who writes about the place falters under the burden of trying to describe what they've seen—a collection of whimsical, odd buildings asssembled over a number of years by Carl Hinshaw's mother, who got into innkeeping and the restaurant business trying to keep body and soul together after being widowed during the Great Depression. I've seen the words "Camelot," "phantasmagoria," "fairy tale," "magical," in the reviews of writers trying to capture the mood of the place. Any and all will do. Staying here is a great giggle for anyone who doesn't like too many straight lines, who enjoys walks and walls

that tilt, and who appreciates the kind of humor represented by a potted geranium atop the ice machine.

We liked in the Orchid Room, a roughly octagonal space where sherry and fruit were set out on a small table between two comfortable chairs. Live plants and fresh flowers were scattered throughout the room and its bath, and the furniture was painted various shades of aqua, cream, and deep orchid. The bath has black-and-gray tile and an improbable little bathtub of brick-colored ceramic tile as well as a shower and a blow dryer to tame your hair.

Chalet Suzanne is famous for its award-winning restaurant, in which the tables are all set with different kinds of china, silver, and glasses collected by the Hinshaws over years of travel. Carl's Romaine soup, Vita's broiled grapefruit garnished with chicken livers, and the shrimp curry are all much-extolled selections, so we tried them all with a nice house wine dispensed in generous servings. We enjoyed everything, including being served by waitresses in costumes that looked Swiss in the Swiss dining room, where European stained-glass windows provide a focal point.

A waitress told me that Carl Hinshaw's soups—which have become so popular that he started a cannery on the premises for people who want to take soup home—have made it to the better gourmet shops and even to the moon with the *Apollo* astronauts—not necessarily in that order.

So there you are, in a wacky, unreal environment, eating multistar-winning food that must be famous by now on the moon, served by waitresses dressed like Snow White, and you're sleeping in a room that looks as though it came out of a Seven-Dwarfs coloring book . . . Is that romantic or what?

How to get there: Chalet Suzanne is 4 miles north of Lake Wales on Highway 27. Signs clearly mark the turns.

Innkeepers: Carl and Vita Hinshaw
Address/Telephone: U.S. Highway 27 (mailing address: 3800 Chalet Suzanne Drive); (813) 676–6011; for reservations, (800) 433–6011
Rooms: 30; all with private bath, TV, and phone, 1 with Jacuzzi.
Rates: $125 to $185, double, EPB. Pets $20 extra.
Open: All year.
Facilities and activities: Lunch, dinner, wheelchair access to dining room. Cocktail lounge, wine cellar open for sampling, gift shop, antiques shop, ceramics studio, swimming pool, lake, soup cannery, air strip. Nearby: golf, tennis, fishing, Cypress Gardens, Bok Tower Gardens.

Glen-Ella Springs
CLARKSVILLE, GEORGIA 30523

I think I'm in love!

Usually country inns are elegant or they are rustic. This one-hundred-year-old place is both. The suites are beautifully finished and furnished with fireplaces; refinished pine floors, walls, and ceilings; local mountain-made rugs on the floors; whirlpool baths; and such niceties as fresh-cut pansies floating in crystal bowls. Some of the less-expensive rooms are simpler, though perfectly comfortable, with painted walls and showers in the bathrooms, but for a romantic interlude I can't think of anything more appealing than one of the suites in this old hotel in the country. Everything about the place invites pleasure.

The fireplace in the lobby is made of local stone, flanked with chintz-covered chairs.

An especially nice swimming pool, surrounded by an extra-wide sun deck that seems posh enough for any Hyatt hotel, overlooks a huge expanse of lawn that ends in woods.

The dining room is what I would call "subdued country," but there is nothing subdued about the food. It is simply spectacular—some of the best I've had anywhere in the South.

Because I sat with a large group for dinner, I had an opportunity to taste many more entrees and appetizers than ordinary. I remember scallops wrapped in bacon served in a light wine sauce; chicken livers in burgundy wine; fresh trout sautéed and then dressed with lime juice, fresh herbs, and toasted pecans; and halibut with Jamaican spices. I sampled desserts the same way and gave my vote to the homemade cheesecake.

The story here is that Barrie, a wonderful cook, had wanted a restaurant for a long time. But the Aycocks also wanted to work and live away from the city. They bought Glen-Ella even though the old hotel needed a tremendous amount of renovating.

They figured that here Barrie could have her restaurant, and since the inn was so far out in the country, lots of guests would spend the night. They do. And lots of other guests, who come for longer stays just to be in the country, enjoy the added pleasure of five-star quality food.

And now one more bragging point for Barrie and Bobby. The hotel has been added to the National Register of Historic Places.

How to get there: Go 8⁷⁄₁₀ miles north of Clarksville through Turnerville on U.S. Route 23/441. Turn left at the GLEN-ELLA sign on to New Liberty–Turnerville Road and continue for 1 mile to the next GLEN-ELLA sign at Bear Gap Road, which is a gravel road. Turn right. The inn is about 1½ miles on the left.

Innkeepers: Barrie and Bobby Aycock

Address/Telephone: Bear Gap Road, Route 3 (mailing address: Box 3304); (404) 754–7295 or (800) 552–3479

Rooms: 16 rooms and suites; all with private bath, some with fireplace and television, some with wheelchair access.

Rates: $75 to $135, double, continental breakfast and EPB Saturday. Inquire about discounts for weeknights and stays of more than 3 nights.

Open: All year.

Facilities and activities: Dining room, with wheelchair access, open to guests and public most days; reservations requested; available for private parties; brown bagging permitted. Gift shop. Swimming pool, 17 acres with nature trails along Panther Creek, herb and flower gardens, mineral springs, conference room. Located in northeast Georgia mountains near historic sites. Nearby: restaurants, golf, horseback riding, boating, rafting, tennis, hiking.

Recommended Country Inns® Travel Club Benefit: Stay two nights, get 50% off third night, Sunday–Thursday; or 10% discount, Sunday–Thursday.

The Gastonian
SAVANNAH, GEORGIA 31401

If you equate romance with opulence, have I got a place for you—The Gastonian! Often an inn of this opulence turns out to belong to absentee owners, or to a group of owners who hire a staff to run the place. A staff may be perfectly competent, but it's not the same as being in an inn with innkeepers who've poured their passion into the property. And that sure describes Hugh and Roberta.

It's not just passion they've poured in, but also money—a million and a half of their own and $900,000 of the bank's, Hugh says, calling it a poor investment but a "hell of a love affair."

How could you not love it? The inn comprises two 1868 historic buildings sitting side by side and a two-story carriage house, joined by a garden courtyard and an elevated walkway.

The guest rooms are filled with English antiques, exotic baths, Persian rugs, and fresh flowers. The most outrageous bath is in the Caracalla Suite (named for a Roman emperor); it has an 8-foot Jacuzzi, sitting on a parquet platform draped with filmy curtains, next to a working fireplace. The fixtures here are of solid brass. In another room, they are of sculptured 24-karat gold. Each bath is unique and styled to complement the theme of its room—French, Oriental, Victorian, Italianate, Colonial American, or Country. All the inn's water runs through a purification system, which means, Hugh says, that you have to go easy on the bubble bath.

The public rooms are equally lavish, furnished with English antiques, satin damask drapes, and Sheffield silver. This kind of thing can easily be intimidating, but not when you're under the same roof with the Linebergers, who figure that having raised five daughters, a history-laden inn is a retirement pushover and jolly good fun at that. And darned convincing romance, too.

How to get there: From I–95, take I–16 to Savannah. Take the Martin Luther King exit and go straight onto West Gaston Street. The inn is at the corner of East Gaston and Lincoln streets.

Innkeepers: Hugh and Roberta Lineberger

Address/Telephone: 220 East Gaston Street; (912) 232–2869 or (800) 322–6603, fax (912) 232–0710

Rooms: 11, plus 2 two-room suites; all with private bath, fireplace, TV, and phone, rooms with wheelchair access.

Rates: $117 to $275, double, full sit-down Southern breakfast or silver-service continental breakfast in your room, afternoon tea, and wine and fresh fruit on arrival.

Open: All year.

Facilities and activities: Sundeck, hot tub, off-street lighted parking, garden courtyard. Nearby: restaurants, carriage tours of historic district, Savannah Riverfront shops.

Little St. Simons Island
ST. SIMONS ISLAND, GEORGIA 31522

This is truly a special place. It is a 10,000-acre barrier island still in its natural state except for the few buildings needed to house and feed guests. You can get there only by boat.

When my husband and I visited, we felt welcomed as though we'd been visiting there for years. For us, the romance was in the sense of adventure and discovery of activities so different from our daily lives.

I still marvel at how much we did in a short time. The permanent staff includes three naturalists. One of the naturalists loaded us into a pickup truck and drove us around the island to help us get oriented. We walked through woods and open areas and along untouched ocean beaches. I saw my first armadillo. I gathered more sand dollars than I've ever seen in one place before. We saw deer, raccoons, opossums, and more birds than I could identify. Serious bird-watchers plan special trips to Little St. Simons to observe the spring and fall migrations.

We rode horseback with one of the naturalists. I was scared to death because I'd never been on a horse before, but they got me up on a mild-mannered old mare, and she plugged along slowly. By the end of the ride, I almost felt as though I knew what I was doing.

We canoed out through the creeks. When a big wind came up, I had a notion to be scared again, but the naturalist directed us into a sheltered spot where we could hold onto the rushes until the weather settled; then we paddled on.

When we weren't out exploring the island, we sat in front of the fire in the lodge, chatting with the other two guests and inspecting the photographs on the walls. They're standard hunting-camp pictures; rows of men grinning like idiots and holding up strings of fish, hunters with rifles grinning like idiots, and people climbing in and out of boats grinning like idiots.

One of the best meals we had while we were there was roast quail, served with rice pilaf and little yellow biscuits. As I polished off an unladylike-sized meal and finished my wine, I realized that *I* was grinning like an idiot.

How to get there: When you make your reservations, you will receive instructions on where to meet the boat that takes you to the island.

Innkeeper: Debbie McIntyre
Address/Telephone: St. Simons Island (mailing address: P.O. Box 21078); (912) 638–7472
Rooms: 2 in main lodge with private bath; 4 in River Lodge, all with private bath; 4 in Cedar House, all with private bath; 2 in Michael Cottage share bath.
Rates: $400, double, AP, wine with dinner, island activities, and ferry service. Minimum two-night stay. Inquire about longer-stay and off-season discounts.
Open: February 1 to November 15.
Facilities and activities: Bar in lodge; collection of books about native birds, plants, animals, and marine life; swimming pool, stables, horseshoes, ocean swimming, birding, naturalist-led explorations, beachcombing, shelling, fishing, canoeing, hiking.

Inn at the Park
LOUISVILLE, KENTUCKY 40208

Combine a truly professional innkeeper with a fabulous old mansion in a nice part of one of the best cities in the South, and you've got sophisticated romance.

Theresa Schuller has had a lot of experience in the hospitality business, working in inns, hotels, and restaurants. When her husband, Bob Carskie, came to Louisville as football coach at the university, Theresa found an 1886 mansion with Richardsonian Romanesque architecture. It has 10,000 square feet of space, hardwood floors, 14-foot ceilings, marble fireplaces, crown moldings, second- and third-floor stone balconies, and an absolutely *awesome* staircase. It's the kind you expect Scarlett, nipped at the waist, flounced,

and hoop-skirted, to come sweeping down.

And the mansion had just been restored in 1985; it looks as it would have when it was new. What's more, it is right by Central Park in the historic district, Old Louisville.

And now it's a delight, a professionally run inn with the comforts of someplace more ritzy than home and breakfasts that guests consistently say are the best they've had anywhere.

Theresa gives you a menu. You choose, then she whips up omelets, Belgian waffles, or shirred eggs, or a yogurt smoothie—on the spot. If you let her know ahead of time, she can accommodate dietary restrictions and the idiosyncrasies of your taste beyond the menu.

Even people who have not learned to stay at inns, especially men who are leery of finding too many frills, like it here—not just because of breakfast, either. With a resident football coach on the scene, you can get into lots of sports talk. Maybe that's not romantic to everybody, but it could be the perfect lure for a partner who likes to get away without losing track of the scores.

But don't get the idea that sports dominate the scene here. In Central Park you can enjoy more cultural activities, such as the Shakespeare in the Park productions. And you can indulge in all the delights of a culturally active city.

How to get there: From I–65, take exit 135A onto West St. Catherine Street. Drive west to Fourth Street and turn left. Go 3 blocks. The inn is the park at the corner of Fourth and Park streets.

Innkeeper: Theresa Schuller

Address/Telephone: 1332 South Fourth Street; (502) 637–6930 or (800) 700–PARK

Rooms: 6; 4 with private bath, all with TV and phone. No-smoking rooms available.

Rates: $65 to $135, double, EPB.

Open: All year.

Facilities and activities: Located in Old Louisville neighborhood near Central Park and 15 minutes from downtown Louisville. Nearby: walking distance to restaurants; University of Louisville; Bellarmine and Spalding colleges; Louisville Zoo; antiques shops on Bardstown Road; Ohio River Cruises on the historic Belle of Louisville sternwheeler.

Recommended Country Inns® Travel Club Benefit: Stay two nights, get third night free, subject to availability.

Shepherd Place
VERSAILLES, KENTUCKY 40383

On five rural acres in the middle of Bluegrass Country, the Yawns keep fifteen sheep. Don't go thinking lamb chops, though; you'd have it all wrong. These sheep are for guests to enjoy watching and petting, for shearing, and for loving. Their wool, as far as Sylvia is concerned, is for spinning and knitting. She shears the sheep only once a year, even though twice a year is possible, so that the wool will be longer and more suited to her handcrafts.

Imagine an interlude in a rural inn with only two guest rooms, where the innkeepers indulge their love of crafts and color and caring by lavishing it on their guests. If romance is caring, this is it.

In busy times you might have to wait to book a night at the inn, too, but the experience is worth the wait.

To give you an idea, an old-fashioned swing sways on the porch. The downstairs parlor once had French doors. These have been converted to floor-to-ceiling windows that let in a glorious amount of light. The light is picked up by 12-inch-high baseboards painted white. Spice-brown walls keep the overall effect from being glaring. Queen Anne–style chairs are set off by formal English sofa lamps, and a red-and-blue oriental rug unifies all the room's elements.

The guest rooms are uncommonly large, 20 feet by 20 feet, with bathroom facilities fitted into alcove rooms in their corners.

As pleasing as all this is, the real kick comes from Sylvia's pleasure with it all. In every way she's thrilled with being an innkeeper in her old Kentucky home. She's proud of the smooth gleam of interior paint Marlin (who used to be a professional painter) has accomplished. She enjoys cooking huge breakfasts, which often include Kentucky ham and such delicacies as whole-wheat pancakes with walnuts. She loves the sheep and working with their wool. And, most significant of all, she enjoys the guests. "We get such *good* guests. We have a bulletin board full of cards and letters they send after they've been here," she said. "This is all even neater than I thought it would be. It's a real blessing."

How to get there: Coming from Knoxville on I–75, take exit 104 onto the Lexington Circle; from Cincinnati, take exit 115. From the Lexington Circle take exit 5B onto U.S. 60. Drive 6 miles to Heritage Road and turn left. The inn is at the corner of U.S. 60 and Heritage Road.

Innkeepers: Marlin and Sylvia Yawn
Address/Telephone: 31 Heritage Road; (606) 873–7843
Rooms: 2; both with private bath, TV available on request. No smoking inside.
Rates: $60, double, EPB.
Open: All year.
Facilities and activities: Pond with ducks and geese. Nearby: restaurants, Lexington, Shakertown.

Madewood

NAPOLEONVILLE, LOUISIANA 70390

Well, fiddle-de-dee, Scarlett would love it here. I know, she was from Atlanta, but she would have loved it here. This is a Rhett-and-Scarlett kind of place, an 1844 Greek Revival mansion with six white columns. Irises grow around the sides of the porches; you can see fields in each direction; pear trees on the property produce fruit for the inn; and the parking area is shaded by established old trees.

The mansion itself is filled with antiques, oriental rugs, and crystal chandeliers, and it has recently been painted and completely refurbished. It is considered one of the important old mansions of Louisiana, with marble fireplaces, a richly carved, unsupported stairway, and elabo-

rate Corinthian and Ionic columns. But Madewood still feels like a home rather than a museum.

Upstairs, one room has been preserved as a dressing room–bathroom, complete with an old scoop-shaped metal bathtub that would have had to be filled and emptied with a bucket. It makes you appreciate the modern bathrooms now available to guests.

And old clothes are displayed in some of the tour bedrooms, laid out and hanging as though someone were just about to put them on.

Be sure you arrange to have Thelma cook dinner for you. She's one of those cooks who can tell you exactly what's in a dish—she just can't give you exact amounts. She stirs things until they "feel right" and cooks them until they "look right." Her menu includes chicken pies and shrimp pies, gumbos, corn bread, green beans, bread pudding, and Pumpkin Lafourche. This is a casserole of apples, raisins, pumpkin, sugar, butter, nutmeg, cinnamon, and vanilla, and don't ask in what proportions or for how long or at what temperature Thelma bakes it. Just enjoy.

As for all that richness and all those calories—fiddle-de-dee, think about it tomorrow!

How to get there: From I–10, take exit 182, cross Sunshine Bridge, and follow Bayou Plantation signs to Highway 70, Spur 70, and Highway 308. The inn faces the highway.

Innkeepers: Keith and Millie Marshall

Address/Telephone: 4250 Highway 308; (504) 369–7151; for reservations, call 10:00 A.M. to 5:00 P.M. weekdays

Rooms: 5 in mansion, 1 cabin and 3 suites in the Charlet House; all with private bath, some with wheelchair access. Inquire about pets.

Rates: $165, double, MAP.

Open: All year except Christmas Eve, New Year's Eve and Day, and Thanksgiving Eve and Day.

Facilities and activities: Nearby: Mississippi River tour boats and tours of plantation homes.

Barrow House
ST. FRANCISVILLE, LOUISIANA 70775

When you have an urge to get away with someone special to enjoy some really spectacular food without having to drive to a hotel after dinner, The Barrow House calls. Listen to this: crawfish salad, Chicken Bayou La Fourche (stuffed with crabmeat), Jambalaya Rice, Pecan Praline Parfait. Served on good china with sterling silver flatware by candlelight on a flower-decorated table in the formal dining room, under the old punkah "shoo fly" fan. Oh, be still my heart!

I can tell you lots more about Barrow House, and I'll get to it, but how can Louisiana food like that, served with such style, come anywhere but first? You have to arrange for such dinners ahead of time, and you select from a number of different possibilities for each course.

"We want people to have a good time here," Shirley said. And they do. Beyond the food there's the house, an 1809 saltbox with a Greek Revival wing added in the 1860s, that's listed on the National Register of Historic Places and furnished with 1860s antiques.

The gorgeous antiques include a rosewood armoire by Prudent Mallard and a queen-sized Mallard bed with a *Spanish moss* mattress. You don't have to sleep in that bed unless you want to, but one man, a doctor with a bad back, said it was the most comfortable bed he'd ever had.

Spanish moss was the traditional mattress filler used in Louisiana for two hundred years.

The Dittloffs' informal tour of the house gives you a chance to learn how the mattress was made and to see all the fine antiques.

Similarly, the professionally recorded Historic District walking tour (with Mozart between stops) the Dittloffs wrote guides you from Barrow House to twenty-three historic stops.

The Dittloffs' inn came to my attention partly through a magazine article on inns in the magazine *Louisiana Life*. Barrow House was included in the article because when a magazine staffer was married in St. Francisville, she dressed for the wedding at Barrow House. By the time she drove off, everybody who should have was crying properly, and Shirley was carrying the bride's train. Shirley was crying, too.

Some people don't want too much personal fuss. Shirley says that she and Lyle have learned to know when guests would rather be left alone. You'll get whatever amount of attention you want—no more.

How to get there: Barrow House is behind the courthouse in the St. Francisville Historic District. You will receive a map after you make reservations.

Innkeepers: Shirley and Lyle Dittloff
Address/Telephone: 524 Royal Street (mailing address: P.O. Box 1461); (504) 635–4791
Rooms: 3, plus 1 suite; all with private bath and TV, phone on request.
Rates: $85 to $90, double; $100 to $115, suite; continental breakfast, wine, and cassette walking tour of Historic District. Full breakfast available at $5 extra per person. Cash and personal checks only.
Open: All year except December 22–25.
Facilities and activities: Dinner for guests by advance reservation. Located in St. Francisville Historic District. Nearby: tour plantations and historic sites.
Recommended Country Inns® Travel Club Benefit: 10% discount, Monday–Thursday.

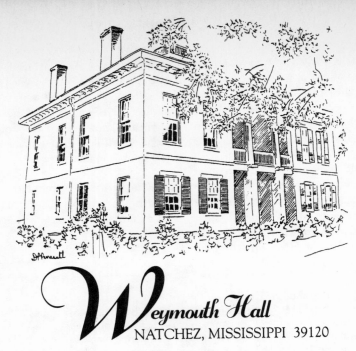

Weymouth Hall
NATCHEZ, MISSISSIPPI 39120

Remember the old notion of lovers' lane? You sit on a hill overlooking the river, head-to-head, holding hands and whispering secrets as the sun sets and the stars come out a few at a time. If the river happens to be the Mississippi and you stay at Weymouth Hall, which happens to sit atop the hill, you have not just romance, but Romance.

Gene calls Weymouth Hall a "gem of Natchez" because of its unique architecture and fine millwork and bridge work, and, most of all, because of its spectacular view of the Mississippi River. Even before we had looked around inside, Gene showed me the backyard of the inn, where guests can sit in the evening to watch the sun set

and the lights come on along the river. "When you've got a view like this, who cares about the house?" he said.

That's a deceptive line. I've never met an innkeeper more involved with the restoration and furnishing of a building than Gene. His collection of antiques by John Belter, Charles Baudoine, and Prudent Mallard is so impressive that even other innkeepers talk about it. The rococo furniture in the double parlor looks as though it had been bought new as a set and kept intact ever since, but Gene spent a lot of time assembling it from wherever he could find it, a piece at a time.

It's worth mentioning that at Weymouth

Hall all the guest rooms (which have showers in the private baths) are in the house, not in adjacent buildings or added wings as is the case with some of the larger tour homes. And breakfast is served at a Mississippi plantation table in the main dining room. Gene says that in conversations many guests have said that "living" in the house is important to them.

On a more frivolous note, Gene keeps a player piano from the 1920s, partly to reflect his sense that the inn should be fun, not a museum.

Nor does Gene's involvement stop with the inn and its furnishings. He knows how to entertain guests. He knows the area well and likes to take guests on little personal tours of outstanding old homes in the area. Some guests find these tours more interesting and less expensive than the larger commercial ones available.

You may decide not to leave the property for any kind of tour, however, once you take in the view of the Mississippi River from Weymouth Hall's backyard. It's unquestionably one of the best vistas in Natchez. And the grounds keep getting more pleasing as the shrubbery and gardens mature. Sitting high on the hill catching the breezes and enjoying the view here can be entertainment aplenty, especially if you're with good company.

How to get there: From Highway 65 and 84 (John R. Junkin Drive) on the south side of Natchez, go north on Canal Street as far as you can. Make a left and a quick right onto Linton Avenue and follow Linton Avenue to Cemetery Road. The inn is directly across from the cemetery, on a small hill.

Innkeeper: Gene Weber
Address/Telephone: 1 Cemetery Road (mailing address: P.O. Box 1091); (601) 445–2304
Rooms: 5; all with private bath, some with wheelchair access. No smoking inn.
Rates: $85, double, full plantation breakfast, house tour, and beverage on arrival.
Open: All year.
Facilities and activities: Nearby: restaurants, Mississippi riverboat tours, tours of many historic Natchez homes.
Recommended Country Inns® Travel Club Benefit: 10% discount, subject to availability.

Hickory Nut Gap Inn
BAT CAVE, NORTH CAROLINA 28710

How about the concept of "laid-back romance."

From this mountaintop inn, elevation 2,200 feet, at the top of Hickory Nut Gorge, you can look out over mountains in all directions and not see another man-made structure. You can sit on the 80-foot screened porch and watch hummingbirds. B. and E.Z. and I were doing that one afternoon as the sun came out toward the end of a rain shower. "I think it will make a rainbow," E.Z. said.

He was right.

When the moment had passed, B. talked about the inn. B. said it was built in 1950 as a mountain retreat by a well-to-do businessman.

She inherited it from a later owner. She and her friend E.Z. have put years of work into refurbishing the place. They've concentrated on keeping such features as the cathedral ceiling and stone fireplace of the great room, and cleaning up the wood paneling throughout. If you know your wood, you'll recognize maple, cherry, poplar, black walnut, and red and white oak, as well as cedar in the closets.

B.'s decorating has grown from her own interests and history and from her respect for what was already in the building. For instance, the eighty-six characters of the Cherokee alphabet, mounted high on the walls, circle the recreation room. They were hand carved in wood by the Cherokee artist Goingback Chiltoskey.

The owner from whom B. inherited the place was part Native American. You find Native American arts and crafts throughout the inn, mixed in with such surprising items as a camel saddle used as a footstool, a trunk used as a coffee table, and an honest-to-goodness hippie dress used as a wall decoration. The dress was B.'s. "Remember when everything we wore had to make a statement?" she said.

This eclectic decor works partly because of B.'s skill in putting things together without overdoing it and partly because of the spaciousness of the building to begin with. The effect is too sophisticated to call rustic and too comfortable to call exotic.

In this inn space, B. and E.Z., two social and articulate people, try to see that you have whatever you need and, at the same time, try to keep out of your hair if what you need most is privacy.

I was searching for a word to describe them and their inn, not having much success. "How would *you* describe it all?" I asked.

They answered almost in union.

"Laid back."

How to get there: In Bat Cave, where Highway 64 splits off from Highway 74 and goes west toward Hendersonville, follow Highway 64 ⁵/₁₀ mile. On the right two pillars made of river rock mark the entrance to the inn. A narrow drive winds ⁷/₁₀ mile up to the inn. You'll know you've made the right turn when you see the inn's small sign about 15 feet up the drive.

Innkeepers: B. and E.Z.
Address/Telephone: P.O. Box 246; (704) 625–9108
Rooms: 4, plus 1 suite; all with private bath. No smoking inn.
Rates: $75, double; $110, suite; continental breakfast.
Open: April through November.
Facilities and activities: Musical instruments; VCR; recreation room with bowling lane, sauna, pool table, Ping-Pong; hiking trails. Nearby: restaurants; crafts and antiques shops; short drive to Chimney Rock and Lake Lure, boating, golf, shopping.

Windsong
CLYDE, NORTH CAROLINA 28721

At Windsong, you'll find romance in the spectacular mountain-top view, in the beauty of the contemporary lodge, and in the whimsy of the theme-decorated rooms. Donna and Gale built the rustic log building specifically to be a small inn and their own home. It has light pine-log walls and floors of Mexican saltillo tile. The rooms are large, with high, beamed ceilings. Skylights and huge windows let in light on all sides. The building perches on the side of a mountain at 3,000 feet, so that looking out the front windows in the direction the guest rooms face, you get a panoramic view of woods and rolling fields below; looking out the back from the kitchen and entry, you see more wilderness

higher up and, closer to the house, the perennial gardens, terraces, and recreational facilities.

In addition to sliding glass doors to let you look down the mountain, each guest room has either a deck or a ground-level patio where you can sit to watch the llamas that the Livengoods keep in some of the lower pastures.

Donna decorated the guest rooms in witty, sophisticated styles, using mostly items her family has gathered living in distant places: hence the Alaska Room with Eskimo carvings and art and a dogsled in the corner; hence the Santa Fe Room with Mexican furniture and a steerhide rug. The Safari Room is especially romantic in the style of *African Queen*. Mosquito netting is draped over the head of the bed, and the room is decorated with primitive artifacts, vines, and bamboo. Dieffenbachia and other junglelike plants flank the big soaking tub in the corner. A little sculptured giraffe with extra-long legs peers out at you from the greenery.

Outside, for some out-of-the-ordinary activity, check out the llama treks. The Livengoods' daughter Sara manages the beautiful herd of llamas, which not only adorn the surrounding hills but also are the focus of gourmet picnic and overnight hikes, a romantic novelty. This is a delightful way to backpack without using your own back.

How to get there: From I–40, take exit 24. Go north on U.S. 209 for 2½ miles. Turn left on Riverside Drive and go 2 miles. Turn right on Ferguson Cove Loop and go 1 mile, keeping to the left. You'll be driving straight up some narrow, unpaved roads. The distance will seem longer than it is.

Innkeepers: Donna and Gale Livengood

Address/Telephone: 120 Ferguson Ridge; (704) 627–6111

Rooms: 5; all with private bath, separate vanity and soaking tub, deck or patio, and fireplace. No air conditioning (elevation 3,000 feet). No smoking inn. One cottage.

Rates: $85 to $99, double; weekly rates 10 percent less; EPB. $130 to $150, cottage.

Open: All year.

Facilities and activities: VCRs and extensive videocassette library, guest lounge with refrigerator and wet bar (brown bagging), piano, pool table; washer and dryer on request; swimming pool, tennis court, hiking trails, llama treks. Nearby: restaurants, Great Smoky Mountain National Park, Asheville and historic sites, Biltmore House, craft and antiques shops, horseback riding.

$\mathcal{L}$a Grange Plantation Inn
HENDERSON, NORTH CAROLINA 27536

"We wanted pampering and that's what we got," my friend said. I recommended this place to my friends the Jacobys and then waited nervously to hear whether they enjoyed it as much as I had. When Jay Jacoby began his report, it didn't sound good. "Everything was so empty as we drove up from Raleigh; I wondered if we were making a mistake."

I started wondering how mad at me he was.

"But then we rang the bell and Jean Cornell opened the door, and the instant we were across the threshold, I knew everything was perfect."

What Jay saw as "empty" I consider "rural," which pleases me. Being more of a city boy, Jay

probably had to adjust. But there's nothing rural inside La Grange Plantation Inn. The Cornells are sophisticated innkeepers (Jean is English) with exquisite taste. The place is furnished with American and English antiques in what Jean calls "relaxed English country style."

The front parlor has a wonderful fireplace, books ranging from current fiction to history and natural studies, and no television to break the mood. The Cornells, who are great readers, count among their enthusiastic guests the owners of a bookstore in Raleigh, so it's no surprise that one outstanding feature of all the guest rooms is a good bedside reading light.

To decorate the guest rooms, Jean made the

window treatments and bed coverings herself, different in each room and elegant—made of rich fabrics, full of flowers, in muted colors.

The private baths are clustered in a central location just outside the rooms; Jean provides plush terry robes for guests to move from their rooms to their bathrooms but allows that you don't have to use a robe "if you'd rather streak!"

Turning La Grange into an inn was a major project. The Historic Preservation Foundation of North Carolina described the inn in an issue of its magazine, *North Carolina Preservation*, as a "two-story double-pile Greek Revival house with Italianate brackets." The oldest part was built in 1770. It took a lot of time and money as well as the expertise of an architect and an architectural conservator working with a contractor to restore the house to historic preservation standards and also make it comfortable. The Cornells did the interior painting and finished the floors themselves. Today the interior and the hospitality are, as my friends the Jacobys found them, pampering and "perfect."

How to get there: From I–85 take exit 214 to N.C. Route 39 North and proceed 4⁴⁄₁₀ miles to Harris Crossroads. There is a state sign pointing right to Nutbush Creek Recreation Area. Turn right and proceed ⁸⁄₁₀ mile to the inn, which is on the left.

Innkeepers: Dick and Jean Cornell

Address/Telephone: State Route 1308 (mailing address: Route 3, Box 610); (919) 438–2421

Rooms: 5; all with private bath, 1 with wheelchair access. No smoking inn.

Rates: $95 first night, $85 consecutive nights, double, full gourmet breakfast in the dining room or continental breakfast in your room.

Open: All year.

Facilities and activities: Swimming pool, lakeside fishing, walking trails, croquet, horseshoes. Nearby: restaurants, golf, boat ramps, swimming beaches, picnic grounds on several state recreation areas; water skiing, sailing, fishing on Kerr Lake.

The Belmont Inn
ABBEVILLE, SOUTH CAROLINA 29620

If your idea of romance involves scenes reminiscent of a show like *The Music Man*, with you and your significant other holding hands as you stroll along the streets nodding to folks, try the Belmont. After you walk the village, you can enjoy a romantic dinner-and-theater evening, all without ever having to step into an automobile (horseless carriage).

The old Spanish-style building was built as a modern hotel in 1902. For years, travelers associated with the railroad, the textile industry, and the Opera House stayed here. But it closed in 1972 and stood empty for eleven years, until Mr. and Mrs. Joseph C. Harden bought it. Restoration took almost a year and involved many peo-

ple in Abbeville. Almost anyone at the inn can tell you stories about bringing The Belmont Inn back to life. Staying here, you feel like a guest not just of the inn, but of the entire community.

The relationship between the Opera House and The Belmont thrives again, too. You can make great package deals including theater tickets, dinner with wine, a drink in the Curtain Call Lounge after the show, your lodging, and continental breakfast the next morning. The package rates are always good, but they vary with the season and so does the show schedule. Activity peaks with summer theater at the Opera House.

Whether it precedes a show or not, dinner in the large dining room with its high ceilings and paddle fans is worth enjoying slowly. The menu tends toward continental cuisine without being self-conscious about it. The chef prepares veal a different way every day. After a nice meal of filleted chicken breasts Dijon with pecans, I let the waitress talk me into a slice of Irish Cream mousse cake.

How to get there: The inn is on the corner of the town square. From Greenwood, take Highway 72 west to Abbeville, turn right onto Highway 20 (Main Street), and go to the first traffic light. Turn right onto Pickens Street. The second building on the right is The Belmont. From I–85, take Highway 28 south into Abbeville where it joins Main Street.

Innkeeper: Janie Wiltshire

Address/Telephone: 106 East Pickens Street; (803) 459–9625

Rooms: 24; all with private bath. Pets allowed by arrangement in special circumstances.

Rates: $67 to $77, double, continental breakfast and wine in room. Inquire about theater packages. Wheelchair access.

Open: All year.

Facilities and activities: Lunch, dinner, lounge, except Sunday. Nearby: theatrical productions at the restored Opera House next door; Russell Lake for fishing, boating, swimming, and water skiing; hunting; gift and antiques shopping in Abbeville.

Ansonborough Inn
CHARLESTON, SOUTH CAROLINA 29401

If I wanted to spend a few romantic days in perfect privacy in Charleston, here's the place I'd choose. Like so many Charleston inns, this one had a different function in its earlier time. It was a three-story stationer's warehouse built about 1900. The building's renovation not only kept the heart-of-pine beams and locally fired red brick, which are typical of the period, but actually emphasized them. The lobby soars three stories high, with skylights; the original huge, rough beams are fully visible, an important part of the decor.

The original plan to use the renovated building as a condo complex didn't work out, which probably was bad news for some in-

vestors; but it's great for inn guests now, because the rooms, which are really suites, are huge. At least one wall in each features the exposed old brick. The ceilings are about 20 feet high. Because all the rooms were fit into an existing shell, no two rooms are exactly the same shape or size. Nothing is exactly predictable. The resulting little quirks, nooks, lofts, and alcoves add a lot of interest.

The living rooms are furnished in period reproductions with comfortable chairs and sofas. What's more, you really can cook in the kitchens. If you ask for place settings and basic kitchen utensils when you make your reservations, the kitchen will be ready when you arrive. The inn is just across the road from an excellent Harris Teeter supermarket housed in an old railroad station. I don't think it would be appropriate to whip up corned beef and cabbage or deep-fried chittlins in this environment, but the arrangement is great for preparing light meals—a good way to save your calories and your dollars for some sumptuous dinners in Charleston's excellent restaurants.

Clearly this isn't the kind of place where everyone sits around the breakfast table comparing notes about dinner the night before, but the continental breakfast (with sweet breads baked at a plantation in Walterboro) and the evening wine and cheese are set up in the lobby so that guests can sit in conversational clusters. But if you don't feel like talking to another single soul, you're entirely welcome to help yourself to wine and cheese and retreat to a private corner or back to your room.

How to get there: From I–25 East, take the Meeting Street/Visitor Center exit. Go 1²/₁₀ miles to Hassel Street. Turn left and go through the next traffic signal. From Route 17 South, take the East Bay Street exit, go 1³/₁₀ miles to Hassel and turn left. From Route 17 North, after crossing the Ashley River, exit to the right and go through the first traffic signal onto Calhoun Street. Drive 1⁴/₁₀ miles to East Bay Street, turn right, and go to the second traffic signal (Hassel Street) and turn left. The inn is on your right.

Innkeeper: Allen B. Johnson; Eric A. Crapse, assistant innkeeper
Address/Telephone: 21 Hassel Street; (803) 723–1655 or (800) 522–2073
Rooms: 37 suites; all with private bath, phone, TV, and kitchen. No-smoking rooms available.
Rates: Spring and fall, $89 to $138, double; summer and winter, $89 to $119, double; continental breakfast and afternoon wine and cheese.
Open: All year.
Facilities and activities: Free off-street parking. In heart of waterfront historic district. Nearby: historic sites, restaurants, shuttle transportation to visitor center. Walking distance to antiques shops and downtown Charleston.

Adams Edgeworth Inn
MONTEAGLE, TENNESSEE 37356

This is romance in the most impeccable taste—museum-quality art, fine antiques, shelves bulging with books, and seclusion on a wooded bit of land in a historical community sometimes called "the Chatauqua of the South."

David and Wendy Adams have a beautiful inn in a three-story Victorian structure built as an inn nearly 100 years ago. You have a couple of different possibilities for suites with private entrances and such niceties as fireplaces, or you can enjoy a room on the second floor.

Outside, if you prefer an active retreat to a sedentary one, the state park and wilderness areas offer lots of privacy and even, David says, some places you can skinny-dip.

Inside, they refurbished and brightened the interior without hiding the wood floors or changing the inn's warm character. They brought a large, eclectic collection of art, as well as antiques and interesting mementos they and their grown children have picked up in world travel. Also, they have some wonderful items from the years Wendy's father spent as a United States ambassador, including the gold-edge ambassadorial china upon which Wendy serves dinner.

Some of the guest rooms have been designed around quilts made by her mother and grandmother that Wendy uses as bedcovers. The library and guest rooms overflow with books.

Classical music deepens the feeling of serenity in the sitting areas and floats out onto the shady porches.

Dinner deserves a write-up of its own. When Wendy dims the lights in the formal dining room, most of the illumination comes from candles, except for small lamps shining over each of the paintings in the room. Often a piano player or guitarist provides music.

We had an appetizer of smoked salmon with Russian black bread and Vidalia onions. Of the several choices of entrees, I especially enjoyed the chicken breast filled with fresh herbs. We had a variety of lightly cooked and sauced fresh vegetables, and a colorful salad of arugula and greens with Camembert. For dessert Wendy served fresh strawberries and kiwi in a custard sauce with a hint of either caramel or maple. Maybe both. The flavors were subtle enough to keep me wondering. If the gods get romantic, they must do it like this.

How to get there: From I–24 take exit 134. Turn right. In the center of the village you will see a steel archway with a Monteagle Assembly sign. Turn right through the arch, once on the grounds turn right at the mall sign and right immediately at Chestnut Hill.

Innkeepers: Wendy and David Adams
Address/Telephone: Monteagle Assembly; (615) 924–4000
Rooms: 13, plus 1 suite with kitchenette and fireplace; all with private bath, some rooms with fireplace or wheelchair access. Smoking on verandas only.
Rates: $65 to $145, double, continental breakfast. Two-night minimum on weekends.
Open: All year.
Facilities and activities: Dinner by reservation. Gift shop. On grounds of Monteagle Assembly. Nearby: golf, tennis, Tennessee State Park, wilderness and developed hiking trails, Sewanee University of the South, Monteagle Wine Cellars.
Recommended Country Inns® Travel Club Benefit: Stay two nights, get third night free, Monday–Thursday, subject to availability.

Von-Bryan Inn
SEVIERVILLE, TENNESSEE 37862

Von-Bryan Inn is on top of a mountain near the Great Smoky Mountains. Not near the top, *on* it. The view includes the Smokies and Wears Valley and treetops in the clouds. The inn is set up to make the most of the view, especially the garden room, a nice protected spot inside from which you can sit in a corner hot tub big enough to hold eleven people and watch the sunset from the windows. The outdoor pool seems to float above clouds and mountains, and from there the view is panoramic. While I was here, I saw men stand in the yard looking across the valleys and deciding, without even going inside, that this was a place to which they must bring their wives.

I hope they do. Not only will they enjoy the romantic view, they'll like the inn, too.

The living room has a stacked-stone fireplace and attractive, unobtrusive furniture grouped for conversation or privacy, as you prefer.

The suite is interesting. It has lots of glass, a pine floor, a queen-sized canopy bed, and a reading loft. Each of the other guest rooms has a special delight, a special view or an unusual bed, for example, but the Red Bud Room is unlike anything I've ever seen. It has a king-sized bed against a natural-paneled wall, windows along another wall, a sitting area with a love seat, and a big cherry red hot tub in the corner. Red simply dominates the room. Jo Ann says that it's one of the most requested rooms and theorizes that folks who would find a red hot tub just too racy at home get a kick out of it on vacation.

Speaking of Jo Ann, if personable innkeepers are important to you, you'll enjoy this inn. Jo Ann is thoroughly competent and produces a gourmet breakfast without a flick of the eyelid, but she's easy, chatty, and comfortable, all at the same time. D. J. has a green thumb and also is a good conversationalist. When I visited, I lingered too long over breakfast because we got to talking about everything from food to our earlier careers, and I couldn't make myself leave.

Among the nice little treats you can arrange for yourself if you stay here are helicopter pickup and delivery to the inn. I didn't experience the helicopter trip, but given the view and the height of the mountain, I think it would be a sensational experience.

One treat you don't have to arrange. Jo Ann unobrusively sets out lemonade, tea, and desserts each evening for all who want them.

How to get there: From Highway 321, turn onto Hatcher Mountain Road (the inn's sign marks the turn) and follow inn signs all the way to the top of the mountain. Ask for a map and more detailed instructions when you make reservations.

Innkeepers: D. J. and Jo Ann Vaughn

Address/Telephone: 2402 Hatcher Mountain Road; (615) 453–9832 or (800) 633–1459

Rooms: 5 in main house, plus 1 three-level suite; all with private bath, some with whirlpool. Separate chalet with whirlpool, 3 bedrooms, kitchen, living room, fireplace, decks, hot tub.

Rates: In main house, $80 to $125, double, EPB and afternoon refreshments. All rates reduced by 10 percent for stays of 2 or more nights Sunday through Thursday. Two-night minimum stay in chalet.

Open: All year.

Facilities and activities: Hot tub, upstairs television lounge in main house, swimming pool. Nearby: restaurants; short drive to Pigeon Forge, Gatlinburg, and Great Smoky Mountains National Park; Glades Crafts Community.

The Midwest

by Bob Puhala

Many people consider the country's heartland nothing more than a tranquil region of family farms and wholesome values akin to something out of a Norman Rockwell painting. In the not-too-distant past, however, the Midwest was a dramatic theater of history filled with legend, lore, and romance.

On the outland border of the Old Northwest, frontiersmen braved both unbroken forests and oceans of tall prairie grasses standing as high as a horse's shoulder to conquer the wilderness and bring civilization to an untamed land. Some of those very log cabins and clapboard buildings that housed early settlers now welcome country inn guests for weekends dappled with history and romance.

Lumber barons hell-bent on clear-cutting virgin pine trees that blanketed North Woods terrain often built elegant mansions as a display of their wealth. Today, many of these same mansions have been converted into luxurious inns that pamper guests during whimsical overnight getaways.

Farmers built lonely homesteads in the midst of flat plains and rolling hills as they tilled the soil, transforming prairie into cropland.

Many of these historic farmsteads have been transformed into country-tinged, out-of-the-way havens for privacy and romance.

Let's not forget Mark Twain's paddle wheelers, churning their way over the Midwest's mighty rivers like the Mississippi, Ohio, and Missouri. Historic inns that catered to riverboat passengers and elegant mansions owned by boat-company magnates have been restored to their former glory, opening their doors to couples looking for a special place to celebrate—whatever.

And if we add Nebraska to this interesting heartland mix, we no longer straddle the borders of wild west frontiers. After all, the Oregon Trail stretches across almost the entire length of the state. And the state's rich traditions include cattle barons, hundreds of thousands of still-open pasturelands, and Native American legacies. You can even overnight in an Indian earth lodge for a romantic experience that really turns back the pages of history.

In fact, two of the most romantic retreats I've ever visited are located in the Midwest. They're included in the pages that follow, pages that offer you a passport to your own romantic fantasies.

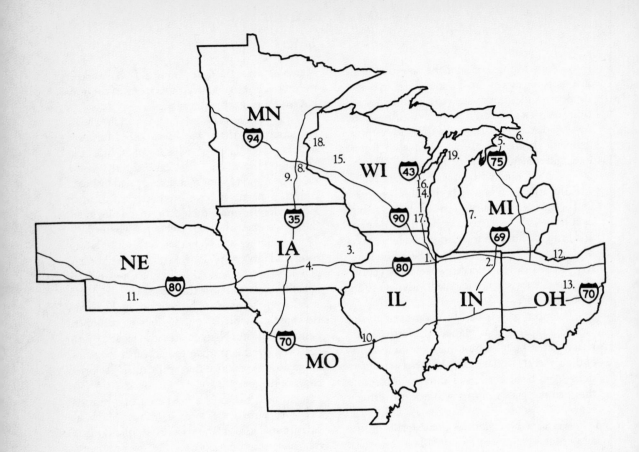

The Midwest

Numbers on map refer to towns numbered below.

The Herrington
GENEVA, ILLINOIS 60134

The Herrington is a handsome inn nestled on the banks of the Fox River. Housed in the restored Geneva Rock Springs Creamery, where milk was kept and chilled along the swift waters of the river in the 1870s, the luxurious day-in-the-country getaway is only about one hour west of Chicago's stress-filled hubbub.

Named for Geneva's first permanent white European settlers (the town sits on a site that the Potowatomie Indians called Big Springs), the inn combines its historic architecture with elegant modern-day fineries—and plenty of opportunities for romance.

Walk inside double doors crested by Palladian windows to a luxurious sitting room, with a fireplace, wing chairs, and nooks and crannies perfect for late-night whispers. An old-fashioned bar climbs the wall on the far end of the room; you can lounge here until your table is ready for gourmet meals prepared by the inn chef.

Some guest rooms have riverside views; others have courtyard vistas (with glimpses of the rushing waters). If you choose to be on the river, your balcony is literally suspended over the water.

While each guest room is individually decorated, they all revel in an understated elegance that includes gracious pampering. We especially liked our room, which featured scrolled brass beds adorned with eyelet lace coverlets, fireplace, ceiling fan, marble-tiled bathroom, and a big whirlpool tub.

And that glass-enclosed riverside gazebo sitting in the middle of the courtyard sports another romantic extra: a large whirlpool tub that allows you to take its soothing waters under the stars with your special someone.

Geneva is one of the most historic little towns in the Chicago exurban area. So if you want to overnight at The Herrington during the town's annual festivals (April's Historic Geneva Days, June's Swedish Days, September's Festival of the Vine, the Riverwalk Octoberfest, and December's Christmas House Walk), be sure to make your reservations far in advance.

How to get there: From Chicago, take the Eisenhower Expressway (I–290) west to I–88 Aurora, exiting at Farnsworth Avenue; go north to Route 38 to the first left past the Fox River Bridge (River Lane).

Innkeeper: Greg Brown, general manager
Address/Telephone: 15 South River Lane; (708) 208–7433
Rooms: 40; all with private bath, whirlpool bath, fireplace, and private balcony or patio.
Rates: $110 to $185, single or double, continental breakfast.
Open: All year.
Facilities and activities: Full-service dining room, high tea, sitting room, bar, riverside spa, outdoor gazebo-enclosed whirlpool tub. Nearby: walk to historic town, shops, boutiques, riverwalk; rent bikes for river trail rides.

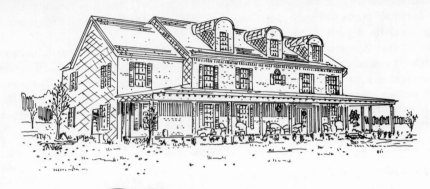

The Checkerberry Inn
GOSHEN, INDIANA 46526

"We wanted to create a European feel to the inn," Susan said. "After all, being surrounded on all sides by Amish farmlands is more than enough country ambience."

The fine appointments of this northern Indiana inn do remind me of intimate, romantic European hotels I've stayed at. In fact, the handsome photographs adorning inn walls were taken by John during his travels in the French Bordeaux region.

Amish straw hats hang over beds, lending a nice regional touch to luxurious guest rooms that boast fine-arts prints, furniture with definite European flair, wide windows that allow views of the rolling countryside, and amenities like Swiss goat's milk soap in the baths. Rooms are named for flowers; my favorite is Foxglove, with its sitting-room fireplace, whirlpool bath, and six windows—an almost perfect lovers' retreat.

Queen Anne's Lace is another handsome room; its most interesting feature is a primitive secretary, made in the 1850s. It consists of 1,200 individual pieces, and it took three years to complete. Its geometric designs put that craftsman far ahead of his time.

The inn's restaurant leans toward country-French cuisine. Four-course meals begin with a fresh garden salad, followed by a fresh fruit sorbet, entree, and dessert. An inn specialty is double duck breast sautéed and served over sweet onions, topped with an orange and port wine sauce, accompanied by *pommes Anna* and a bouquet of fresh vegetables. The vegetables, herbs, and spices are grown specially for the inn. Other favorites include chicken basil, veal medallions, and rack of lamb served off the bone with herb cream-and-garlic cheese.

Checkerberry sits on one hundred acres, so there's plenty of quiet and relaxation. It's just a walk through French doors to the swimming pool, and the woods contain numerous hiking trails. And the inn provides Indiana's only professional croquet course. So now is the time to perfect your game.

Unless you're too busy enjoying each other.

How to get there: From Chicago, take the Indiana Toll Road (I–80/90) to the Middlebury exit (#107). Go south on Indiana 13, turn west on Indiana 4, then go south on County Road 37 to the inn. It's 14 miles from the toll-road exit to the inn.

Innkeepers: John and Susan Graff, owners; Shawna Koehler and Jane Erickson, assistant managers

Address/Telephone: 62644 County Road 37; (219) 642–4445

Rooms: 13, including 3 suites; all with private bath and air conditioning. Wheelchair access.

Rates: $75 to $240, weekdays; $100 to $300, weekends; continental breakfast.

Open: May through December; limited time February through April.

Facilities and activities: Full-service dining room, swimming pool, arbor, croquet course, tennis court, hiking trails, cross-country ski area. In the midst of Amish farmlands; offers horse-drawn buggy tours of Amish surroundings, sleigh rides in winter. Near Shipshewana auctions, Middlebury festivals.

$\mathcal{S}$quiers Manor
MAQUOKETA, IOWA 52060

Nothing prepares you for the splendor of this 1882 house, listed on the National Register of Historic Places.

The handsome Queen Anne home boasts fine wood everywhere. There's a walnut parlor, a cherry dining room, and butternut throughout the rest of the house.

Fine antiques are everywhere, too; some, such as the 1820s Federal four-poster mahogany bed in the Harriet Squiers Room, are of museum quality.

That's not surprising, since Cathy and Virg also own a nationally renowned antiques store just a few miles out of town.

Romantics should try the Jeannie Mitchel

Bridal Suite. Its canopied brass bed stands more than 7 feet tall. (Note the mother of pearl on the footboard.) And the Victorian Renaissance dresser with marble top is another treasure.

Did I mention that the suite has a double whirlpool bath?

So does the J. E. Squiers Room; there a green marble floor creates a path leading to a cozy corner whirlpool for two. What better way to spend an evening on a romantic getaway.

And Opal's Parlor (named after a longtime resident of the manor when it rented its rooms as apartments) features not only 1860s antiques and hand-crocheted bedspreads but also a Swiss shower that acts "like a human car wash," said

Cathy. Maybe not especially romantic, but it sure does get you squeaky clean.

Every common room bespeaks luxury and splendor. The parlor's fireplace, with tiles depicting characters in Roman mythology, is unusual. Look at the fabulous hand-carved cherry buffet in the dining room. The dining room's 10-foot-tall, hand-carved jewelers' clock is another conversation starter.

And the library, an enclave done entirely in butternut paneling and graced with its original fireplace, is flat-out gorgeous.

Not only do you get great atmosphere; Cathy's breakfasts are terrific, too. Consider pumpkin pecan muffins, black-walnut bread, eggs Katrina, pecan-stuffed French toast, seafood quiches, apple pudding, and more.

But the newest wrinkle is "candlelight evening desserts." Imagine nibbling on Cathy's chocolate bourbon pecan pie, delicious tortes, or Grandma Annie's bread pudding, a guest favorite. Other kinds of nibbling is optional.

How to get there: From Dubuque, take U.S. 61 south to U.S. 64, then turn east into town. One block past the second stoplight, turn right, then go 1 block to the inn.

Innkeepers: Cathy and Virg Banowetz
Address/Telephone: 418 West Pleasant Street; (319) 652–6961
Rooms: 6, including 1 suite; all with private bath and air conditioning.
Rates: $65 to $95, single or double; $125, suite; EPB.
Open: All year.
Facilities and activities: Library, parlor, porch. A short drive to Mississippi River towns; Dubuque, site of low-stakes riverboat casino gambling; and Galena, Illinois, a Civil War–era architectural wonderland.
Recommended Country Inns® Travel Club Benefit: Stay two nights, get third night free, Monday–Thursday, except seven days before or after holidays, subject to availability.

$\mathcal{L}$a Corsette Maison Inn
NEWTON, IOWA 50208

My wife, Debbie, and I sat in front of a roaring fire in an elegant parlor, enjoying a romantic gourmet-style breakfast.

First Kay brought us a delightful fresh fruit compote of pink grapefruit, mandarin orange slices, grapes, and kiwi. Her home-baked apple muffins with strudel were next. (We could have eaten four apiece, they were so delicious.)

We sipped on raspberry and orange juice, which washed down authentic English scones, another of Kay's specialties. Then came a wonderful frittata with two cheeses—and some special La Corsette French bread.

It was one of the ultimate bed-and-breakfast experiences.

No wonder food at Kay's inn has received a 4½-star rating from the *Des Moines Register* and has been hailed as a "gleaming jewel in the crown of fine restaurants."

The mansion itself is a 1909 Mission-style masterpiece built by an early Iowa state senator. Not much has changed in the intervening years. Gleaming mission oak woodwork, Art Nouveau stained-glass windows, and other turn-of-the-century architectural flourishes make La Corsette a special place.

We overnighted in the Windsor Hunt Suite; the massive bedchamber has a huge four-poster bed (you use a stepstool to reach the high mattress), and the sitting room boasts its own fireplace—which we used for a romantic end to the day—as well as a two-person whirlpool bath.

Other rooms are imbued with their own particular charms. The Penthouse bedchambers, for instance, are located in the tower and surrounded by beveled-glass windows. Use your imagination here.

Kay's romantic five-course gourmet-style dinners, prepared by both herself and a new chef (a graduate of the Culinary Institute of America, by the way), are renowned. The first person to make reservations for the evening sets the night's menu. Choices include the likes of French veal in cream, broccoli-stuffed game hen with Mornay sauce, and roast loin of pork with prune chutney.

How to get there: From the Quad Cities, take I–80 to Newton (exit 164), and go north until the second light (Highway 6); then turn right and continue 7 blocks to the inn.

Innkeeper: Kay Owen

Address/Telephone: 629 1st Avenue; (515) 792–6833

Rooms: 5, including 2 suites; all with private bath and air conditioning. No smoking inn.

Rates: $55 to $75, single or double; $75 to $165, suites; EPB. Multi-night minimum during Pella, Iowa, Tulip Festival and some other special events. Pets allowed by pre-arrangement.

Open: All year.

Facilities and activities: Two sitting rooms with fireplace; porch. Nearby: Maytag Company tours, tennis courts, golf courses, horseback riding, cross-country skiing. A short drive to Trainland, U.S.A.; Prairie Meadows Horse Track; Krumm Nature Preserve.

Kimberly Country Estate
HARBOR SPRINGS, MICHIGAN 49740

Ronn and Billie's inn could be a romantic showcase for *House Beautiful*.

That's not surprising, I guess; Ronn, an interior designer, has transformed this Southern plantation–style home into an elegant retreat that offers some of the most extraordinarily luxurious inn surroundings possible.

We got the red-carpet treatment (literally) as we mounted steps to the house, set atop a gentle hill and surrounded by fields and farms.

Inside, Chippendale and Queen Anne–style furniture, Battenburg linens, Laura Ashley fabrics, and exquisite antiques collected by the innkeepers over forty years add to the elegance.

The Lexington Suite is the epitome of romanticism, with its four-poster bed and Battenburg linens lending touches of sophistication; this room also has its own sitting area, wood-burning fireplace, and Jacuzzi.

Le Soleil is another of our favorites, with its walls of windows, sunny yellow color, and hand stenciling. And four of the rooms open onto a shaded veranda overlooking the inn's 22-by-40-foot swimming pool.

The library is a most stunning common room. It's entirely paneled with North Carolina black walnut—milled on the spot as the house was built, Billie told me.

Pampering is legion here. Guests find a decanter of sherry in their rooms upon arrival, with an invitation to join Ronn and Billie for afternoon tea and hors d'oeuvres—sometimes at poolside in good weather. At night they return to their rooms to discover beds turned down and chocolate truffles on the pillows.

Weekend breakfasts are another Southern-tinged plantation treat. Billie might serve fresh fruit compote, scrambled eggs, smoked turkey sausage, home-baked muffins, and more.

If you want to experience the "estate of the art" in romantic country inn living, make your reservations now.

How to get there: From Petoskey, take U.S. 31 north to Michigan 119, continue north toward Harbor Springs; turn right at Emmet Heights Road, then left on Bester Road, and continue to the inn.

Innkeepers: Ronn and Billie Serba
Address/Telephone: 2287 Bester Road; (616) 526–7646 or 526–9502
Rooms: 6, including 3 suites; all with private bath. Wheelchair access.
Rates: $135 to $225, single or double, EPB and afternoon tea. Two-night minimum on weekends. No smoking inn.
Open: All year.
Facilities and activities: Library, lower-level entertainment room, terrace, swimming pool. Nearby: golf, biking, hiking; sailing and other water activities on Little Traverse Bay. A short drive to chic shops in Harbor Springs, downhill skiing at Boyne Highlands and Nubs Nob.

Grand Hotel
MACKINAC ISLAND, MICHIGAN 49757

The Grand Hotel, built in 1887, has been called one of the great hotels of the railroad and Great Lakes steamer era. Its location high on an island bluff provides magnificent vistas over the Straits of Mackinac waters. And it also was the location for one of the most romantic period movies ever made—*Somewhere in Time*—which still draws fans to the historic hostelry.

Its incredible, many-columned veranda is 660 feet long (it claims to be the longest in the world) and is decorated with huge American flags snapping in the wind, bright yellow awnings that catch the color of the sun, and colorful red geraniums hanging everywhere. Many guests simply sit in generous rockers, sip on a drink,

relax, and enjoy cooling lake breezes. We also like to admire the hotel's acres of woodland and lawns, finely manicured with exquisite flower gardens and greenery arrangements.

At the Grand Hotel, guests feel immersed in a long-ago era of luxury and romance. Even the attire of hotel attendants harkens back to a long-ago era; they're dressed in long red coats and black bow ties. Once Debbie and I rode the hotel's elegant horse-drawn carriage (the driver wore a black top hat and formal "pink" hunting jacket) from the ferry docks, up the long hill, to the grand portico. That was one of the most romantic journeys we've ever taken.

Inside, the hotel boasts Victorian-era colors

and decor—greens, yellows, and whites, with balloon draperies on the windows, high-back chairs and sofas everywhere in numerous public rooms, and a healthy dash of yesteryear memorabilia hanging on hallway walls. (One 1889 breakfast menu especially caught my eye, listing an extraordinary selection of foods, including lamb chops, lake fish, stewed potatoes in cream, and sweetbreads.)

Special services are legion and include complimentary morning coffee, concerts during afternoon tea, romantic horse-drawn-carriage island tours, hold-me-close dinner dances, and much more. It seems as if the pampering never stops.

Many of the guest rooms have spectacular lake views that induce lots of lovey-dovey musings. Rates include breakfast and candlelight dinners, with Lake Superior whitefish an evening specialty. A dessert treat—the Grand pecan ball with hot fudge sauce—is a sweet confection best shared with your special honey. The rest of the evening's romantic bliss is up to you.

How to get there: From either Mackinaw City from the Lower Peninsula or from St. Ignace on the Upper Peninsula, a thirty-minute ferry ride brings you to Mackinac Island. Dock porters will greet your boat. There's an island airstrip for chartered flights and private planes.

Innkeeper: R. D. Musser III, corporation president
Address/Telephone: Mackinac Island; (906) 847–3331
Rooms: 317; all with private bath.
Rates: $135 to $245, per person, May through mid-June; add $15, mid-June through late October.   Special packages available.
Open: Mid-May to late October.
Facilities and activities: Main dining room, Geranium Bar, Grand Stand (food and drink), Audubon Bar, Carleton's Tea Store, pool grill. Magnificent swimming pool, private golf course, bike rentals, saddle horses, tennis courts, exercise trail. Carriage tours, dancing, movies. Expansive grounds, spectacular veranda with wonderful lake vistas. Nearby: museums, historic Fort Mackinac, Mackinac Island State Park, and other sites, guided tours; specialty shops. There are no motor vehicles allowed on historic Mackinac Island; visitors walk or rent horses, horse-drawn carriages and taxis, and bicycles.

The Shiloh
WHITEHALL, MICHIGAN 49461

If you've ever had dreams of sailing the open seas in a tall ship, here's your chance.

Howard and Cheryl, who for more than twenty years have skippered sails across the Great Lakes and the Caribbean, have decided to let us experience the luxury and romance of a real high-seas adventure that includes "cruising waters under billowing sails, supping on a gourmet repast, then being lulled to sleep by waves lapping against the bow of your vessel."

All you've got to do is climb aboard their boat, *The Shiloh*, a 46-foot, double-headsail ketch, whose classic beauty and luxury may be unequaled on Lake Michigan.

Officially named Tanbark Sailing Adven-tures (for the distinctive tanbark colors of the sails on the ebony-hulled boat), the Coast Guard–licensed world-class yacht glides over the clear waters of the Great Lakes, prompting a feeling of exhilaration and freedom like nothing you've ever experienced before.

The luxurious accommodations of *The Shiloh* include rich teak interiors. The main salon and dining areas are spacious and airy, with opening ports and hatches and a traditional open skylight that allows cooling breezes in during the day and moonlit stargazing opportunities at night.

Two private double staterooms are equally luxurious, with teak interiors, hanging locker, and plenty of drawer space. No reason for anyone, even landlubbers, to get claustrophobic in here. And the head . . . er, bathroom, includes a hot shower, another uncompromising standard of luxury cruising.

The special overnight bed-and-breakfast sail includes a sunset cruise, overnight anchor in a tranquil cove (where the romance of moonlight on the high seas can spark all sorts of lovey-dovey fireworks), and spectacular sunrise. The ship's breakfast is a buffet-style affair, with fresh fruits, juices, coffee cakes, and more.

Of course, there's plenty to do on board. Relax in the main salon, watch television, listen to music, read a good book. Or hang in a hammock topside, under the heat of the sun washed by cool breezes, while sailing home into port.

There's a swimming ladder if you'd like to take a dip in the drink. And a dinghy allows plenty of opportunities for beachcombing small islands and sandy beaches.

The biggest treat, however, might be sailing *The Shiloh* yourself. Just ask Howard or Cheryl if you can take over the helm for a few minutes. You'll see how much fun skippering can be.

How to get there: From Muskegon, take U.S. 31 north to the Whitehall exit; get off at Business U.S. 31 (called Colby Road), and continue west to Mears Street; turn left (south) and go to Slocum Street; turn right, then follow to Lake Street and continue to Crosswinds Marina.

Innkeepers: Howard and Cheryl Whelan, captains
Address/Telephone: 302 South Lake (dock) (mailing address: 11588 Pond Road, Montague 49437); (616) 894–5084
Rooms: 2 double-berth staterooms share 1 shower and bath.
Rates: Overnight bed and breakfast sail: $380, 1 couple, $455, 2 couples; 2-day sail: $797 up to four people; 3-day sail: $1,162; week's sail: $2,054.
Open: Early April through mid-October.
Facilities and activities: Lunch and dinner, including topside barbecue, available; music library, book collection, game locker, AM/FM stereo cassette, microwave oven, refrigerator/freezer, swim ladder, dinghy.

Rosewood Inn
HASTINGS, MINNESOTA 55033

This handsome Queen Anne, built in 1878, now houses one of the most romantic getaways imaginable. That's not really surprising, since Pam and Dick's other Hastings hideaway (the Thorwood Inn) reflects similar pampering-inspired luxuries.

As soon as you see Rebecca's Room, you'll get the idea. This is a stirring romantic retreat, with a marvelous all-marble bathroom highlighted by a double whirlpool bath resting in front of its own fireplace. There's a second fireplace opposite an inviting four-poster antique bed. And a four-season porch offers views of the inn's rose garden.

Or consider the Vermillion Room, with a see-through fireplace that warms both an ornate brass bed and a sunken double whirlpool bath.

If you want shameful opulence, try the Mississippi Room. As large as an apartment, it offers skylights over a sleigh bed, its own fireplace, baby grand piano, bathroom with both a copper tub and double whirlpool—and a meditation room where "people can either relax or be creative," said the innkeeper. "We've even had several guests do paintings here." A collection of some of those works are hanging about the room.

The breakfasts are added treats. And the mealtime flexibility is unusual: They'll serve whenever guests are hungry, between 6:00 and 11:00 A.M. Eat in one of the dining areas, on the porch, in your room, or in bed—the choice is yours.

The feast might include homemade breads and blueberry muffins, cheese strata, wild-rice gratiné, cherry strudel, raspberry coffee cake.... Aren't you hungry just thinking about all this food?

Another chance to feast: The inn offers gourmet dinners in the formal parlor—or in your own room. The meal might feature delights such as beef Wellington and a raspberry strudel with chocolate and vanilla sauce. The cost is $44.70 to $56.70 per couple.

The innkeepers are also happy to arrange an in-room "hat box" supper, or to package a delightful evening with dinner at one of the town's fine restaurants, including limousine service. And they occasionally arrange dinner at the inn featuring Minnesota-accented recipes accompanied by live chamber music.

How to get there: From the Twin Cities, take U.S. 61 south into Hastings and exit at Seventh Street; then turn left and proceed 1½ blocks to the inn.

Innkeepers: Pam and Dick Thorsen
Address/Telephone: Seventh and Ramsey; (612) 437–3297
Rooms: 8, with 4 suites; all with private bath and air conditioning; TV and phone upon request. No smoking inn.
Rates: $75 to $195, single or double, EPB. Two-night minimum on weekends. Special packages available.
Open: All year.
Facilities and activities: Dinner by reservation. Sitting room, parlor, library, porch. Nearby: historic river-town architecture, arts and crafts, stores, antiques shops, specialty boutiques, Mississippi River water activities, bluff touring on bikes and hikes, St. Croix Valley Nature Center, Alexis Bailly vineyard winery, downhill and cross-country skiing, snowshoeing, golf.

Thorwood Inn
HASTINGS, MINNESOTA 55033

Perhaps Thorwood's ultimate romantic retreat is the Steeple Room, with its see-through fireplace and double whirlpool—set in the house's steeple. The steeple rises 23 feet above the tub and boasts a ball chandelier hanging from the pinnacle. Ooh, la la!

Others swear by Sarah's Room, with its bedroom-sized loft, window views of the Mississippi River Valley, and skylight over a queen-sized brass bed. Or Maureen's Room, with its unusual rag-rug headboard, fireplace, country-quilted bed, and double whirlpool bath.

However, my favorite lovers' lair is Captain Anthony's, named for the original owner's son-in-law, who operated a line of steamboats on the Mississippi. It has a canopied four-poster brass bed and Victorian rose-teal-and-blue Laura Ashley fabrics. Though the Lullaby Room (the house's historic nursery) with its double whirlpool bath is a close runner-up.

The house itself, fashioned in ornate Second Empire style and completed in 1880, is a testament to the innkeepers' restoration prowess and romantic notions. When I saw the marble fireplaces, ornate rosettes and plaster moldings on the ceilings, and elegant antiques and surroundings, it was difficult to imagine that the house had once been cut up into several apartments. For more fine detail, just look to the music room. Pam said that maple instead of oak was used for flooring because it provided better resonance for live piano concerts, popular with society crowds at the turn of the century.

There's lots of special pampering, too. A complimentary bottle of wine from the local Alexis Bailly vineyards and snacks of fruits and pastries await guests. Then there are those breakfast baskets.

"People seem to enjoy the morning breakfast baskets more than anything else," Pam told me as we sat in the parlor of her gracious inn. "It has grown into quite a tradition." Once when she mentioned to a repeat couple that she'd been thinking of changing that practice, "They immediately spun around, with dismayed looks on their faces, and said, 'You wouldn't.' I knew right then we could never change."

Lucky for us. The breakfast basket, delivered to the door of your room, is stuffed with platters of fresh fruits, omelets or quiches, pull-apart pastries and rolls, home-baked breads, coffee, juice, and more. As Dick says, "Pace yourself."

How to get there: From LaCrosse, take U.S. 61 north to Hastings; then turn left on Fourth Street and proceed to inn.

Innkeepers: Pam and Dick Thorsen

Address/Telephone: Fourth and Pine; (612) 437–3297

Rooms: 7; all with private bath and air conditioning. Wheelchair access. No smoking inn.

Rates: $75 to $145, single or double, EPB. Can arrange for pet sitters. Special package rates available.

Open: All year.

Facilities and activities: "Hat box" dinners in your room. Nearby: walking tour of historical area just blocks away. Quaint Mississippi River town with specialty and antiques shops, several good restaurants. Parks and nature trails; also river, streams, lakes, and all sorts of summer and winter sports.

Schumacher's New Prague Hotel
NEW PRAGUE, MINNESOTA 56071

Anyone stepping into Schumacher's New Prague Hotel is immediately transported into the romantic era of Old World Bavaria.

In fact, it looks similar to many European country hotels I've stayed at. A peaceful air of rich handiwork, fine craftsmanship, wonderful imported Old World antiques, and a deep commitment to dining excellence are what make Schumacher's one of the best there is.

Built in 1898, the hotel has an ornate European-style lobby, with pressed-tin ceilings, rich floral wallpaper, fine European antiques, and oriental rugs that cover original maple floors. A wonderful front desk is original, too.

John commissioned renowned Bavarian folk artist Pipka to design the graceful stenciled scenes that enliven guest, lobby, and restaurant rooms.

Upstairs are eleven individually decorated guest rooms, named in German for the months of the year, and furnished with Old World trunks, chairs, beds, and wardrobes. Better yet, several have fireplaces, and all boast double whirlpool baths. More authentic touches include eiderdown-filled pillows and comforters, and 100-percent-cotton bedding and tablecloths, which were purchased in Austria, Czechoslovakia, and Germany.

August is my favorite, with its king-sized bed, primitive Bavarian folk art, and a red wildflower theme carried out in stenciled hearts on the pine floor and on an ornately decorated wardrobe. You'll feel as if you've been transported to southern Germany.

And *Mai* has a high-canopied double bed, reached by a small ladder; the design inside the canopy features storybook-style figures from newlyweds to senior couples. John places a complimentary bottle of imported German wine and two glasses in each room, just one of the many thoughtful touches.

Guess who's the chef? John is a classically trained cooking-school graduate who specializes in excellent Old World cuisine—with a Czech flair. His extensive menu features more than fifty-five equally tantilizing dinner entrees.

"What's your pleasure? I'll cook you a feast!" he said. A typical Central European meal includes *romacka* (cream of bean soup with dill) and Czech roast duck served with red cabbage, potato dumplings, and dressing, with apple strudel for dessert. Then you might head upstairs for your own Old World–style recipes for romance.

How to get there: From Minneapolis, take 35 W south; exit on County Road 2. Continue to Minnesota 13 and turn south; proceed directly into New Prague; the hotel is on the left.

Innkeepers: John and Kathleen Schumacher
Address/Telephone: 212 West Main Street; (612) 758–2133
Rooms: 11; all with private bath, air conditioning, and phone, some with gas fireplace and hair dryer.
Rates: $104 to $120, single or double, Sunday through Thursday; $130 to $155, single or double, Friday through Saturday; EP. Special packages and senior citizens' rates available. Personal checks from Minnesota only.
Open: All year except Christmas Eve and Christmas Day.
Facilities and activities: Full-service restaurant with wheelchair access. Bavarian bar, European gift shop, travel agency. Nearby: drive to cross-country and downhill skiing, swimming, golf, boating, fishing, biking, hiking, orchard, museums, racetrack, amusement park.

St. Charles House
ST. CHARLES, MISSOURI 63301

Open the door to this re-created 1800s brick building within sight of the lazing Missouri River, and you step back into an air of nineteenth-century luxury and romance.

The inn sits on Main Street of Missouri's first state capital, a street lined with more than one hundred historic brick buildings dating to the late nineteenth century (and today largely inhabited by arts and antiques shops).

It's a lovingly restored retreat from the bustle of visitors that can overwhelm the tiny hamlet. The replica house looks fit for a prosperous frontier businessman, sporting spacious rooms, fine antiques, and elegant surroundings.

"All of our antiques pre-date 1850," said Patti. Many were purchased in Denver, some right in town. Especially noteworthy is a massive Austrian buffet with intricate hand carving and a 9-foot-tall French walnut armoire.

The house's open floor plan includes a four-columned foyer and a bedchamber complete with oak hardwood floors, queen-sized canopy bed, and original Mary Gregory table lamp.

An elegant sitting area offers oriental-style rugs and a place to relax. There's even a mini-refrigerator in an antique side buffet along with a small wet bar.

Walk downstairs to reach the bath. Behind handsome double doors is a claw-footed tub under a crystal chandelier in a huge room decorated in pink and blues. Just outside is another Victorian-style sitting room. (Insert your own fantasies here.)

The innkeepers also own a guest cottage located a few doors down Main Street. This 1850s house is charming, outfitted in English country antiques that include a Welsh cupboard dating to 1813. Its two rooms offer pencil-post and four-poster cannonball beds, antique claw-footed tubs, and more fabulous antiques.

Hard to believe, but "it took only three days to buy all our pieces," Patti said. "We went on an antique-buying spree, and every place we stopped just happened to have exactly what we wanted."

But it's the St. Charles House's main residence that's best suited for "getting-to-know-you" adventures.

How to get there: From St. Louis or Kansas City, exit I–70 at First Capital Drive, and follow that north, then east to Main Street; turn right and continue to the inn.

Innkeepers: Patricia and Lionel York

Address/Telephone: 338 South Main Street; (314) 946–6221 or (800) 366–2427 via town Tourism Center

Rooms: 1 suite with sitting room, porch overlooking Missouri River, and private bath. One 2-bedroom guest cottage with 2 baths, dining room, small porch.

Rates: $90 weekdays, $115 Friday and Saturday for suite; $75 weekdays, $90 weekends for each room in cottage; deluxe continental breakfast.

Open: All year.

Facilities and activities: Walk to quaint shops, restaurants, riverboat cruises, tours of the first state capital. A short drive to downtown St. Louis and the Arch, St. Louis Art Museum, restored Union Station, Opera House, Powell Symphony Hall, and Fox Theatre.

Dancing Leaf Earth Lodge
STOCKVILLE, NEBRASKA 69042

A back-to-nature adventure conjures up its own special brand of romance. That's what I was thinking as the wind blew ferociously at about forty-five miles per hour when we arrived at Dancing Leaf, located on the banks of Medicine Creek, in a setting of rolling hills that once hosted farming ancestors of the Pawnee Tribe.

And the surrounding cottonwoods were really dancing, raising the noise level from their usual polite ballet to that of a stampeding crowd.

Les took us to one of the earth lodges, which appear much as they would have more than 1,000 years ago when built by the Upper Republican Culture in this region's prehistoric times. He explained that it took every bit of 400 hours to construct the dwelling.

"First, you have to cut the timber, in this case about 300 ash, cedar, and hackberry trees, and cure it months before you start to build," he explained. "Then we excavate a 20-foot-by-20-foot living floor and set native trees in holes to provide support for the walls and roof." These are made from more than 200 rafter poles, which are layered with sandbar willows and prairie hay to provide protection from the elements for this igloo-shaped dwelling.

Another unique characteristic of the lodge is its long, low entryway. We had to bend almost in half to traverse the walkway.

"This acts as a chimney for the cold and

heat," Les said. In fact, if you keep the lodge flap down, temperatures inside stay at 75 degrees during summer. Heat from the central fire hearth (with smoke escaping through a smokehole) keeps things toasty enough in winter.

But Dancing Leaf is much more than an opportunity to experience a facet of prehistoric culture. "Guests tell us that this place often prompts a personal spiritual reawakening, a chance to get in touch with the renewing power of nature and to learn more about themselves," Les said.

Such profound experiences occur most often after introduction to the sweat lodge, Les explained. Like I said—a different kind of romance, one that calls on the renewal of the spirit itself.

How to get there: From North Platte, exit I–80 and go south on U.S. 83; turn left (east) on Nebraska 23/18 at Maywood, and proceed to Curtis; then follow Nebraska 18 east into Stockville. Go into town; at the intersection with the county fairgrounds on the corner, turn left (there is a sign here), go past the fairgrounds, past the brick schoolhouse, and over the switchback bridge crossing Medicine Creek to the earth-lodge office. It's about 1½ miles north of Stockville.

Innkeepers: Les and Jan Hosick
Address/Telephone: Box 121; (308) 367–4233
Rooms: 2 authentic Native American earth lodges; portable bathroom provided.
Rates: $25 per adult; EP. $40 per adult; EPB (may include some nontraditional meals).
Open: All year.
Facilities and activities: Native American sweat lodge, nature trails, primitive living skills classes, calendar pole and medicine wheel, prehistoric garden, spiritual-bonding points, council areas, Medicine Creek mud slides (swimming), canoeing, fishing. Also explore lodge's archeological sites, museum, gift shop. Less than 1 hour's drive to Lexington antiques shops and Buffalo Bill's Scout's Rest Ranch in North Platte.

Sweet Valley Inn
KELLEYS ISLAND, OHIO 43438

After just one day at this charming 1892 Victorian home on romantic Kelleys Island (whose entire 2,800 acres are listed on the National Register of Historic Places), I realized that this was one of the Midwest's best inns.

But first, some history. Here's how the inn got started: Bev noticed a FOR SALE sign on the house when she returned to the island more than 30 years after she'd attended 4-H camp here. Paul had only been to the island once in his entire life.

"It'd make a perfect bed and breakfast," she told him.

The rest, as they say, is history.

Paul and Beverly have fashioned a turn-of-the-century showplace at their pretty yellow house. Grand double front doors with original stained glass open to an elegant foyer. Tour the house and you'll discover that it has beautiful woodwork: cedar (from the island) in the dining room, butternut in hallways, oak in the kitchen, and pine on the second floor.

There are four working fireplaces. And a handsome butternut stairway, leading to upstairs guest rooms, is lighted by more original stained-glass treatments.

Every guest room features fine antiques, transporting guests back into a long-ago period of elegance. Our bedchamber offered antique pine-plank floors, floral Victorian-style wall treatments, and beautiful window views of the property.

Romantics might ask Paul to hitch up Firmy to the inn's Amish-custom-made surrey for an afternoon ride along the Lake Erie shoreline. (He'll even pick up guests at the ferry docks, if requested.)

You can spend some evening time in the Sun Room, which enjoys views of Bev's beautiful gardens, talking with the innkeepers and other guests. Morning took us into the dining room, itself a showplace with its Empire buffet, black marble fireplace, and plank floors.

Only breakfast surpassed the fine surroundings. First we delighted in a fruit dish dappled with sour cream and brown-sugar sauce. Next came hot apple cinnamon muffins—nobody could get enough of these delicious treats. Then deviled eggs with mushroom sauce.

And for the final course: homemade waffles smothered with berries, walnuts, powdered sugar, and whipped cream.

"Whipped cream for breakfast!" one guest exclaimed. "This really is a great place."

I'll second that notion.

How to get there: From the ferry docks, "follow the traffic into town" (it's not hard to find, believe me) and look for Division Street. Turn north and continue about 1 mile down the road until reaching the inn, which is on the left side of the road.

Innkeepers: Paul and Beverly Johnson
Address/Telephone: 715 Division Street (mailing address: P. O. Box 733); (419) 746–2750
Rooms: 4 share 2 baths. No smoking inn.
Rates: $75, single; $85, double; EPB. Special packages available.
Open: All year.
Facilities and activities: Family room, enclosed sunporch, garden with pond, lawn with tree swings, horse barn and corral. Carriage rides and bike rentals available. Swimming, picnics, fishing, sailing, hiking, biking. A short drive to Glacial Grooves, ferry ride to Cedar Point Amusement Park.

The Inn at Honey Run
MILLERSBURG, OHIO 44654

"Just look at that," Marge said, pointing to a black Amish carriage clip-clopping down a winding country road just below a room deck of The Inn at Honey Run. "That's why I love spring, fall, and winter here. You can still see sights like that through the trees. It takes you back to the 1800s."

To get here I had driven down a hilly, twisting road that I thought would never end. "We're hard to find," Marge admitted. Her graceful inn is situated on sixty hilly, wooded acres in the middle of Ohio Amish country. Its wood-and-stone construction blends magnificently with the gorgeous landscape.

"Birding here is great," Marge said, as she pointed to countless feeders surrounding the inn. "Visitors have recorded about thirty different species."

I was anxious to see the rooms, and I wasn't disappointed. They're done in a potpourri of styles: Early American; contemporary with slanted ceilings and skylights; and Shaker—my favorite—with many pegs on the walls to hang everything from clothes to furniture.

Marge uses Holmes County folk art to highlight each room; handmade quilts adorn walls and beds (which are extra long); and there are comfy chairs with reading lamps.

More surprises: Twelve "Honeycomb Rooms" are the "world's first commercial earth-shelter rooms," built under and into Holmes County hills. "It's the perfect place for overstressed executives," Marge said of these almost cavelike retreats, which feature wood-burning fireplace, whirlpool bath, and breakfast delivered to the door. And there are two wonderful cabins perched high on a hill, with panoramic views of Holmes County landscapes; these are, perhaps, the inn's most romantic getaway retreats.

Inn food is made from scratch, with pan-fried trout from Holmes County waters a dinner specialty. Marge's full country breakfast features juice, eggs and bacon, French toast with real maple syrup, and homemade breads.

Then you might take a romantic hand-holding hike of the grounds. But don't be surprised if you're followed by Luke, the inn's coon hound, or by Sandy, the beagle.

How to get there: From Millersburg it is 3.3 miles to the inn. Go east on East Jackson Street in Millersburg (Routes 39 and 62). Pass the courthouse and gas station on the right. At the next corner, turn left onto Route 241, which makes several turns as it twists out of town. Nearly 2 miles down the road, while proceeding down a long, steep hill, you'll cross a bridge over Honey Run. Turn right immediately around another small hill onto County Road 203, which is not well marked. After 1 mile, turn right at the small inn sign. Go up the hill to the inn.

Innkeeper: Marge Stock

Address/Telephone: 6920 County Road 203; (216) 674–0011; toll-free in Ohio (800) 468–6639

Rooms: 36, with 1 suite and 2 cabins; all with private bath and air conditioning, most with TV.

Rates: $79 to $150, rooms; $200 to $275, cabins; single or double, continental breakfast. Two-night minimum Friday and Saturday. Special winter rates.

Open: All year.

Facilities and activities: Full-service dining room (closed Sunday) with wheelchair access. BYOB. Meeting rooms host movies and table tennis on weekends, library, game room, gift shop. Hiking trails, sheep and goats in pastures, nature lecture and walks most weekends, horseshoes, croquet, volleyball. Nearby: Holmes County antiques and specialty stores, cheese factories, quilt shops, 9-hole golf course. A short drive to Roscoe Village canal-era town and Warther Wood Carving Museum.

Recommended Country Inns® Travel Club Benefit: 10% discount, Monday–Thursday, subject to availability.

The Washington House Inn
CEDARBURG, WISCONSIN 53012

Cedarburg is a historic woolen-mill town, with many rare "cream city" brick and stone buildings dating from the mid-1800s. In fact, the downtown area alone contains more historic structures than any other city west of Philadelphia!

One of these is The Washington House Inn, a country-Victorian "cream city" brick building completed in 1886. The tall front doors and authentic frontier ambience are softened by a long lobby sprinkled with Victorian furnishings, rich parquet floors, brass chandeliers, and a marble fireplace.

I looked at the original hotel register, which recorded visitors during the months of 1895.

How did anyone ever have the time to write in that fancy scroll? I also noticed an unusual display: a "wedding brick" discovered during recent restoration with the date "1886" and the names of the happy couple scratched on it.

The guest rooms are named for leading citizens of historic Cedarburg. The country-Victorian decorations are absolutely charming, with floral wallpapers, fancy armoires, cozy down quilts, fresh flowers, and more. I really like the leaded-glass transom windows of some rooms.

In the newly restored rooms, there's more of a plain country feeling, but there's nothing plain about the decor. The exposed brick walls and beamed ceilings are spectacular.

Then there are some very deluxe quarters; my favorite romantic retreat has country-style antiques, loft beds cozied by their own fireplace, and another loft area that boasts a 200-gallon spa tub warmed by a second fireplace. Now that's really something special!

Or perhaps you'd like a room at the inn's other building, the 1868 Schroeder House, located about four doors down from the main inn; cozy fireplaces are part of the romance here.

It's fun to eat breakfast in a dining room with white pressed-tin ceilings, oak tables and chairs, and tall windows that wash the room in light. (Of course, you may have breakfast in bed, too.) Home-baked breads, cakes, and rolls are made from recipes found in an authentic turn-of-the-century Cedarburg cookbook. Cereal, fresh fruit, and beverages also are offered.

One of Wendy's favorite times of the day is the afternoon social hour in the dining room, with an opportunity to share with guests her love of this historic town. A manteled fireplace with Victorian sofas and chairs just off the main dining area makes things more cozy.

How to get there: From Chicago, take I–94 to I–43, just north of Milwaukee, and get off at the Cedarburg exit. This road eventually changes to Wisconsin 57; follow it into town (where it becomes Washington Street). At Center Street, turn left and park in the lot behind the hotel.

Innkeeper: Wendy Porterfield, manager
Address/Telephone: W62 N573 Washington Avenue; (414) 375–3550 or (800) 369–4088
Rooms: 34, including 15 suites; all with private bath, air conditioning, TV, and phone; 31 rooms with whirlpool bath. Wheelchair access.
Rates: $59 to $159, single or double; $119 to $159, suites; continental breakfast. Special packages available.
Open: All year.
Facilities and activities: Situated in heart of historic Cedarburg; walk to restaurants and Cedar Creek Settlement: old Woolen Mill; Stone Mill Winery; antiques, crafts, specialty shops. A short drive to Ozaukee Pioneer Village, Ozaukee Covered Bridge (last remaining covered bridge in Wisconsin).
Recommended Country Inns® Travel Club Benefit: 50% off $99 to $159 rooms.

Canoe Bay Inn & Cottages

CHETEK, WISCONSIN 54728

Dan and Lisa's inn, already one of the "Top Ten" country inns in the Midwest, just keeps getting better. Take a look for yourself.

They've added four luxurious and romantic cottage suites, featuring Frank Lloyd Wright's signature Prairie-style architecture along with "every possible creature comfort with the ultimate in privacy." Even Canoe Bay's exterior spaces have received what Wright called "organic architecture" treatment, with natural prairie, woodland grasses, and wildflowers designed and installed by a nationally renowned consulting ecologist.

The innkeepers spared no expense in re-creating the great architect's distinctive style.

For example, the Oak Park Suite boasts a 14-foot wall of casement windows overlooking a lake; the Wood Grove Suite allows guests to observe natural surroundings from their platform two-person Jacuzzi through wraparound windows. Also count on river-rock fireplace, stereo TV/VCR/CD, wet bar with refrigerator and microwave oven, huge private deck, and more.

The main building centerpiece is a great room, with soaring natural-cedar cathedral ceilings, a wall of windows, and a 30-foot-tall, hand-constructed fieldstone fireplace.

Dan (former TV weatherman for WFLD-Channel 32 in Chicago) and Lisa built their inn on the shore of crystal-clear Lake Wahdoon, a fifty-acre spring-fed body of water surrounded by 280 acres of private oak, aspen, and maple forests. The inn provides breathtaking views, incomparable service, and complete privacy besides the many opportunities for outdoor recreation and relaxation, including wildlife watching.

Mornings bring pampering, with breakfast baskets delivered to your room or brought out to the patio overlooking the lake, where you can enjoy scores of chirping songbirds. Meals might include fresh grapefruit and juices; freshly baked cranberry bread, croissants, and homemade preserves; a delicious egg soufflé and cheese plate; and beverages. Canoe Bay's commercial kitchen also offers dinner featuring Northern Wisconsin cuisine to guests.

Later, you can wander along Canoe Bay's 2 miles of nature trails, which double as cross-country ski paths in winter. One trail leads to a bridge connecting one of the lodge's two islands to the mainland.

The inn's standout season could be autumn, with its incomparable colors, but holidays receive special treatment, too. Thanksgiving and New Year's Day guests can enjoy guided cross-country ski tours, ice skating, ice fishing, and a 14-foot-tall Christmas tree with all the trimmings. Not to mention a free, personal weather forecast from prognosticator Dan, who's often heard to say, "If there's a better place on Earth, I don't know it."

Forget Earth. This is heaven.

How to get there: Once in Chetek, Highway 53 is named Second Street. Follow that through town, over a bridge, and turn right on County D (there's a cemetery at this intersection); go about 1½ miles to Hogback Road (look for a CANOE BAY sign here); turn left and continue for about 7 miles to the inn.

Innkeepers: Dan and Lisa Dobrowolski
Address/Telephone: W16065 Hogback Road; (715) 924–4594 or (800) 568–1995
Rooms: 8, including 4 main lodge luxury suites and 4 luxury cottage suites; all with private bath, whirlpool bath, and air conditioning.
Rates: Weekdays: $89 to $129, lodge rooms; $119 to $159, cottage suites; EPB.
  Weekends: $109 to $159, lodge rooms; $149 to $189, cottage suites; EPB. Gourmet dinners $50 per couple.
Open: All year.
Facilities and activities: Sitting room, video room, book library. Located on private 280 acres: 2 private lakes, hiking paths, nature trails, cross-country ski trails, fishing, swimming, canoes, rowboats, and more. About 45 minutes west of St. Paul, Minnesota.
Recommended Country Inns® Travel Club Benefit: 10% discount, subject to availability.

The American Club
KOHLER, WISCONSIN 53044

Just 4 miles from the shoreline of Lake Michigan, amid tall pines, patches of white birch, scrubbed farmhouses, and black soil, is one of Wisconsin's most romantic retreats. It's The American Club, a uniquely gracious guest house.

There's an uncommonly European ambience at this elegant inn. With its Tudor-style appointments of gleaming brass, custom-crafted oak furniture, crystal chandeliers, and quality antique furnishings, The American Club looks like a finely manicured baronial estate. It's also the only five-diamond resort hotel in the Midwest.

Built in 1918 as a temporary home for immigrant workers of the Kohler Company (a renowned plumbing manufacturer, still located across the street), the "boarding house" served as a meeting place where English and citizenship classes were taught—a genuine American Club.

Talk about romance: Some rooms feature a four-poster canopied brass bed and huge marble-lined whirlpool bath. Special suites contain a saunalike environmental enclosure with a push-button choice of weather—from bright sun and gentle breezes to misty rain showers. And consider other guest pamperings: fluffy bathrobes, twice-daily maid service, daily newspapers—the list goes on!

The inn's showcase restaurant is The Immigrant, a romantic hideaway where we dined on a four-course gourmet meal that included smoked Irish salmon. The wine list is impressive, too. For dessert we walked to the Greenhouse, in the courtyard. This antique English solarium is a perfect spot for chocolate torte and other Viennese delights.

Not to mention your late-night rendezvous with your special sweetie.

How to get there: From Chicago, take I–94 north and continue north on I–43, just outside of Milwaukee. Exit on Wisconsin 23 west (exit 53B). Take 23 to County Trunk Y and continue south into Kohler. The inn is on the right.

From the west, take I–94 south to Wisconsin 21 and go east to U.S. 41. Go south on 41 to Wisconsin 23; then head east into Kohler.

Innkeeper: Susan Porter Green, vice-president; Alice Hubbard, general manager
Address/Telephone: Highland Drive; (414) 457–8000 or (800) 344–2838, fax (414) 457–0299
Rooms: 160; all with private whirlpool bath, air conditioning, TV, and phone. Wheelchair access.
Rates: May 1–October 31: $155 to $575, single; $185 to $575, double; EP. November 1–April 30: $120 to $525, single; $150 to $525, double; EP. Two-night minimum on weekends from Memorial Day through Labor Day, and December 30 through January 2.
Open: All year.
Facilities and activities: Nine restaurants and full-service dining rooms. Renowned for extravagant buffets, special-event and holiday feasts; large Sunday brunch. Ballroom. Sports Core, a world-class health club. River Wildlife, 500 acres of private woods for hiking, horseback riding, hunting, fishing, trapshooting, canoeing. Cross-country skiing and ice skating. Also Kohler Design Center, shops at Woodlake, Kohler Arts Center, Waelderhaus. Nearby: antiquing, lake charter fishing, Kettle Moraine State Forest, Road America (auto racing).

Inn at Pine Terrace
OCONOMOWOC, WISCONSIN 53066

Cary O'Dwanny and his wife, Christine, two of the inn's principal owners, greeted Debbie and me outside their inn, an impressive three-story Victorian mansion built in 1884 by the Schuttler family, well-known wagon makers from Chicago. In fact, two Schuttler sons married girls whose families used those wagons to haul barrels of beer for their breweries; one was an Anheuser, another a Busch.

As soon as I stepped inside the massive double doors of the tiled foyer, accented with stained and etched glass, I knew the inn would be quite special.

The restoration, which took more than two years to complete, is an accomplished one. Cary spent more than $750,000 in millwork alone to bring back the elaborate butternut and walnut moldings that are everywhere. Furniture, done in antique Eastlake style, was custom made especially for the inn. A curving walnut handrail that crowns the three-story staircase is valued at $55,000. Most bathrooms have a marble-lined two-person whirlpool bath; guest-room doors have brass hinges and hand-carved wooden doorknobs; custom wall coverings and brooding Victorian paint colors evoke the period as almost no other inn has before.

Once the town was an exclusive vacation spot for wealthy Southern families escaping the summer heat. "The mansion was the 'in' place to be," Cary said. "Five U.S. presidents were guests here, beginning with Taft." Other notables included the likes of Mark Twain and Montgomery Ward.

Elegant guest rooms are named for historic residents of Oconomowoc. Most are huge by inn standards, with the first-floor beauty perhaps the romantic showpiece. It features a massive bedroom area with a crowning touch: marble steps leading to a marble platform, upon which sits a white-enamel, brass-claw-footed bathtub illuminated by a bank of three ceiling-to-floor windows—shuttered for privacy, of course.

Rooms on the third floor are smaller, since these are the old servant's quarters; however, they are no less attractive. Our room, named for Captain Gustav Pabst, was a charming hide-away with slanting dormer ceilings that created a small sitting-room alcove; its brass lighting fixtures, rich woodwork, deep green wall coverings, double whirlpool tub, and tiny window offering a view of Lac La Belle made it one of our favorites.

A breakfast buffet, served in the dining room on the lower level, means cereals, fresh fruits, home-baked muffins, and coffee. Later you can lounge at the inn's swimming pool, or take a dip in the refreshing water while already making plans for your return visit here.

How to get there: From Milwaukee, take I–94 west to U.S. 67. Exit north and continue through town to Lisbon Road. Turn right; the inn is just down the street.

Innkeeper: Mary Quissek, manager
Address/Telephone: 371 Lisbon Road; (414) 567–7463
Rooms: 13; all with private bath, air conditioning, phone, and TV, 6 with double whirlpool bath. Wheelchair access. Well-behaved pets OK.
Rates: $69.50 to $119.50, single or double, continental breakfast.
Open: All year.
Facilities and activities: Sitting room, conference room, swimming pool. Short walk to Lac La Belle for swimming, fishing, boating, and three beaches. Restaurants and Olympia Ski Area, with downhill and cross-country skiing, a short drive away.
Recommended Country Inns® Travel Club Benefit: 15% discount, Sunday–Thursday.

St. Croix River Inn
OSCEOLA, WISCONSIN 54020

This eighty-plus-year-old stone house is poised high on a bluff overlooking the scenic St. Croix River. It allows unsurpassed, breathtaking views while providing one of the most romantic lodgings in the entire Midwest.

I'm especially fond of a suite with a huge whirlpool bath set in front of windows, allowing you to float visually down the river while pampering yourself in a bubble bath.

"The house was built from limestone quarried near here," Bev said. "It belonged to the owner of the town's pharmacy and remained in his family until a few years ago."

Now let's get right to the rooms (suites, really), which are named for riverboats built in Osceola. Perhaps (and this is a *big* perhaps) Jennie Hays is my all-time favorite inn room. It is simply exquisite, with appointments that remind me of exclusive European hotels. I continue to rave about a magnificent four-poster canopy bed that feels as good as it looks and a decorative tile fireplace that soothes the psyche as well as chilly limbs on crackling-cool autumn or frigid winter nights.

Then there is the view! I'm almost at a loss for words. A huge Palladian window, stretching from floor to ceiling, overlooks the river from the inn's bluff-top perch. It provides a romantic and rewarding setting that would be hard to surpass anywhere in the Midwest. The room has a whirlpool tub, and there's a private balcony with more great river views.

The G. B. Knapp Room is more of the same: a huge suite, with a four-poster canopy bed adorned with a floral quilt, tall armoire, its own working gas fireplace, and a whirlpool tub. Then walk through a door to the enclosed porch (more like a private sitting room), with windows overlooking the river. There are also exquisite stenciling, bull's-eye moldings, and private balconies.

Pampering continues at breakfast, which Bev serves in your room or in bed. It might include fresh fruit and juices, omelets, waffles, French toast, or puff pastries stuffed with ham and cheese, and French bread and pound cake.

Bev also delivers to your room a pot of steaming coffee and the morning paper a half hour before your morning meal. She can recommend a great place for dinner. But you simply may never want to leave your quarters.

Let's face it: This is one of the Midwest's most romantic retreats—pure grace and elegance.

How to get there: From downtown Osceola, turn west on Third Avenue and follow it past a hospital and historic Episcopal church (dating from 1854, with four turreted steeples). The inn is located on the river side of River Street.

Innkeeper: Bev Johnson
Address/Telephone: 305 River Street; (715) 294–4248
Rooms: 7; all with private bath and air conditioning, 2 with TV.
Rates: Friday and Saturday, $100 to $200; Sunday through Thursday, $85 to $150; single or double, EPB. Gift certificates available.
Open: All year.
Facilities and activities: Outdoor porch, sitting room overlooking St. Croix River. Nearby: several antiques shops, canoeing, fishing, downhill and cross-country skiing at Wild Mountain or Trollhaugen. A short drive to restaurants and Taylors Falls, Minnesota—a lovely little river town with historic-homes tours and cruises on old-fashioned paddlewheelers.
Recommended Country Inns® Travel Club Benefit: Stay two nights, get third night free.

White Lace Inn

STURGEON BAY, WISCONSIN 54235

Bonnie and Dennis call their inn "a romantic fireside getaway." I can't think of a better place to spend a cozy, pampered weekend for two.

And things have only gotten better since my last visit. Now the White Lace Inn resembles a private Victorian-era park, with three handsome historic buildings connected by a red-brick pathway that winds through landscaped grounds filled with stately trees, wildflower gardens, and a rose garden featuring varieties dating from the 1700s. You will also enjoy the Vixen Hill gazebo, a great place to pause among the inn's many gardens; it is a beauty from Pennsylvania.

The Main House was built for a local lawyer in 1903; what's surprising is the extensive oak woodwork put in for a man of such modest means. Stepping into the entryway, I was surrounded by magnificent hand-carved oak paneling.

Bonnie has a degree in interior design and has created guest rooms with a warm romantic feel, mixing Laura Ashley wallpaper and fabrics with imposing, yet comfortable, antique furnishings like rich oriental rugs and high-back walnut and canopied beds. Fluffy down pillows are provided, handmade comforters and quilts brighten large beds, and lacy curtains adorn tall windows.

The 1880s Garden House has rooms with

their own fireplace. They're done in myriad styles, from country elegant to the grand boldness of oversized Empire furniture.

This time my wife and I stayed in the Washburn House, the third and newest "old" addition to the White Lace. All rooms here are luxurious; ours had a canopy brass bed with down comforter, fireplace, and two-person whirlpool. It was graced with soft pastel floral chintz fabric and white-on-white Carol Gresco fabrics that tell a story (in fact, some of her work is part of the Smithsonian Design Institute's collection). The bath's Ralph Lauren towels are heavenly.

Back in the main house, Bonnie's homemade muffins are the breakfast treat, along with juice, coffee, and delicious Scandinavian fruit soup (a tasty concoction served cold) or old-fashioned rice pudding. Blueberry soup and apple crisps are summer specials. It's a great time to swap Door County stories.

But we couldn't wait to get back to our room.

How to get there: From Milwaukee, take U.S. 41 north to Wisconsin 42, toward Sturgeon Bay. Just outside the city, take Business 42/57 and follow it into town, cross the bridge, and you'll come to Michigan Street. Follow Michigan to Fifth Avenue and turn left. White Lace Inn is on the right side of the street. Or you can take the 42/51 bypass across the new bridge to Michigan Street. Turn left on Michigan, go to Fifth Avenue, and take a right on Fifth to the inn.

Innkeepers: Bonnie and Dennis Statz

Address/Telephone: 16 North Fifth Avenue; (414) 743–1105

Rooms: 15, in 3 historic houses; all with private bath and air conditioning, some with fireplace, whirlpool, TV, and wheelchair access.

Rates: $68 to $148, single or double, continental breakfast. Special winter or spring fireside packages available November through May.

Open: All year.

Facilities and activities: Five blocks to bay shore. Close to specialty and antiques shops, restaurants, Door County Museum, Miller Art Center. Swimming, tennis, and horseback riding nearby. A short drive to Whitefish Dunes and Potawatomi state parks, Peninsula Players Summer Theater, Birch Creek Music Festival. Cross-country skiing and ice skating in winter. Gateway to the peninsula.

The Southwest

by Eleanor S. Morris

Ah, romance! Who can define it?

Dictionaries try. *Webster's* defines romance as "extraordinary life, not real or familiar," adding "colloquially, to make love." *Thorndike Barnhard* agrees; its definition reads, "a love affair, an interest in adventure and love." *Collins Gem* (a French dictionary) declares it *"poesie"* and *"idylle,"* and *Cassell's New Compact French Dictionary* says romance is not only *"amourette"* and *"aventure"* (love and adventure), it is also *"inventer a plaisir"*: to imagine a pleasure, a delight.

So, is it more of a feeling we bring to a place, or can the place itself be romantic, engendering romantic feelings in us? I think it's both; I like the way the French say that romance means to invent a delight. Imagination inspires us to look for surroundings that will complement and enhance romance.

Herein are twenty inns of the Southwest that provide a delightful ambience of *"idylle et poesie."* Although they help keep romance alive, part of their magic comes from what you bring along with you. Whether it's romance amid the opulence of a Victorian mansion, in an eagle's aerie in the mountains, or in the pampered Southern comfort of an antebellum plantation, these inns provide the perfect setting for a wonderful experience of romance.

The rest is up to you.

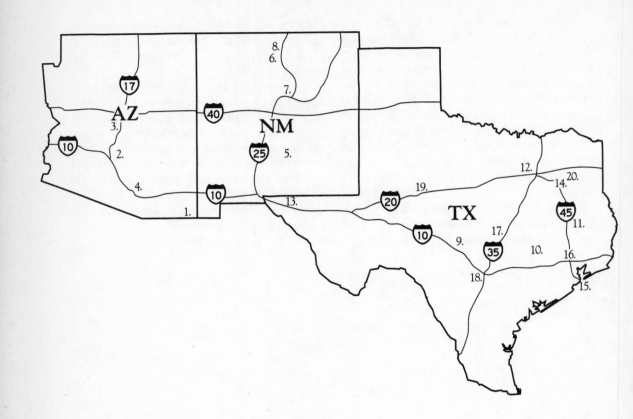

The Southwest

Numbers on map refer to towns numbered below.

Bisbee Grand Hotel
BISBEE, ARIZONA 85603

Opulence, extraordinary almost-out-of-the-world opulence, is what we found at the well-named Bisbee Grand. Grand is a perfect adjective for this inn—so is elegant. From the red velvet Victorian Suite to the other-worldly Oriental Suite, exotic luxury abounds in this posh, treasure-filled inn.

The modest, small black marquee over the double doors, squeezed in between two storefronts, hardly prepared us for what awaited as we climbed the red-carpeted stairs leading from the narrow entrance to the second floor and the inn rooms. Once there, faced with an iridescent stuffed peacock at the head of the stairs, we found ourselves in a world we certainly had never expected in the quaint and charming Old West mining town of Bisbee.

Each of the seven guest rooms is a world in itself, full of beautiful furniture and decorative details. "These antiques were collected for thirty years," innkeeper Bill said with justifiable pride. As for the three suites, they are extravaganzas, excitingly imaginative, full of unexpected appointments, such as a working fountain next to a lovely, large flower arrangement in the Garden Suite.

The Oriental Suite is unashamedly opulent, with walls covered in black, pink, and gold fabric depicting Chinese scenes. The brass bed is adorned with onyx and alabaster. "It's a unique, one-of-a-kind honeymoon bed," Bill explained. It's wide and high, with an oval mirror and paintings, while bronze dragon vases and black lacquer vie with other choice collectibles in the room.

The Victorian Suite is dripping with deep red-velvet hangings, not only on the windows but also making a cozy nest of the canopied bed. The Garden Suite is a bower of flowers; as for the rest of the rooms, like the Coral and the Gray rooms, Deer Springs and Crow Canyon, well, any one is an outstanding setting for romance.

On the main floor, adjacent to the Grand Western Saloon, the inn's old-fashioned Victorian parlor has an antique piano that we played. Fun was sitting at the saloon's 35-foot bar, which came from Wyatt Earp's Oriental Bar by way of the Wells Fargo Museum.

Breakfast will satisfy both the most eager gourmet and the health food aficionado. "All our food is from Tucson Cooperative Warehouses," Bill noted, "and we recycle and compost everything." The fruit course consisted of watermelon, cantaloupe, pineapple, and green grapes; the delicious quiche was full of cheese and mushrooms, with ham on the side; the homemade bread was delicious; and for sweets, there were cheese Danish and cinnamon rolls.

"We treat our guests very special, with all the grace and elegance of the best of a Victorian mining town," Bill said, in case we hadn't noticed! Morning coffee, hot tea, iced tea, and a plateful of ginger snaps, lemon bars, and peanut butter and chocolate chip cookies were available in the saloon practically 'round the clock. And not the least of the pleasures of this small, elegant inn was watching the sunset, or the rainbow after it rains, over the mountains facing the front balcony.

How to get there: From Highway 80 east take Tombstone Canyon Road for approximately 2½ miles until it becomes Main Street. You can't miss the Bisbee Grand on the left.

Innkeeper: Bill Thomas

Address/Telephone: 61 Main Street (mailing address: P.O. Box 825); (602) 432–5900 or (800) 421–1909

Rooms: 11; 7 with private bath. No smoking inn.

Rates: $50 to $75, double; $95, suites; EPB.

Open: All year.

Facilities and activities: Grand Western Saloon with complimentary snacks, pool table, large TV screen, and Ladies' Parlor; Murder Mystery weekends. Nearby: Old Bisbee Tour, City Mine Tour, Bisbee Mining and Historical Museum, antiques shops, art galleries.

The Inn at the Citadel
SCOTTSDALE, ARIZONA 85255

"Everything has family meaning," Kelly Keyes said of this posh, family-built inn in chic Scottsdale, at the foot of outstanding Pinnacle Peak. "It's all been built in threes and fives; those three arches over there are for three daughters—me and my two sisters."

The sentiment goes beyond the immediate family. Kelly pointed out that the brands decorating the Marque Bar were those of everyone who had anything to do with the building of the inn. "Architects, builders, my parents—theirs is the flying double K," she explained. We thought such sentiment was pretty romantic.

The inn had a propitious beginning. Built on Hopi Indian land, the Hopis were invited to a blessing of the land, and everyone, even the children, came. It was a black-tie-and-jeans event, jeans and boots.

This is a pretty sumptuous establishment for the casual Southwest, more like a fine European-style hotel than a country inn, but "we try to put guests at their ease," Adam Wilson told us. "Sometimes they're a little taken aback, awed by the location." This is grand country, with Pinnacle Peak just overhead.

Kelly's mother, Anita Keyes, is an interior designer, and each of the eleven rooms is decorated with careful detail, down to the smallest item. Original artwork by such artists as Jonathan Sobel and Armond Laura hang on the walls, and antiques are used extensively. The armoires in six of the rooms were painted by local Arizona artists Liz Henretta, Skip Bennett, Sherry Stewart, and Carolyn Baer.

Rooms have safes, robes, hair dryers, bath amenities, and an honor bar, stocked with not only premium liquors, wine, and champagne, but also playing cards, along with the expected soft drinks, crackers, and candy bars.

Fresh hot coffee comes along with the complimentary newspaper each morning and each room has cable TV with HBO. It was tempting to just curl up and lounge and never come out!

The larger rooms are more like suites, with big sitting areas and desks. The king-sized beds are covered with quilted satiny spreads, and the pillow shams match the dust ruffles.

Actually, the Citadel is not only an inn. It's a restaurant and shopping complex in a shady courtyard complete with a pond and a bubbling waterfall. The continental breakfast is served either in The Market or in your room, whichever you prefer. Fresh-squeezed orange juice is followed by a large serving of seasonal fresh fruit—we had raspberries—and then moist zucchini, bran, or corn muffins, and, of course, coffee or tea.

At The Market we found everything from blue-corn waffles to hamburgers, pastas, salads, and enchiladas, all deliciously fresh and nicely served. The award-winning 8700 at the Citadel really goes all out, with the finest regional American cuisine. One of chef Leonard Rubin's specialties is roast rack of black buck antelope. "It's pretty popular," Adam said. The menu also features 8700 Mixed Grill, poached salmon, and coffee toffee crunch cake.

How to get there: From I–17 take Bell Road 30 miles east to Scottsdale Road, then go north 4 miles to Pinnacle Peak Road and east 2 miles to the inn.

Innkeepers: Kelly Keyes, Jane De Beer, and Adam Wilson
Address/Telephone: 8700 East Pinnacle Peak Road; (602) 994–8700 or (800) 927–8367
Rooms: 11; all with private bath; wheelchair accessible. No smoking inn.
Rates: $195 to $265, double, continental breakfast.
Open: All year.
Facilities and activities: Two restaurants, piano bar, limo tours of the desert, health and beauty spa facilities, banking, banquet and catering facilities, boutiques. Nearby: hiking to Pinnacle Peak; golf.

Saddle Rock Ranch
SEDONA, ARIZONA 86336

This luxurious home is not we expected from a place that calls itself a ranch. While the historic homestead, built in 1926, is on the edge of a residential area, it sits on three acres of hillside overlooking Sedona, and it has starred in many Old West films.

"I just saw a late-night 'thirties movie, *Angel and the Bad Man*," Dan told us, "and there was our whole house! It was a dude ranch back then, and the wife of the owner always played an Indian princess in the films," he added with a laugh.

Fran and Dan, who met while both were employed at a prestigious California hotel, are experts in providing special attention to guests.

What we found was the same VIP treatment that they gave to many of the "rich and famous." And before that Dan had a rather adventurous career: My spouse recognized recognized his name; he played football for the Pittsburgh Steelers.

"He's lived every man's fantasy," Fran said. "He also raced with Mario Andretti on the Indy circuit." They moved to Sedona for the climate, and now Dan and Fran are having an adventurous time innkeeping. "Our guests are wonderful, outstanding, and we want them to have the same total experience throughout their visit. It's a point of pride to us that our guests get the best of not only what we have to offer, but what Sedona has to offer as well," Dan said, and we reveled in the full concierge service with restaurant reservations at Sedona's finest. If we'd wanted we could have had reservations for concerts, theater, tours, and anything else we could think of.

Guest rooms are elegantly comfortable, as is the living room. Large Saddle Rock Suite has a country French canopied bed and a rock fireplace; furniture in the Rose Garden Room was Dan's great-great-grandfather's, and the room has its own private, walled rose garden; The Cottage in back, with wood-paneled walls, is surrounded by panoramic vistas. Robes, nightly turndown, chocolates, bottled water, afternoon snacks, guest refrigerator and microwave oven—we made ourselves at home in this just-about-perfect inn.

There are cuddly teddy bears everywhere, and it's Dan who collects them! "I was born at home, and the doctor brought a bear when he delivered me—I still have it," he said. It lives in retirement with other teddy bears on a daybed that belonged to his great-great-grandfather.

Breakfast is served in the large and sunny dining room. Specialties are heart-shaped peach waffles and individual Dutch babies (pancakes) filled with apples and vanilla ice cream or yogurt. "I like to use our local Sedona apples, peaches, and pears," Fran said. Orange juice is always fresh-squeezed, and if you prefer tea to coffee, as I do, there are sixteen different ones to choose from.

At the rear of the property, a national forest shelters wildlife; deer come to the salt lick, and quail abound. The inn has tamer specimens in Diana and Fergie, miniature schnauzers. "But guest quarters are off-limits to them," Fran said, "unless you particularly request some puppy love!"

How to get there: Take Highway 89A (Airport Drive) to Valley View; go south 1 block to Rock Ridge Drive, left to Forest Circle, and right to Rock Ridge Circle; continue beyond Rock Ridge Drive and take the gravel road on the left up the hill to Saddle Rock.

Innkeepers: Fran and Dan Bruno
Address/Telephone: 255 Rock Ridge Drive; (602) 282–7640
Rooms: 3; all with private bath. No smoking inn.
Rates: $110 to $130, double; EPB and afternoon snacks. Extended-stay specials; two-night minimum stay.
Open: All year.
Facilities and activities: Swimming pool and spa, concierge service, Sedona airport transportation. Nearby: restaurants, shops, hiking, fishing, horseback riding, Hopi Mesa tours.

The Suncatcher
TUCSON, ARIZONA 85748

"I've tried to take all the qualities of a first-class hotel and put in the charm of a bed and breakfast," Dave said of his luxurious inn. A sure clue was the name of each guest-room name: There's the Connaught, the Four Seasons, the Regent, and the Oriental. With the hotels as his inspiration, Dave gave up his law practice to become an innkeeper.

"I was traveling a lot and I was ready for a change," he told us. "I began thinking about other things I could do." Now Dave likes to open the door wide and call, "Welcome to The Suncatcher!" He was delighted with our surprise, which was just what he has learned to expect.

"I see the guests' eyes open," he said, "and

it's such a pleasure. As for the name, The Suncatcher, why do people come to Tucson?" he asked. "The sun, the dry heat, the desert," he answered himself. "And I thought, what do I want my place to be? A retreat, a getaway—so I invented the name." Dave also created the inn emblem, bright little terra-cotta faces that are on the walls and elsewhere.

The huge common area (70 x 70 feet), with its soaring ceiling, has several focal points. In one corner there's a large, copper-hooded fireplace; in another, a mirrored mesquite bar. A centerpiece is the grand piano that Dave's parents bought for him when he was fifteen. "I play a little," he said modestly; he'd rather encourage guests to entertain. Display cases contain many personal treasures he collected on his travels.

The room is done so well we assumed it was decorated by a professional—it would make a beautiful spread in a fashionable home-decorating magazine. But Dave said he did it all himself, and he's pretty proud of that. The entire area—sitting, dining, kitchen—is open, and we watched chef Dave prepare breakfast, beginning with grapefruit halves, juices and coffee, on to cold cereals, egg strata, bagels, and honey date muffins. He asked the night before what time we'd like breakfast, which we thought was pretty accommodating. Any time is fine, and late in the day there are complimentary hors d'oeuvres. "My pleasure is sitting down and speaking with my guests," he said.

One guest room opens off the huge airy and spacious common area, two have French doors opening off the pool, and a fourth is around the corner with its own entrance.

The Connaught (London) is furnished with Chippendale-style furniture in gleaming dark mahogany; the Four Seasons with a formal canopied bed; the Regent (Hong Kong) has lovely original oriental scrolls. We chose the Oriental (Bangkok), the largest room, which had, among other splendors, its own Jacuzzi. All have at least one comfortable chair, writing desk, original artwork, and fresh flowers.

How to get there: The inn is on the edge of Saguaro National Monument. From I–10 and downtown Tucson, take Broadway east, crossing as a last landmark Houghton. Continue on to Avenida Javelina, bearing in mind that Avenida Javelina is beyond the DEAD-END sign on Broadway. Turn north on Javelina, and the inn is on the left in the middle of the block.

Innkeeper: David Williams
Address/Telephone: 105 North Avenida Javelina; (602) 885–0883 or (800) 835–8012
Rooms: 4; all with private bath, phone, TV, and VCR; wheelchair accessible. No smoking inn.
Rates: $125 to $145, double, EPB. Two-night minimum stay.
Open: All year.
Facilities and activities: Heated pool and spa, bicycle. Nearby: restaurants, tennis and health club, hiking, horseback riding, Saguaro National Monument; 15 minutes to downtown Tucson.

Casa de Patron
LINCOLN, NEW MEXICO 88338

Innkeepers Cleis (pronounced Cliss) and Jeremy used to camp in nearby Lincoln National Forest, and she fell in love with the little town of Lincoln.

"I told Jerry I *had* to live here," Cleis told us with a laugh. "He thought I was bananas; this house was a wreck. But it had great charm, and after it was fixed, we decided to share it with others."

The historic nineteenth-century house was the home of Juan Patron, born in 1855. The Jordans decided to name the inn after his family, who lived in the house and kept a store there during the mid-1800s. Young Juan lost his father in an 1873 raid on Lincoln, forerunner of the Lincoln County Wars. Billy the Kid, Sheriff Pat Garrett, murders, and rival mercantile establishments—these are the ingredients of the bloody Lincoln County Wars. We could hardly wait to visit the museums and hear the story; we figured it was pretty wild in Lincoln back then.

But we found plenty of peace and tranquillity in the beautiful forested country, the calm broken only by the many festivals and pageants in the tiny town and in nearby Capitan (home of Smokey the Bear) and Ruidoso.

Each guest room in the spanking white adobe-and-viga house is decorated with collectibles and antiques like the 1800s spinning wheel from Jerry's family back in Deerfield,

Illinois. The number 1 Southwestern Room has twin beds and a full bath; number 2 Southwestern Room has a queen bed and washbasin and private bath around the corner; the Old Store has a queen bed, private bath, and outside entry to a patio. The casitas are completely private, and the Jordans are understandably proud of the fact that they built them from scratch. Casa Bonita has a cathedral ceiling in the living area and a spiral staircase winding up to the loft bedroom; we liked that a lot.

For our breakfast, Cleis baked an egg soufflé and served it with strawberry walnut muffins, home-fried potatoes, and fresh fruit—in the clear mountain air our appetites were hearty. The huge kitchen has a wonderful collection of washboards, those old-fashioned thingamajigs for scrubbing clothes. Our refreshing drinks in the evening were enhanced by music, with Cleis at the baby grand in the parlor or at the real live pipe organ in the dining room. The music was professional—Cleis has a master's degree in organ music.

As for dinner, you can drive to La Lorraine in Ruidoso, Chango in Capitan, or Tinnie's Silver Dollar in Tinnie; but, Cleis said, "that's one of the reasons why we went into the dinner business (by prior arrangement only): People said, 'What, you mean we have to get in the car and drive 12 miles?'"

A Salon Evening might be a night of ragtime and American cuisine, or German specialties accompanied by suitable music if you're feeling sociable. We went for a walk in the cool mountain air.

How to get there: Casa de Patron is located at the east end of Lincoln on the south side of Highway 380, which runs between Roswell and I–25. The highway is the main and only road through the tiny town.

Innkeepers: Cleis and Jeremy Jordan
Address/Telephone: P.O. Box 27; (505) 653–4676
Rooms: 3, plus 2 two-room casitas; 3 rooms with private bath, casitas with private bath, hide-a-bed, and kitchen; no air conditioning (elevation 5,700 feet). No smoking inn.
Rates: $73 to $93, double; EPB for main house, continental for casitas; afternoon drinks and snacks.
Open: All year.
Facilities and activities: Dinner by advance reservation. VCR, special entertainment such as German Evenings and musical Salon Evenings. Nearby: Billy the Kid country with state monuments and Heritage Trust museums, Lincoln National Forest, hiking, skiing, horse races at Ruidoso Downs, soap-making and quilting workshops.

Adobe & Pines Inn
RANCHO DE TAOS, NEW MEXICO 87557

Even the innkeepers admitted that if we weren't watching for the orange, blue, and turquoise poles that mark the road to the inn, we'd miss the turn-off. But, like us, you can always turn around and look again. And once you find it, you'll get a friendly welcome from Rascal, the cocker-terrier, who, said Charil, "along with our horse Desi, requests no other pets at the inn."

And what an inn; it's full of beauty, beginning with the lovely mural at the end of the 80-foot-long portale, a 1950s scene of the famous Taos Pueblo. "We didn't come into this blind," Charil said. "We even hired a consultant who told us what to expect from innkeeping." She laughed.

"We've had our eyes opened more ever since."

Like so many happy innkeepers, they were looking for a lifestyle different from their hectic one in San Diego. They sold everything they owned and traveled in Europe for a year. "We didn't know we were doing our homework," Chuck said. They landed in Taos because Chuck had a birthday and Charil surprised him with tickets to the balloon festival in Albuquerque. While there they chanced to look at an advertisement on business opportunities. "Taos was not a plan, but we fell in love, made an offer.

"Then we had three and a half months of intense renovation," Chuck added ruefully of the 150-year-old adobe home on four acres of fruit and pine trees. He brightened up. "But it's all Charil's decor. She does a dynamite gourmet breakfast, too!"

This was true. It was so gorgeous we left the table to get our camera for photos before we destroyed the 4-inch-tall puff pastry hiding banana yogurt and the German pancakes smothered with fresh raspberries and golden raisins.

Chuck is no slouch, either, when it comes to muffins. Lemon poppyseed, apple cinnamon . . . "Guests dub them Chuck's killer muffins," Charil said. They've had so many requests for recipes that Chuck has compiled their own Southwest cookbook.

Rooms are beautiful, too. Two open off the portale: Puerta Azul, a blue room with an antique writing desk and a hand-painted kiva fireplace, and Puerta Verde, green and rust colors with a romantic canopied bed and sitting area by the fireplace. The one hundred-year-old 'Dutch' doors open at the top for a view outside without opening the entire door.

Puerta Rosa, off the courtyard, conceals a surprise under vaulted ceilings: an oversized, sunken bathroom with Mexican tiles surrounding a large cedar sauna (and a separate shower). There's a fireplace to warm the room and another in the bedroom by the sitting area. Puerta Turquesa, a separate guest cottage off the courtyard, has a jet whirlpool bath as well as two fireplaces. There's a kitchen here, too; it was tempting to stay a while and make ourselves at home.

During afternoon hors d'oeuvres, we relaxed and asked about the underground tunnel built for escaping from Indians.

How to get there: The inn is off Highway 68 in Rancho de Taos, a small settlement between Santa Fe and Taos. The turn-off to the inn, which is on the east side of the road, is marked by orange, blue, and turquoise poles $\frac{3}{10}$ mile south of St. Francis Plaza and 4 miles north of the Steakout Restaurant. Both landmarks are on the east side of the road.

Innkeepers: Charil and Chuck Fulkerson
Address/Telephone: P.O. Box 837; (505) 751–0947 or (800) 723–8267, fax (505) 758–8423
Rooms: 5; all with private bath, 1 with TV. No smoking inn.
Rates: $85 to $145, double, EPB and afternoon snacks.
Open: All year.
Facilities and activities: Jet tub. Nearby: Historic Church St. Francis de Assisi; shopping; art galleries; seven minutes from Taos with its historic Plaza, galleries, shops, and restaurants; historic Taos Pueblo; Kit Carson House; Rio Grande Gorge; Taos Ski Valley.

Dos Casas Viejas
SANTA FE, NEW MEXICO 87501

Santa Fe seems to be a happy place for people to embark upon new careers. Back in San Francisco, Jois (pronounced "Joyce") was an interior designer and Irving had retired as a dentist.

"We wanted to be in Santa Fe, but we still wanted to work," Jois said. "This is absolutely perfect for us. We like to decorate, cook, entertain, talk with people—we've taken our favorite hobbies and turned them into a business."

It took two years of hunting to find what they were looking for, and what they found was not quite what they expected: not one, but a pair of 1860s adobe buildings! Which is how the inn called Dos Casas Viejas was born: the name means "two old houses."

Jois didn't exactly say they were in bad shape, but "as a designer, I saw them the way they would be, not the way they were." Irving was optimistic, too, when she said, "We could fix them up." He loved it: "Goody, I get to do some work." What a husband!

But it wasn't all a bed of roses (although Irving is quite a rose gardener). There are strict regulations in Santa Fe when it comes to historic property. "You keep everything the way it is" is the edict, which presents quite a challenge.

The historic buildings lie within a half-acre compound enclosed by walls 18 inches thick. It was exciting, passing through the gate into the courtyard, like driving into the narrow street of a pueblo in Old Mexico. The walls of the courtyard blend into the thick walls of the buildings, and we were surrounded by pink adobe; the only thing missing was cobblestones.

To the right was the main house, with its long, shaded portale containing the lobby/library and dining room. Straight ahead and a little to the left was the second house, which houses the guest rooms. Each one has a private entrance off the secluded courtyard.

Guest rooms are furnished with authentic Southwest antiques, and you know Jois and Irving had a great time seeking them out. All have original vigas (beams) and great lighting; the mirrors are flattering. Jois said, "A good decorator knows how to take care of these things." There were flowers, bath sheets, and a woodburning kiva fireplace in case of chilly days and nights. On warm, sunny days guests like to sit outside by the heated lap pool (and exercise in it,

of course) and listen to the fountain cascading into the far end of the pool; for us the weather was ever accommodating, and we were at the pool whenever we wished.

Breakfast can be served there, or in the dining room, or as we chose to do, you can carry a basket back to the privacy of your room. It's a continental meal, but more than just coffee and doughnuts—fresh-squeezed orange juice, fresh raspberries or blackberries, chocolate yogurt coffeecake, or maybe pistachio yeast bread.

Irving does the yeast breads, Jois the others, and they pride themselves on never repeating with the same guests. "We have twenty-eight different recipes," they brag.

How to get there: From I–25 north take the St. Francis exit, and go 3⁸⁄₁₀ miles into town. At Agua Fria Street, turn right. The inn is 2 blocks on the right, next to Guadalupe Inn. There is a sign.

Innkeepers: Jois and Irving Belfield
Address/Telephone: 610 Agua Fria Street; (505) 983–1636
Rooms: 5; all with private bath, phone, and TV, 1 with wheelchair access. No smoking inn.
Rates: $125 to $185, double, EPB.
Open: All year.
Facilities and activities: Lap pool. Nearby: Governor's Palace; Santa Fe Plaza, with shops, galleries, and restaurants; Fine Arts Museum; St. Francis Cathedral; Mission of San Miguel; Santa Fe Opera; Institute of American Indian Arts Museum; Santuario de Guadalupe; Loretto Chapel; Cross of the Martyrs; Indian pueblos.

Casa Europa
TAOS, NEW MEXICO 87571

Marcia and Rudi list young son Maximilian as one of the innkeepers; he is a fine host.

Rudi and Marcia are the hospitable models their son patterns himself after. Both are used to the public and enjoy entertaining. Before coming to Taos, they were proprietors of a fine restaurant in Boulder, Colorado, for many years.

"But," Rudi told us, "I needed to do something with people again."

"He needs to work about eighteen hours a day," Marcia added with a fond laugh.

"Well, we get our guests started, we introduce them, and then they are fine," Rudi explains. We certainly were fine, our only problem being one of indecision at teatime; should

we choose the chocolate mousse–filled meringue or the raspberry Bavarian? Or perhaps the Black Forest torte or one of the fresh fruit tarts? (We really wanted one of each, all made by chef Rudi, who was trained at the Grand Hotel in Nuremberg, Germany.)

Breakfast was another such feast prepared by chef Rudi. We had fresh fruit salad, a mushroom-and-asparagus quiche, lean bacon edged in black pepper, home-fried potatoes, and fresh homemade Danish that absolutely melted in our mouths.

The house itself is a treasure, with fourteen skylights and a circular staircase to the gallery above the main salon, displaying the paintings, pottery, and sculpture of local artists as well as wonderful Navajo rugs. The inn appears deceptively small from the outside; inside, the large common rooms (but very uncommon!), both upstairs and down, lead to six exceptionally spacious and elegant guest rooms. It's also very comfortable. The wood floors are graced with oriental rugs; the white stucco walls are hung with original art. The front courtyard is bright with flowers around the Spanish fountain; the European garden in back offers quiet relaxation.

The English Room is a departure, with fine antique English furniture.

How to get there: Driving into Taos from the south on Highway 68, take Lower Ranchitos Road left at the blinking-light intersection just north of McDonald's and south of Taos Plaza. Go 1½ miles southwest to the intersection of Upper Ranchitos Road, which will be on your right. (For a landmark, there's a James Mack Studio on the right-hand corner.)

Innkeepers: Marcia, Rudi, and Maximilian Zwicker
Address/Telephone: 157 Upper Ranchitos Road; (505) 758-9798
Rooms: 6; all with private bath, several with built-in bancos that convert to twin beds; no air conditioning (elevation 7,000 feet). No smoking inn.
Rates: $80 to $110, double, EPB and afternoon tea.
Open: All year.
Facilities and activities: Swedish sauna, hot tub, three private courtyards for play. Nearby: historic Taos Plaza with restaurants, shops, and art galleries; hiking, horseback riding, and winter skiing; Taos Indian Pueblo and museums.

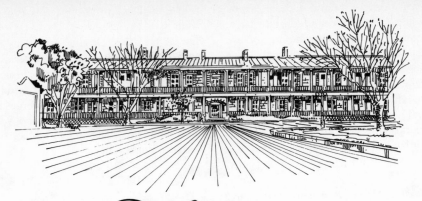

Ye Kendall Inn
BOERNE, TEXAS 78006

Back in the early days of Texas, there was no hotel for travelers to these parts until Erastus and Sarah Reed bought a parcel of land for $200 in 1859. They began renting out their spare rooms to horsemen and stagecoach travelers, and from being known as The Reed House, the building changed its name through the years to The King Place and the Boerne Hotel. It wasn't called Ye Kendall Inn until 1909. Today the old two-story building, of Hill Country stone, fronted by white-railed porches 200 feet along its length on both upper and lower floors, is alive again as an inn, facing the large open spaces and white gazebo of the town square.

The romantic old place is full of mysteries.

"The cellar goes into a tunnel," said Sue. "It goes to the building way down on the corner; I guess it was for stagecoach passengers to hide from the Indians." (But too bad, it's not open to the public. Never mind, there's another mystery.)

"We have a ghost who lives here," Sue confided. "I haven't seen it, but my mother says she has. She heard boots and a man's voice, and then she saw a floaty shape going up the stairs."

Perhaps it's the quiet that leads to fanciful—or real?—visions. We loved the inn because it was so quiet. Sue said it's the Hill Country quiet—there are not even dances here on Saturday night. But there's plenty to do all the same, with quite a few festivals held in Main

Plaza out front, like a yearly Fun Fair with arts and craft shows, dances and pig races in town, and famous Hill Country caverns nearby.

High up along the walls in the upstairs rear of the building are what Sue called "shoot-out" windows, possibly used to defend against those same Indians the stagecoach passengers were hiding from in the tunnel.

The entire lobby and rooms opening off it contain boutiques with antiques and designer clothing, but the huge upstairs hall is for inn guests, with comfortable lounge chairs, a large dining table, and double doors opening off the long porches both front and back. The view to the front is of the green square; in the back there's a large courtyard with white tables and chairs, where we enjoyed the Hill Country breeze under the tall old trees.

Guest rooms are furnished with English and American antiques, and each has a unique per-sonality. The Erastus Reed Room is masculine with trophy heads mounted on the wall; the Sarah Reed Room is feminine in soft yellow and white. Fascinating are the old-fashioned bath-room fixtures, right there in the rooms, although the footed tubs and the commodes are screened off; Sarah Reed's screen is of white lace.

Breakfast, supervised by Bobbie, is juice and coffee, fresh fruit, sweet rolls, and quiche, so it's more than plain continental. And the Cafe at Ye Kendall Inn has more gourmet fare, from fet-tucine Alfredo to chicken Cordon Bleu. (We couldn't resist trying the Boerne Special, chicken-fried steak with country gravy.)

How to get there: I–87 goes right down the mid-dle of Boerne, and the inn is at the west end of Main Square, on Blanco, which crosses the high-way.

Innkeepers: Bobbie and Don Hood and Sue Davis
Address/Telephone: 120 West Blanco; (210) 249–2138 or (800) 364–2138
Rooms: 11, including 1 suite; all with private bath and TV, 1 with wheelchair access. No smoking inn.
Rates: $80 to $125, double, continental breakfast.
Open: All year.
Facilities and activities: Cafe serving breakfast, lunch, and dinner; boutiques. Nearby: Agricultural Heritage Center; Cascade Caverns; Cave Without a Name; Guadalupe River State Park; 15 miles from San Antonio.

The Browning Plantation
CHAPPELL HILL, TEXAS 77426

We felt like Scarlett O'Hara and Rhett Butler, driving up to this beautiful antebellum mansion hidden in the woods. This elegant mansion easily could be awed by its own splendor; but with Dick and Mildred as innkeepers, the spirit of fun rules instead.

"We have a good time," Dick said. "People don't want to hear how the house was put together or how old Browning died. Mildred and I tell them all *our* troubles, and we have a good laugh instead."

Still, the Ganchans have made an entertaining story of the resurrection of the old Browning plantation, which was truly a formidable undertaking. Mildred was looking for a cute little Victorian house to move to their property elsewhere when they made the mistake of stopping by to see a place that "needed a little attention." What they saw was a completely ruined mansion left over from cotton-and-slavery days.

Listed on the National Register of Historic Places, the inn once again has the fake wood graining that was the height of elegance back when the house was built in the 1850s. Daughter Meg Ganchan Rice spent ages practicing the technique as her contribution to the family restoration effort.

Upstairs guest rooms in the big house have 12-foot ceilings and massive windows and are furnished with nineteenth-century antiques, including plantation and tester beds.

Where to relax is a choice that can be difficult: the parlor, the library, or the south veranda, with its beautiful view over the vast acres of green farmland? For an even more breathtaking scene, we climbed the three flights to the rooftop widow's walk that crowns the house.

And there is more. One son-in-law is such a train buff that he has built a model railroad on the property, and if he's in residence, you may be able to cajole him into a ride.

"He has more rolling stock than the Santa Fe," Dick bragged as he proudly showed off the new two-room "depot" he designed, a replica of a Santa Fe original. Guest rooms inside the depot have horizontal pine paneling and blue-striped-

ticking curtains and bedspreads.

You'll feel like Scarlett and Rhett all over again at breakfast around the huge dining table, eating dishes like the inn's Eggs Sardou accompanied by a hot fruit compote. But first there's an Orange Julius eye-opener, and maybe there will also be hot biscuits. There's a social hour with snacks before dinner, too.

How to get there: From U.S. Highway 290 east of Brenham, take FM 1155 south until you come to a short jog to the left. Immediately to your right you'll see a dirt road. Turn right onto it; continue south across the cattle guard and under the arch of trees until you reach the plantation house.

Innkeepers: Mildred and Dick Ganchan
Address/Telephone: Route 1, Box 8; (409) 836–6144
Rooms: 6 in main house and Model Railroad Depot; 2 with private bath, 2 with TV. No smoking inn.
Rates: $85 to $110, double; $75 weeknights; EPB and evening snacks. No credit cards.
Open: All year.
Facilities and activities: Swimming pool, model train with 1½ miles of track, 220 acres of natural trails, fishing in lakes on property. Nearby: historic sites in Washington-on-the-Brazos and Independence, Star of the Republic Museum, miniature horses at Monastery of St. Clare; good restaurant in Brenham.

Warfield House
CROCKETT, TEXAS 75835

Crockett is a delightful small town (about 7,000) filled with friendly people, unique shops and restaurants, and many historic sites. "Being the fifth oldest town in Texas, it has a special place for history buffs. We're certainly a visitor-friendly town and enjoy the opportunity to show off," Judy said.

Well, showing off is a Texas trait, and we enjoy it. The Warfield House is one of Crockett's lovely older homes, built by a Minnesotan who came to town in 1897. He took three years to complete the house, built Minnesota-style with twelve rooms, a third-floor attic, and a three-room cellar. Put together of rough-cut heart of pine, and square-head nails, it was built to last.

"I moved here from Houston when I was nine, and Jerry moved here with the General Telephone Company, and with these perfect old homes, we thought Crockett needed an inn," Judy said. "Jerry and I had this dream for four years."

The town didn't think so at first and resist-ed, but Judy was aided and abetted by her friend Alma Turner Sevier, who served as Judy's con-tractor, decorator, plumber, and designer. "She was 86 when she did the house," Judy said. "She made the drapes, made and covered the benches at the foot of the beds, did the magnolia paint-ings on the walls. She did so much there was no way I could completely repay her. So since the only thing she can't do is cook, I promised to give her breakfast for the rest of her life."

Alma comes often, and with good reason. We had what Judy calls a "historical" egg casserole, with bacon, biscuits, homemade "asphodel" bread, strawberry muffins, and fruit compote, and were enthralled by Alma's entertaining tales of Crockett past and present.

But first, morning coffee and tea were placed on a window seat so that we could help ourselves when we woke up.

Of course there's an Alma Room, "named in honor, as well, of all the ladies who really cared about the house," said Judy. A violet-and-green color scheme and a four-poster bed make it both regal and romantic.

Ruth & Leela's Room, named for the Warfield daughters, has twin beds covered in periwinkle blue. The walls are sunny yellow, and the songbirds along the ceiling border and on the drapes are planned to invite the outdoors in.

Marlene's Room, decorated so that you feel it's "your friend's home," Judy said, is in honor of another friend who helped make the inn dream come true. "My friend and her husband wanted to sell their home—this one—but didn't want to put it on the market until they consulted us. 'We want you to have it,' they said, so Jerry and I figured this was meant to be our inn."

Judy is proud of the nineteen quilts she has inherited from her mother and grandmother. All the needlework in the inn is her mother's, too. She found some photographs of her great-great-grandfather and his twin in an old trunk and learned that they fought barefoot in the snow at Shiloh—another great story at this romantic inn.

How to get there: Entering town on Highway 287 or Highway 21 (Old Camino Real), follow the road into downtown. From downtown Courthouse Square, the inn is 3 blocks east on Houston.

Innkeepers: Judy and Jerry Teague
Address/Telephone: 712 East Houston Avenue; (409) 544-4037
Rooms: 4; all with private bath. No smoking inn.
Rates: $68 to $98, double, EPB.
Open: All year.
Facilities and activities: Swimming pool and hot tub. Nearby: Davy Crockett Memorial Park, Visitor Center-Museum, Fiddler's Festival, Davy Crockett National Forest, and Mission Tejas State Historic Park.

Hôtel St. Germain

DALLAS, TEXAS 75201

For sheer luxury, unabashed, unashamed Sybaritic living, the small and elegant Hôtel St. Germain takes the prize. Well, it's already taken several prizes, like the *Inn Business Review*'s naming the St. Germain "One of the outstanding inns of 1992."

The inn, a beautiful residence built in 1906, is architecturally imposing. The white, three-story structure has two balconies on the left and two curved porches on the right, with black wrought-iron railings, which also frame two sets of stairs to the curved driveway in front. French doors lead out, and in the stairwell, there's a huge twenty-four-paned window crowned with a glass arch.

With its impressive foyer, 14-foot ceilings, sumptuous parlor, stately library, and lavish suites, it takes all the adjectives in *Roget's Thesaurus* to describe this inn adequately. The antique pieces alone are a feast for the eyes.

"My mom was an antique dealer," Claire said, taking us on a tour of the mansion. "We serve on antique Limoges—my grandmother's heavy gold china—Waterford crystal, and sterling." She alternates eight different sets of china; they're stored in the china cabinet in the small dining room.

The large dining room has bay windows of decorative glass, topped with an extravagant valence over Austrian shades. The crystal chandelier is palatial. Beyond is a romantic New

Orleans–style walled courtyard. Our tête-a-tête breakfast there took on another dimension: The chive-and-cheese quiche and blueberry muffins tasted like nectar and ambrosia.

Soft classical music played in the library; there is a grand buffet piano for more personalized music. The original wallpaper is charming, and we enjoyed looking at the before-and-after-renovation photographs in the hall.

Suite One, a huge room decorated in rose and gray, has a rose spread and a high canopy over the bed. Suite Three has what appears to be a larger-than-life king-sized bed, which can be divided into two twins. The sitting room has a lovely antique Belgian sofa, and there's a separate dressing room. Suite Four boasts a Jacuzzi as well as a Mallard bed, a huge armoire, and a sitting area with a sofa and fireplace.

The Dangerous Liaison Suite is 600 square feet of blue, green, and gold. Besides the bed, there's a bed-lounge in the wall, a Cheval mirror, and antique Mallard furniture. In the sitting area are a fireplace and a sparkling chandelier.

The Smith Suite, on the third floor, overlooks downtown Dallas. The Napoleon sleigh bed has a crown canopy, and there is a Victorian sitting area, complete with fireplace. The padded cloth walls are another example of sheer luxury, an atmosphere that the Jacuzzi in the bath does nothing to dispel.

Hôtel St. Germain is really a taste of another world!

How to get there: From Central Expressway exit at Hall Street and turn right to Cole. At Cole turn left onto Cedar Springs, take a left onto Maple Avenue and go half a block. From North Dallas Toll Road, heading south, pass the Wycliff exit and veer to the left as you curve around to the first traffic light, which is Wolf Street. Turn left for 2½ blocks to Maple, turn right, crossing Cedar Springs to the inn, the large white mansion with a curved driveway.

Innkeeper: Claire Heymann
Address/Telephone: 2516 Maple Avenue; (214) 871–2516, fax (214) 871–0740
Rooms: 7; all with private bath, TV, and radio. Smoking permitted except in dining room.
Rates: $225 to $600, double, EPB.
Open: All year.
Facilities and activities: Dinner, lunch for 6 or more, bar service, room service, valet parking, guest privileges at The Centrum Health Club. Nearby: downtown Dallas, with Dallas Museum of Art, Kennedy Memorial, Old City Park, Reunion Tower, West End Historic District, Farmer's Market, more.

Sunset Heights Inn

EL PASO, TEXAS 79902

Built in 1905 up in the high and mighty area of El Paso overlooking downtown, this inn on the National Register of Historic Homes is a three-story corner house of dark-yellow brick surrounded by an iron fence. Tall palm trees wave over it, and the large grounds of almost an acre are graced by roses blooming much of the year. "Twenty-nine bushes," Richard said, while he confessed that he doesn't take care of it all by himself.

Food, gourmet food, is his specialty, and we weren't able to predict what he would feed us for breakfast because "I don't decide what to serve until I look at my guests the evening before," he said. This statement brought forth a contented groan from an earlier guest, who was recovering from the morning-before feast in a corner of the beautifully decorated parlor.

The five-to-seven-course meal was more like a lunch or dinner buffet than a breakfast. It began with prunes in cream and went on to quiche served with kiwi and purple grapes; then came Cordon Bleu chicken on rice with tomato and avocado, and eggs Benedict with papaya and star fruit, followed by angel-food cake with blueberry yogurt. This took us through the day until the champagne and late-night snacks.

Richard, late of the military, raised three daughters by himself and learned to cook in self-defense. "We entertained a lot and couldn't afford a cook, so we all learned to cook. When the girls were small, sometimes we had sit-down dinners for thirty." But he prefers buffet because "people circulate better." Now at Sunset he has a helper in daughter Kim, responsible for many of the gourmet meals they serve.

Roni, who is a practicing physician, displayed a second talent in the decorating of the inn. She did most of the pleasing color selections, while much of the furnishings are antiques from Richard's family. The parlor has a Victrola dating from 1919, and it still plays. Although the old table radio is a replica, the kerosene lamp is one Richard studied by when he was a boy on a farm in Oklahoma. "We didn't have electricity," he said. "That old lamp got me through school." But what we admired the most was the wonderful Coromandel screen behind the old sewing machine in the parlor. Richard told the story of how he was able to get it out of China—back when we weren't speaking to China—by shipping it through Panama.

The inn is a decorator's dream, with beautifully coordinated fabrics and wall coverings, mirrored doors, and sybaritic bathrooms. The Oriental Room has another Coromandel screen as well as a brass bed. The bathroom, with brass fixtures and a huge bathtub, is on what was once a porch. But not to worry: All the windows are now one-way mirrors.

How to get there: From I–10 West take Porfiro Diaz exit and turn right for 2 blocks to Yandell. Turn right for 6 blocks (count the ones on the right, not the left) to Randolph, and the inn is on the far corner to the left.

Innkeepers: Richard Barnett and Roni Martinez
Address/Telephone: 717 West Yandell; (919) 544–1743 or (800) 767–8513
Rooms: 10, 6 in main house, 4 in annex across the street; all with private bath, telephone, and TV; wheelchair accessible (electric chair lift from first to second floor). No smoking inn.
Rates: $80 to $165, double, EPB.
Open: All year.
Facilities and activities: Dinner for minimum of six people; pool and Jacuzzi. Nearby: many museums and historic fort, old Spanish missions, Tigua Indian Reservation, zoo, scenic drive, Ciudad Juárez in Mexico just across the Rio Grande.
Recommended Country Inns® Travel Club Benefit: 10% discount each night; or stay two nights, get third night free, holidays excluded; subject to availability; not good with other offers or special rates; offer good for one year from publication.

Raphael House
ENNIS, TEXAS 75119

The Raphael House has stood in central Ennis since 1906, and since 1988 Danna has restored it to all its former glory, which was glorious indeed. Yet she confesses to acquiring the house as sort of a lark. Visiting her family after a buying trip to New York (she was a buyer for several Austin stores), she came to look at the house "before it was torn down or burned. Once Ennis Avenue was lined with big houses like this, but this is the only one left." She returned three times and finally made an offer to buy from the last of the Raphaels, a patient in a nursing home. Before she knew it, she was the new owner of the wonderful old house and was fortunate to be able to buy much of the original furniture.

"I feel as if I adopted a family," she told us as she showed off the many family photographs that she "inherited." The walls are covered with Raphaels, one of the first families in Ennis back at the turn of the century, when they built the first department store, the Big Store. Rooms are named for the Raphael family members who lived in them. Julia's Room has its original set of white French furniture from 1918, bought by sister Wilhelmina, but kept by her parents. "They wouldn't let Wilhelmina take the set with her because they didn't like the man she married," Danna was delighted to explain.

Ernest's Room has a beautiful tiger-oak chest, hidden under a coat of paint when Danna acquired it. "I was having it stripped—I was going to sell it. But the strippers called me and said, 'We think you ought to have a look at this.'"

The library is stocked with old and new books, magazines, a television, and a VCR. The entry is so huge that it holds a large grand piano, which Danna encourages guests to play. "Sometimes they'll sing," she says, "and it's so nice to come in at night and hear them."

Breakfasts are as rich as the house, and we feasted on French toast stuffed with strawberries and cream cheese and what Danna calls her Tex-Czech breakfast with local Kolabasse sausage and marvelous strudel stuffed to the rim with apples, pears, pecans, and coconut.

We decided that if we couldn't be romantic here, we'd have been pretty hopeless!

How to get there: Ennis is on Highway 287, which becomes Ennis Avenue. Raphael House is at the northwest corner of Ennis, at Preston Street.

Innkeepers: Danna Cody Wolf and Brian Wolf
Address/Telephone: 500 West Ennis Avenue; (214) 875–1555
Rooms: 6; all with private bath; TV available. Smoking in sunroom and on porches.
Rates: $68 to $150, double; $10 less weekdays; EPB.
Open: All year.
Facilities and activities: Lunch, dinner, tea, and receptions by reservation, cooking classes spring and fall. Nearby: Colonial Tennis and Health Club, shopping area's than 100 antiques shops, Landmark Commission driving tour, spring Bluebonnet Trail, Railroad Museum.
Recommended Country Inns® Travel Club Benefit: 10% discount, Monday–Thursday, subject to availability.

The Gilded Thistle
GALVESTON, TEXAS 77550

We asked innkeeper Helen Hanemann to explain The Gilded Thistle's name, because it seemed to me to be a contradiction. Helen, very much into the island's history, said that like native thistle, sturdy Texas pioneer stock sank deep and lasting roots into the sandy island soil, building a Galveston that flowered into a gilded age of culture and wealth, a most romantic city in its heyday.

Her home was part of those people and their times—in the late 1800s Galveston's Strand was known as "the Wall Street of the West"—and The Gilded Thistle is a lovely memorial to Galveston's past.

The beautiful antiques throughout the house make it an exceptionally elegant place to stay, but the atmosphere is so homey that our awe melted away to pure admiration. Helen is on duty at all times, and we joined the other guests in her kitchen, watching her arrange the fresh flowers that fill the rooms.

It wasn't hard to get used to being served on fine china, with coffee or tea from a family silver service. Breakfast, Helen told us, is "whenever you want," so we could sleep late and then eat lazily on the L-shaped screened porch around the dining room, especially enjoying Helen's specialty, "nut chewies," and her crispy waffles. There's always a bowl filled with apples or other fruit on the sideboard.

Tea and coffee are available at all times, and we loved it when our morning began with orange juice and a pot of boiling water for coffee or tea at our bedroom door.

The evening snack tray could almost take the place of dinner; there are strawberries and grapes and other fruit in season, ham and cheese and roast beef sandwiches, at least four kinds of cheese, and wine. And if after that you don't feel like going out, Pat will rustle up something gourmet, like a bowl of his seafood gumbo with special rice and French bread, compliments of the house.

The Gilded Thistle has been gilded horti-culturally: In recent years the inn's landscaping has won two prizes, the Springtime Broadway Beauty Contest and an award for a business in a historic building. But it's never easy; that's the reason for the Texas saying that if you don't like the weather, wait a minute, it'll change. "A few years ago we had that bitter winter," Helen said. "Now we've put in lawn sprinklers and wouldn't you know—too much rain."

How to get there: Stay on Highway 45 South, which becomes Broadway as soon as you cross the causeway onto Galveston Island. The inn is just beyond 18th Street, on the right.

Innkeepers: Helen and Pat Hanemann
Address/Telephone: 1805 Broadway; (409) 763–0194 or (800) 654–9380
Rooms: 3; 1 with private bath, all with TV and TTD for hearing impaired. No smoking inn.
Rates: $125 to $175, per room, EPB and snack tray in evening.
Open: All year.
Facilities and activities: Nearby: historic Ashton Villa and the Bishop's Palace; the historic Strand, with Galveston Art Center, Galveston County Historical Museum, Railroad Museum, shops and restaurants; the Seawall and Gulf Coast beaches, Moody Gardens Rainforest Pyramid, Texas Seaport Museum.

La Colombe d'Or
HOUSTON, TEXAS 77006

We didn't have to go to France for romance; this very special inn is patterned after one of the same name in St. Paul de Vence, France, where many famous French painters traded their work for lodging. Houston's La Colombe d'Or ("the golden dove") is hung with fine art, too, and each suite has a name we recognized.

We stayed in the Van Gogh Suite, named for one of our favorite Impressionist painters. Others are named for Dégas, Cézanne, Monet, and Renoir; the largest suite, up at the top, is called simply The Penthouse. Although there are no original works, the suites are decorated with reproductions of each master's work.

So we hardly missed the originals, so swathed in beauty and luxury were we in this prince of an inn. On our coffee table we found fruit, Perrier water, and wine glasses waiting to be filled from our complimentary bottle of the inn's own imported French wine.

Owner Steve Zimmerman has succeeded in bringing to La Colombe d'Or the casual elegance of the French Riviera. European and American antiques, as well as his own collection of prominent artists' works, are set in the luxurious house that was once the home of Exxon oil man Walter Fondren and his family.

The twenty-one-room mansion, built in 1923, is divided into suites. Each consists of a huge bedroom with a sitting area and a glass-enclosed dining room where Queen Anne furniture, china plates, linen napkins, and cutlery are in readiness for breakfast. As soon as we rang in the morning, a waiter arrived with a tea cart from which he served a very French-style plate of sliced kiwi fruit, raspberries, and strawberries; orange juice; coffee; and croissants with butter and jam. We ate this artistic offering surrounded by the green leafy boughs waving outside our glass room.

You may have luncheon or dinner served in your room, too, but we feasted downstairs on meunière of shrimp and lobster, cream of potato and leek soup, the inn's Caesar salad, and capon Daniel; and as if that weren't enough, we ended with crème brûlée!

The inn is a member of *Relais et Châteaux*, a French organization that guarantees excellence, and we absolutely soaked up the hospitality, tranquillity, and luxury.

How to get there: 3410 Montrose is between Westheimer and Alabama, both Houston thoroughfares.

Innkeeper: Steve Zimmerman

Address/Telephone: 3410 Montrose Boulevard; (713) 524–7999

Rooms: 6 suites; all with private bath; wheelchair accessible.

Rates: $195 to $575, per suite, EP.

Open: All year.

Facilities and activities: Restaurant, bar. Nearby: within five minutes, Houston central business district, Houston Museum of Fine Arts, Rice University, and Menil Art Foundation; the Astrodome.

Gruene Mansion

NEW BRAUNFELS, TEXAS 78130

Sharon and Bill not only wanted a resort, they wanted one with a history. They found it in the Gruene Mansion, set on a historic cotton plantation on the banks of the Guadalupe River.

The inn is located within the Gruene (pronounced "green") Historic District on the northern edge of New Braunfels' city limits. "Bill and I really like the history of Gruene Mansion," Sharon said. "It was built by Henry Gruene back in the mid-1800s, as was Gruene Dance Hall, just down the street." This is the oldest dance hall in Texas.

Sharon spoke of the original owner as though she knew him. "Henry built the hall for the closeness and warmness of his friends. He also had a little house where travelers could come and stay; they just had to replace the logs for the fire. He was kind to strangers, and we wanted to live that way. It's the best way to meet people."

All the cottages have little porches overhanging the river, and they are furnished with antiques and handmade quilts; each room is different. Sharon had a great time decorating—imagine having seventeen rooms to design!

We loved Fireside Lodge #2 with it's slanted ceiling and pretty flowered wallpaper of pink and blue flowers on a black background. You can imagine the interesting contrast that makes with the rough wood paneling, made from both poplar and yellow pine. The fireplace wall is white stone; the brass bed has a colorful patchwork quilt and a crocheted afghan laid across the foot. (Feet can get chilly during cool Hill Country nights.)

But tempting too was Bluebonnet Lodge with huge bluebonnets painted on the walls, both bedroom and bath. The shower curtain in the bath is an old quilt (protected by a liner, of course) and dolled up with a pointed lace valance—Sharon has many original ideas. Walls in the Grand River Lodge are painted bright blue between the wood strips, and stenciled with red and yellow stylized tulips.

We wandered down to Gruene Dance Hall for a beer and some Texas two-stepping—we were thrilled to find live music. We dined next door at the Grist Mill Restaurant, housed in the ruins of a hundred-year-old cotton gin beneath a water tower on the banks of the Guadalupe River, with its pretty little rapids and its happy white-water rafters, many floating down from Canyon River when the water's right.

How to get there: From I–35 take exit 191 (Canyon Lake) and go west on Highway 306 for 1½ miles, following the Gruene Historical signs. Turn left into Gruene and go to the end of the road. The inn is on the right as you turn left onto Gruene Road.

Innkeepers: Sharon and Bill McCaskell

Address/Telephone: 1275 Gruene Road; (210) 629–2641 or –8372, fax same or (800) 299–8372

Rooms: 17, in assorted cottages on the river; all with private bath and TV. No smoking inn.

Rates: $85 to $200, double; breakfast $5 extra. No credit cards.

Open: All year.

Facilities and activities: Nearby: Grist Mill Restaurant; Gruene Dance Hall; antiques; museums: Hummel, Sophienburg, Handmade Furniture, and Children's; Schlitterbahn Water Park; rafting, tubing, and swimming on Guadalupe and Comal rivers; bicycling; horseback riding; golf; tennis; Natural Bridge Caverns and Wildlife Ranch; Canyon Lake, with fishing, boating, swimming, and waterskiing; discount shopping malls.

The Ogé House
SAN ANTONIO, TEXAS 78204

The Ogé House (pronounced "oh-jhay"—it's French) is one of the most magnificent homes to be found in San Antonio's historic King William District of fine homes. It was built in 1857 for Louis Ogé, a pioneer cattle rancher and a Texas Ranger. It's set on large, lovely grounds at the end of the block, facing the street, while the rear of the house overlooks San Antonio's famous river.

Like many old beauties, the home had become an apartment house, but it was just waiting for Sharrie and Patrick to find it. They had been looking, driving up the East Coast for six weeks, before they realized that this was where they wanted to be.

"I used to redo old houses back East," Sharrie said. "And we'd been collecting antiques for ten, twelve years." Visiting her father here, they heard that the old house might be available, and the rest is history.

The house is huge. There are two guest rooms opening off the majestic lobby, which is actually the second floor, since we climbed a total of eleven steps up to the front door. Once there, we admired the antique French set of two settees and two chairs. "They're from a private suite in the Waldorf Astoria in New York," Patrick said.

The Library, at the rear of the house, is relaxing, with soft yellow walls, white woodwork, satin-striped sofas, and books. The brass bucket in The Library is filled with menus from the city's many fine eating places.

Upstairs (third floor) the Giles and Mathis suites both open onto the porch across the front of the house, while Riverview, off the landing by the back stairs, is intensely private, with its own porch and view of the river, and that's the one we chose.

Down below, on the main level, the Mitchell Suite has a platform canopy bed and a daybed, while the Bluebonnet Room is done in Texas antiques, with a four-poster rolling-pin bed and the desk of an old Texas judge. But that's all we found of Old-West Texas.

"We're not a Texas country inn," Sharrie said. "We have more of the flavor of a small European hotel or an English country manor house."

Interesting pieces are fun to discover. I admired a small pretty I-didn't-know-what: "It's papier-mâché and mother of pearl—it was a Victorian sewing case," Patrick explained, lifting the lid to show me the compartments inside.

Sharrie's "Deluxe Continental Breakfast" began with poached pears and went on to such delicacies as pecan log roll, apple torte, cherry cheesecake, and fruit pasties.

You can join everyone for breakfast in the dining room or take it out on the front veranda, but we elected to go out on the grounds and sit overlooking the river. The in is on one and a half acres, and with all the trees leafed out, we couldn't see any of the neighboring houses. We couldn't believe we were in downtown San Antonio!

How to get there: From I–35 take 281 south and exit at Durango. Turn right and go through three traffic lights to St. Mary's. Take the first left to Pancoast, and the inn is head on at the end of the street.

Innkeepers: Sharrie and Patrick Magatagan
Address/Telephone: 209 Washington; (210) 223–2353 or (800) 242–2770, fax (210) 226–5812
Rooms: 10; all with private bath and TV. No smoking inn.
Rates: $125 to $195, double, deluxe continental breakfast.
Open: All year.
Facilities and activities: Parking. Nearby: Downtown San Antonio, with The Alamo, La Villita, Convention Center, museums, RiverCenter Mall, El Mercado.
Recommended Country Inns® Travel Club Benefit: 20% discount, Monday–Thursday, subject to availability.

Mulberry Manor
SWEETWATER, TEXAS 79556

It was exciting to discover a mansion like Mulberry Manor in a town the size of Sweetwater (about 12,000 population). It was built in 1913 for banker, businessman, and rancher Thomas Trammell—and the architect was John Young, father of movie star Loretta Young.

Which adds to the Hollywood glamor of this showplace, with its glass-domed atrium, filled with green plants and sunshine, in the center of the house. The inn's rooms surround the atrium, and the formal French parlor to the right of the entry is furnished in authentic Louis Quinze. The tailored parlor on the left also contains lovely pieces, garnered from all over.

"Just about everything is from estate sales and antiques shops," Beverly said. "We bought everything in this house on weekends." This gave them something to do while the house was being restored. "Auctions are really the best buy," was her advice.

The house had a checkered life after the Trammells were gone. To give you some idea of the size, in 1923 it became Sweetwater and Nolan County's only hospital. Then, like many old homes, the 9,800-square-foot house was divided into apartments. Eventually, in case having been designed by Loretta Young's father wasn't romantic enough, it somehow became part of the estate of the brother of General Clair

Chennault of the famous Flying Tigers.

The house has three downstairs guest rooms and a vast suite upstairs. The separate barroom has an oversized television screen and a sitting area. The formal dining room is impressive, but so is the so-called breakfast room, with its brocaded French chairs, a beautiful mirrored sideboard, and an oriental rug on the polished wood floor.

But most exotic is the upstairs suite, which Beverly described as "Neo-Classical." To give you an idea of the size, originally it was a ballroom. "It was an apartment, and it was horrible," Beverly shuddered. On the huge expanse of white carpet, the furniture is gold and black, with green plants. A group of statuary, busts of classical figures, occupies a corner. Adding to the glamor, the adjoining bath is suitably sybaritic.

Breakfast was as opulent as the manor. Fresh fruit compote, eggs Benedict or quiche, hash browns, sausage or ham, biscuits and gravy, cinnamon raisin biscuits, strawberry cream cheese on croissants. And there was a big snack tray with the beverage of our choice in the afternoon; our treat was cream puffs filled with ham salad. Who does all this? "Me. I'm the cook!" Beverly said.

Her dinners are spectacular seven-course meals, too. And to cap it all off, Raymond takes guests for a fun ride in that shiny 1929 Model A Ford out front.

How to get there: Take exit 244 off I–20 and go north 4 blocks to Sam Houston Street and number 1400. There's a sign on the model A Ford out in front.

Innkeepers: Beverly and Raymond Stone

Address/Telephone: 1400 Sam Houston Street; (915) 235–3811 or (800) 235–3811

Rooms: 4, plus 1 two-bedroom, 1½-bath guest house; 2 rooms with private bath; wheelchair accessible.

Rates: $60 to $200, double, EPB and afternoon snacks.

Open: All year.

Facilities and activities: Dinner by reservation, hot tub. Nearby: horseback riding; golf; Pioneer City–County Museum; lakes Sweetwater, Trammell, and Oak Creek Reservoir with fishing, boating, and water sports; World's Largest Rattlesnake Roundup (March).

Charnwood Hill Inn
TYLER, TEXAS 75701

We found it pretty romantic to experience the style of living enjoyed by an old-time Texas oilman. Although Charnwood Hill Inn was built around 1860 by a Professor Hand, who was headmaster of a school for girls, the mansion passed through several hands until it was purchased by oil tycoon H. L. Hunt in the early 1930s.

"The Hunt family extensively remodeled," Don said, as we wandered through the tall-ceilinged rooms full of opulent furnishings.

We weren't sure what sort of furnishings the Hunts had when this gorgeous mansion was their home, but it would have to be something to equal Patsy and Don's collection. "We spent seventeen years collecting and didn't want to get rid

of it," Don said. They needed to find a place worthy of such beautiful antiques, and Charnwood Hill shows them off to perfection. Patsy and Don bought the home in 1978.

A pair of curved steps leads up to the white-columned entrance. The large foyer and living room are stately. The dining room is impressive, with a handmade table and ten chairs of solid pecan, a Chinoiserie breakfront displaying antique Meissen china, an oriental rug, and a delicate chandelier. It makes a contrast to the bright breakfast room, although even that, in its way, is formal, with its glass tables, chairs covered with summery floral fabric, bricked floor, and branched chandelier.

We were in a mansion, all right. Common areas of the inn include the formal living room, library, TV room, the Great Hall on the first floor and the Lodge on the second floor, the Garden Room, the Gathering Hall, the front and east balconies, screened swing porch, front porches, the arbor, and the beautiful east and west gardens. "Tyler's famous Azalea Trail starts right outside of this house," Don said.

Tyler considers itself "Rose Capital of the World," and the annual Texas Rose Festival is an important local event. Margaret Hunt was Rose Queen in 1935; and JoAnne Miller, daughter of the then-owner of the home, was Rose Queen in 1954. Both times the Queen's Tea was held in the gardens.

The 1,500-square-foot Art Deco Suite on the third floor was constructed for the two Hunt daughters; the gray carpet makes a perfect foil for the Chinoiserie pieces and the print fabric on a black background. The second-floor sleeping porch and one bedroom were converted into what is now called the Lodge, which has a bar, TV, and lots of room for meetings.

Our breakfast was a full gourmet feast. Eggs Benedict was served with an inn specialty—a tasty breakfast potato casserole—and a mélange of mixed fruits, and juices, coffee, and tea. If you wish, at 4:00 P.M. Patsy will serve a Lemon Tea of cheesecake with fresh fruit.

Dinners are as you like, also, with Texas steak a specialty.

How to get there: From I–20 take Highway 69 south to North Broadway, which becomes South Broadway at Tyler Square. Continue south 4 blocks to Charnwood and turn left. The inn is on the right, and there's a sign.

Innkeepers: Patsy and Don Walker
Address/Telephone: 223 East Charnwood; (903) 597–3980, fax 592–3980
Rooms: 7, including 1 suite; 5 with private bath, 5 with TV. No smoking inn.
Rates: $95 to $175, double, EPB.
Open: All year.
Facilities and activities: Tea and dinner by reservation, elevator, gift shop. Nearby: Municipal Rose Garden & Museum, Brookshire's World of Wildlife Museum and Country Store, Hudnall Planetarium, Caldwell Zoo, Azalea Trail, Texas Rose Festival, East Texas State Fair.
Recommended Country Inns® Travel Club Benefit: 10% discount, subject to availability.

Rocky Mountain Region

by Doris Kennedy

In an attempt to select the most romantic inns from the many hundreds I have visited, I first asked myself what I would look for when choosing such an accommodation for my husband and myself. Next I interviewed friends and colleagues, questioning them as to the qualities they would seek in their ideal hideaway for two.

I discovered most of us pretty much thought the same, with the main difference being in the order of preference.

As for me, I would look for a secluded place, private, with soothing sounds in the form of birdsong, the steady chirp of crickets, the rush of a river, or the distant call of coyotes at dusk.

Luxurious or rustic, either would be fine; but if a turret room were available, I would absolutely have to have it, for here we would leisurely sip morning coffee and take turns reading aloud. I would like a fireplace and perhaps a four-poster canopied in ruffles and lace, or one made of rough-hewn logs and covered with billowy quilts.

No phones, please. And if a television must be present, let it be hidden away in an armoire.

Blessed is the innkeeper who is attentive yet discreet. Guests seeking a romantic rendezvous want to be greeted warmly, then graciously left alone. Let the innkeeper spin his or her magic by leaving treats and morning coffee outside the door and, while we are out, a fresh rose on the bed, a pitcher of ice water spiked with floating fresh strawberries, and a love poem or a sachet of potpourri under the pillows.

Flowers, candles, adjustable soft lighting, and a nearby wood or a park for wandering hand in hand would be nice.

Most of all, let it be peaceful, where hushed conversations proceed without interruption, where secrets are shared and promises made, and where cherished memories have their beginnings.

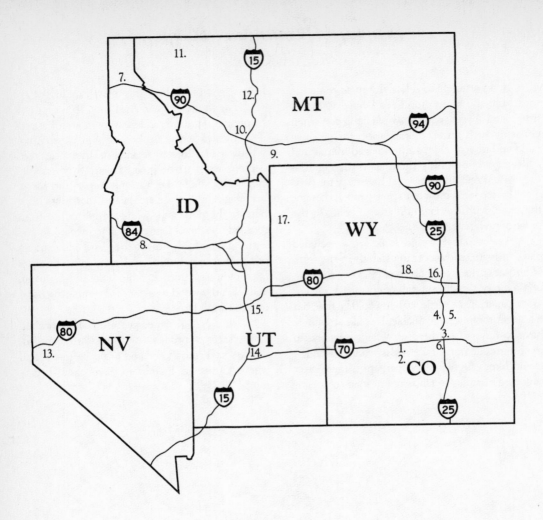

Rocky Mountain Region

Numbers on map refer to towns numbered below.

Sardy House
ASPEN, COLORADO 81612

If your ideal romantic getaway leans toward turreted, Victorian mansions, perhaps this is the inn for you: a red-brick masterpiece with original oak staircases and sliding parlor doors, round reading rooms tucked away in a turret, gourmet breakfast set upon pearl gray linen centered with fresh flowers, and fine dining in the evenings as well.

Soft plum carpeting with pale pink roses, made in Ireland especially for the Sardy, is used throughout the building, and wallpaper of subdued gray cloaks the walls. The guest rooms have thick terry his and her robes, heated towel racks, down comforters with Laura Ashley duvets, and televisions hidden in walls or armoires. Except for two units with antique tubs, all have whirlpool baths.

We have a thing about carriage houses, and that is where we chose to stay, in a beautifully appointed complement to the main mansion. Our room had a vaulted, many-angled ceiling; natural wicker table, chairs, and writing desk; a cherry-wood, high-off-the-floor bed with feather-filled comforter and five fluffy pillows; and a bay window that looked out on Aspen Mountain and the ski slopes. The almond-scented lotion, shampoo, and bath gel were another nice touch. If you add just a few drops of bath gel to your whirlpool bath, you'll both disappear into a myriad of boundless bubbles!

Our breakfast was a Brie-cheese omelet topped with sautéed cinnamon apples, nut bread, a garnish of fresh fruit, coffee, and orange juice. Crabtree & Evelyn preserves from London were on every table.

With the glow of candlelight reflecting softly off the silver, crystal, and china, our evening meal featured filet mignon with a sauce of pink peppercorns and cream and Colorado rack of lamb with fresh herbs, an extensive wine list, unusual hors d'oeuvres, and fancy desserts. For those who prefer the privacy of their room, the Sardy House will serve either or both breakfast and dinner in your guest room.

The Sardy House is a popular place for small weddings, receptions, and private dinners. It has been awarded the Mobil 4 Star rating: "Outstanding . . . worth a special trip."

How to get there: Sardy House is on the corner of Main and Aspen streets in downtown Aspen.

Innkeeper: Jayne Poss

Address/Telephone: 128 East Main Street; (303) 920–2525 or (800) 321–3457

Rooms: 20, including 6 suites; all with private bath and TV, most with whirlpool bath, suites with VCR, stereo, and dry bar. No air conditioning (elevation 7,908 feet).

Rates: $150 to $420, single or double, summer; $239 to $549, single or double, winter; EPB. High-end rates are for suites. Rates will vary, depending on season. Romance package includes 3-night stay, champagne upon arrival, and one candlelight dinner for two. Inquire about rate.

Open: Mid-June to mid-October and from Thanksgiving to mid-April.

Facilities and activities: Dining room open to public for breakfast, dinner, and Sunday brunch. Bar, heated outdoor pool, sauna, Jacuzzi. Nearby: restaurants, shopping, art galleries, free ski shuttle, all within walking distance; summer music festivals, hiking, fishing, river rafting, downhill skiing (Aspen Mountain, Snowmass, Aspen Highlands, and Buttermilk), cross-country skiing, ice skating.

Crested Butte Club Victorian Hotel & Spa
CRESTED BUTTE, COLORADO 81224

A stay at the Crested Butte Club is a taste of luxury that everyone should experience at least once and, preferably, many, many times. All the guest rooms are beauties, but the romantic elegance of the Presidential Suite is nonpareil. I had decided on this room, sight unseen, when making a reservation by phone. I couldn't have made a better choice.

As I opened the door, I caught my breath—it was that overwhelming. A rich royal blue carpet, strewn with peach and yellow roses and gold curlicues, spread before me. A French Provincial four-poster, which I later discovered to be an exceptionally comfortable waveless waterbed, stood against the far wall. Fresh flowers graced the coffee table in front of a white brocade love seat.

Ah, but there was even more opulence to discover. In the bathroom, dark wood wainscoting met cream-colored wallpaper sprinkled with tiny blue flowers; twin pedestal sinks, imported from Italy, sat beneath oak cabinets; an oak pull-chain commode hid in one corner; and, best of all, a sloped-to-fit copper tub with hammered-brass feet beckoned me to break out the bubble bath. Later, imagine lying in bed and watching the flickering firelight glimmer against the brass and candlestick chandelier.

Other rooms feature oak or white-iron–brass beds; televisions hide in armoires or above fireplace mantels; two rooms have decks; and all chambers have gas fireplaces and copper tubs.

The Crested Butte Club has a first-class spa with complimentary use for inn guests. It also is open to the public, but guests have private after-hours privileges.

Honeymooners and anniversary couples receive champagne, with a choice of labels. In addition, newlyweds are given a gift copy of the *Colorado Cookbook*, with a personal note of congratulations and best wishes. Horse and carriage rides from the hotel to one of many romantic restaurants can be arranged by the innkeeper.

Couples desiring a unique getaway should inquire about Joe's "Ski and Sea" package—several days at the Crested Butte Club followed by a stay at the inn's luxurious property on the beaches of Mazatlán, Mexico.

How to get there: From Gunnison, about 220 miles southwest of Denver, take Highway 135 north to Crested Butte. When you reach Crested Butte, take Elk Avenue into town. Turn left onto Second Street. The inn is on the left.

Innkeeper: Joe Rous

Address/Telephone: 512 Second Street (mailing address: P.O. Box 309); (303) 349–6655

Rooms: 7, including 1 suite; all with private bath, cable TV, phone, and working fireplace. No air conditioning (elevation 9,000 feet). No smoking inn.

Rates: $75 to $225, double, depending on room and season, continental breakfast and Happy Hour. Seniors, 10 percent discount. Spa and "Ski and Sea" packages available.

Open: All year.

Facilities and activities: Sports Pub, weight gym, lap pool, three whirlpools, two steam baths, two massage rooms, climbing wall, "Pilates" instruction, personal weight trainers. Nearby: restaurants, shopping, shuttle to ski slopes, hiking, mountain biking, wildflower meadows, championship golf course, tennis, horseback riding, jeep tours, downhill and cross-country skiing, Aerial Weekend (hot-air ballooning, skydiving, hang gliding, stunt pilots), Chamber Music Festival, Slavic Harvest Festival, wildflower and photography workshops.

Castle Marne

DENVER, COLORADO 80206

For those of us not lucky enough to grow up in a castle amidst opulence and grandeur, the Castle Marne provides a wee glimpse of what we missed. The exterior is stunning. For years, passersby have paused to admire the medieval-looking rusticated stone structure. Now they come to spend the night.

Inside, one can't help but marvel at the glowing woodwork, original fireplaces, and exquisitely decorated rooms. The parlor, blessed with a baby grand piano and treasured family antiques, lends itself nicely to the intimate Victorian tea served each afternoon on heirloom porcelain china and silver.

There's something hopelessly romantic about climbing the stately oak staircase, past the resplendent beveled-crystal and stained-glass Peacock Window, to your guest room. Our favorite chamber is the Presidential Suite, an elegant affair featuring a king-sized brass–white-iron tester bed with rose bed cover peeping through ecru lace. This room is further enhanced by a tiny fireplace, an antique gentleman's dresser, and a cozy turret room surrounded by five lace-paneled windows. French doors lead to a private solarium with a large whirlpool tub and a balcony overlooking downtown Denver.

The Conservatory also caught our fancy. This light and airy room has a queen-sized bed, a wicker armoire and love seat, and creamy walls sprinkled with cabbage roses.

Imagine a private candlelight dinner in the Castle Marne's formal dining room amid the gracious ambience of days long past. Soft music accompanies your conversation, and you scarcely notice the striking of the wall clock as you dine on chilled marinated shrimp and Cornish game hen with apricot glaze and fruit and nut stuffing, followed by chocolate mousse and café au lait. Later you climb that wonderful oak staircase, soak in the oversized Jacuzzi with balcony doors open to the stars and, eventually, sip a cup of wine or tea in your own tiny turret hideaway. Every couple should have just such an evening at least once in their lifetime. Hopefully, many, many times.

Extraordinarily good breakfasts come from Jim and Diane's kitchen, too. A fresh fruit plate is followed by wonderful homemade breads, muffins, and cinnamon sticky buns. Perhaps you will choose one of their many waffle varieties with real maple syrup, an innovative quiche, or a hot-from-the-oven breakfast casserole.

How to get there: From East Colfax Avenue, turn north onto Race Street. Proceed for almost 1 block. Inn is on southeast corner of Race Street and Sixteenth Avenue.

Innkeepers: Jim and Diane Peiker

Address/Telephone: 1572 Race Street; (303) 331–0621

Rooms: 9; all with private bath and phone; 3 with jetted whirlpool tubs for two on private balconies. No air conditioning (not needed; walls are 20 inches of solid stone). No smoking inn.

Rates: $90 to $180, double, EPB plus Victorian tea.

Open: All year.

Facilities and activities: Concierge service; Victorian luncheons and candlelight dinners available with prior arrangement; game room with pool table and exercise equipment; gift shop. Nearby: business and financial districts, Colorado State Capitol, U.S. Mint, Center for the Performing Arts, restaurants, convention center, museums, recreation centers, shopping facilities, professional sporting events, golf, tennis, hiking, fishing, biking; downhill and cross-country skiing approximately 50 miles away.

Queen Anne Inn
DENVER, COLORADO 80205

The two side-by-side Victorians that make up the exceptionally romantic Queen Anne Inn reign amid a row of lovely old homes in downtown Denver's Clements Historic District. While you relax in the beautifully appointed parlor, you are apt to witness a breathless couple arriving by horse and carriage, she still in her long, white wedding dress, he nervously trying to avoid stepping on same. Or the newest arrivals might be a middle-aged pair, with bottle of champagne in hand, bent on escaping their lawn-mowing, car-polishing neighbors for a romantic weekend getaway. They've come to the right place.

Every guest room is different, and each one is special in its own way. The Fountain Room, overlooking Benedict Fountain Park, boasts a four-poster with frilly, white-ruffled arched canopy, soft peach walls, a blue-and-peach love seat, and a black-tiled sunken tub tucked away in one corner. A more romantic room would be hard to find.

While the Tower Room, with European carved king-sized bed and bay window love seat, is exceptionally inviting, the Aspen Room is definitely the most unusual. Located in the turret, it features a hand-painted, wraparound mural of an aspen grove. If you lie on the bed and look up at the ceiling, you will gradually see the forest come alive until the aspen leaves seem to quake in the alpenglow.

The grounds are positively lovely. A series of latticework arbors leads to an enclosed backyard garden bordered by brick and flagstone planters filled with flowers and greenery. Ornate, white iron tables and chairs and a center fountain beckon couples to linger awhile.

According to Tom, "This inn is known for providing 'White Lace Romance.' The Queen Anne hosts an average of two honeymoon couples, two anniversary couples and three couples on a 'getaway' per week." When I asked him what he thinks makes his inn so romantic, he replied, "The fresh flowers, chamber music, champagne upon arrival, candlelight dinners, antique brass beds and canopied four posters, claw-footed tubs and soaker tubs-for-two, lights on dimmer switches, direct-dial phones to call friends with happy news, and late checkout. And then there's the private garden, perfect for a secluded breakfast or evening glass of wine."

Numerous publications, including *Bride's* magazine, *Romantic Hideaways*, *Bridal Guide*, *Country Inns*, *Travel Holiday*, and *Vacations* agree. All have raved about the Queen Anne's romantic qualities.

How to get there: From East Colfax Avenue, take Logan Street north to 20th Avenue. Turn left onto 20th Avenue and proceed to 21st Street. Turn right onto 21st Street and then immediately right again onto Tremont Place. Inn is on the left.

Innkeeper: Tom King

Address/Telephone: 2147-51 Tremont Place; (303) 296–6666 for information; (800) 432–INNS for reservations

Rooms: 14; all with private bath, phone, air conditioning, and stereo chamber music. No smoking inn.

Rates: $75 to $125, double; $135 to $155, suite; EPB and afternoon refreshments. Special rates for airline employees, travel agents, entertainers, and members of AAA. Inquire about rates for Romance Package.

Open: All year.

Facilities and activities: Innkeeper will arrange horse-and-carriage rides, catered candlelight dinners, musicians for private serenading, and just about anything else your imagination (or his) can come up with. Nearby: Colorado State Capitol, U.S. Mint, Center for the Performing Arts, museums, shopping, restaurants (several five-star), all within walking distance; hiking, fishing, biking; downhill and cross-country skiing approximately 50 miles away.

River Song Inn
ESTES PARK, COLORADO 80517

If planning a formal wedding is not to your liking, you may want to check out the River Song's three-night Elopement Package. Included are a full breakfast each morning, one therapeutic massage per person, a gourmet picnic lunch, and a candlelight dinner for two. The bride and groom can take their vows, performed by innkeeper Gary Mansfield, either at the inn or, during winter, on snowshoes amongst breathtakingly beautiful surroundings in Rocky Mountain National Park.

The River Song recently added a wonderfully secluded two-unit cottage, with guest quarters separated by a foot-and-a-half-thick wall to ensure privacy. Named "Wood Nymph" and "Meadow Bright," the two chambers are nestled on the mountainside (easily accessible) near a rushing stream and tranquil, trout-filled pond, with a spectacular view of the snow-capped peaks of Rocky Mountain National Park. Both have fireplaces, canopied beds (Wood Nymph's is handmade of river birches, and Meadow Bright's is a massive hand-hewn log affair), decks, and radiant-heated floors. Wood Nymph has a Jacuzzi whirlpool tub and Meadow Bright features a fireside jetted tub and a waterfall shower. Both rooms have wheelchair access.

But, if you are looking for something unique and also romantic, you really should ask for the River Song's most requested accommodation:

Indian Paintbrush. A charming cottage sequestered among tall pine trees, it is tastefully done in Southwestern decor and features a love seat, handwoven Navajo wall hangings, an oversized bathtub, and, best of all, a swinging, queen-sized bed suspended from the ceiling by heavy white chains in front of a rose-tiled fireplace.

Sue is an excellent cook and makes many delectables such as apple pandowdy, blueberry cobbler served with vanilla yogurt, and corn fritters topped with genuine Vermont maple syrup. Elegant candlelight dinners, served in style with heirloom silver, crystal, and china, are available with prior notice.

Plush off-white couches and a soft blue carpet add luxuriance to the living room, where one entire side is a window with a magnificent view of tall pines and mountains. Books line two walls, a warm fire crackles in the fireplace, and the grandfather clock periodically chimes the hour. All's well at River Song.

How to get there: Going west on Elkhorn Avenue, Estes Park's main street, turn left onto Moraine Avenue and proceed 4 blocks. At first stop sign, turn right onto Highway 36. At stoplight (1⅓ miles) turn left onto Mary's Lake Road. Watch for River Song Inn mailbox just across bridge. Turn right and proceed for ⅘ mile. The road ends at River Song.

Innkeepers: Gary and Sue Mansfield

Address/Telephone: Mary's Lake Road (mailing address: P.O. Box 1910); (303) 586–4666

Rooms: 4 in main inn, 1 carriage house suite, 4 deluxe cottages; all with private bath. Two rooms in 1 cottage with wheelchair access. No air conditioning (elevation 7,522 feet). No smoking inn.

Rates: $95 to $195, double, EPB. Inquire about rates for three-night Elopement Package.

Open: All year.

Facilities and activities: Candlelight dinner and box lunches by reservation. Located on twenty-seven acres of land with easy hiking trails. Nearby: Rocky Mountain National Park, restaurants, shopping, hiking, fishing, sailing, mountain climbing, golf, tennis, wildlife seminars, cross-country skiing, snowshoeing.

The Lovelander Bed & Breakfast Inn
LOVELAND, COLORADO 80537

Loveland, Colorado, is known nationwide as the Sweetheart City, where one can send his or her valentines to be postmarked by hand and mailed from "Loveland." What better way to impress that special someone?

The Lovelander Bed and Breakfast Inn fits right into the scheme. Its Victorian elegance definitely lends itself to romance. Here guests whisper sweet promises in the garden, sip sherry on the porch, and take a tea tray to the privacy of their room. Want more? How about a soak in an antique footed tub filled to the brim with passion fruit–scented bubbles?

A wide veranda wraps around the front and one side of this lovely circa-1902 inn; inside,

gleaming woodwork, an ornate organ from the late 1800s, a corner fireplace, and plush overstuffed furniture add to the inviting glow of the parlor.

Lace-curtained bay windows spread soft light into the dining room, where one can always find coffee or tea and genuine, homemade Victorian vinegar cookies on the sideboard. Breakfast is served either at tables set for two or at the large oval dining room table.

And the two of you are in for a treat when you come down to breakfast. Baked eggs Florentine, cinnamon-raisin breakfast pudding, stuffed French toast with strawberry-tangerine sauce, almond scones, banana-oatmeal pancakes, gingered melon with honey, and strawberry-banana smoothies are only a few of the specialties Marilyn cooks up in her kitchen.

The private and secluded guest rooms are tucked away in downstairs corners and upstairs gables. Sloped ceilings and lots of nooks and crannies, along with antique writing desks, armoires, carved walnut and oak and brass and iron beds, and claw-footed bathtubs, add to the charm of these chambers.

Among our favorites are the Country Garden Room, with its queen-sized bed covered with a pale aqua floral spread, oak desk, and indoor window box filled with cheerful wooden tulips, and the Columbine, with king-sized bed, writing desk, love seat, and elegant bath with 6-foot whirlpool tub.

The Lovelander dedicates the entire month of February to romance. Guest chefs create gourmet candlelight dinners, musicians entertain, and lovers receive commemorative valentines and complimentary boxes of chocolates. During the rest of the year, Marilyn will arrange romantic dinners for two at area restaurants, with limousine service, if desired.

How to get there: From I–25, turn west onto Highway 34 to Garfield Avenue. Turn left onto Garfield to West 4th Street. Turn right onto West 4th Street. Inn is on the right.

Innkeepers: Marilyn and Bob Wiltgen
Address/Telephone: 217 West 4th Street; (303) 669–0798
Rooms: 11; all with private bath, air conditioning, and phone, some with whirlpool bath. No smoking inn.
Rates: $84 to $125, double, EPB and beverages and snacks. Seniors, 10 percent discount.
Open: All year.
Facilities and activities: Meeting and reception center. Nearby: restaurants, shopping, art galleries, museums, concerts, performing arts, lectures, theater, outdoor and indoor swimming pools, outdoor and indoor Jacuzzis, golf, tennis, hiking, biking, fishing, boating, cross-country skiing, llama farm, Rocky Mountain National Park.
Recommended Country Inns® Travel Club Benefit: Lovelander coffee mug.

Meadow Creek Bed & Breakfast Inn
PINE, COLORADO 80470

Our idea of a perfect couple of days would be to hide away in this inn's Room in the Meadow, a delightful cottage set in a grassy meadow and blessed with a fireplace, Jacuzzi for two, brass king-sized bed, private deck, microwave, and fridge. We would spend time outdoors, too, wandering through the woods in search of wildflowers and forest critters, listening to the wind rustle through the aspen, fir, and pine, and having afternoon lemonade in the gazebo, all the while absorbing the peace and quiet of the countryside.

Or your choice might be the new Colorado Sunshine Suite, a dream-come-true love nest with a king-sized bed, see-through, double-hearthed fireplace, private hot tub, sauna, and patio. From above, skylights spread moonbeams and stardust over all.

This inn was once the summer home of a prince, and in my opinion it's still fit for a king and queen. The two-and-a-half-story stone structure was built in 1929 for Prince Balthasar Gialma Odescalchi, a descendant of nobility from the Holy Roman Empire. When the prince left Colorado in 1947, the residence was absorbed into a 250-acre ranch; more recently, it has been transformed into a lovely country inn.

Among other guest accommodations are the Wild Rose Room, where a lop-eared cousin of Flopsy, Mopsy, and Cottontail, dressed in pink taffeta, sits on a queen-sized bed covered with white lace, and the cheery Sun Room, featuring a white wicker bed and love seat.

I recommend that you make dinner reservations at the time you book your room. The night we were there, the fare was marinated, grilled chicken with mandarin orange sauce, homemade bread, tossed green salad, pecan pie, ice cream turtle pie, and, an inn specialty, mountain mud slide, a cookie crust filled with layers of cream cheese and chocolate mousse, whipped cream, and chocolate bits.

A full breakfast is provided at the inn, or a couple may take a continental-style repast of homemade pastries, fruit, and juice to their room the night before if they don't care to come down to the inn for breakfast in the morning.

How to get there: Take Highway 285 (Hampden Avenue) south from Denver to Conifer. From the traffic light at Conifer, continue on Highway 285 for exactly 5³⁄₁₀ miles. Turn left, follow road past school and take next left onto Douglas Drive at Douglas Ranch. Turn right onto Berry Hill Lane and continue to inn.

Innkeepers: Pat and Dennis Carnahan, Judy and Don Otis

Address/Telephone: 13438 U.S. Highway 285 (Barry Hill Lane at Douglas Ranch); (303) 838–4167 or (303) 838–4899

Rooms: 7, including 1 luxury cottage; all with private bath, 3 with private hot tub, fireplace, king-sized bed and private entry. Limited wheelchair access. Air conditioning in Grandma's Attic and Colorado Sunshine Suite (elevation 8,200 feet).

Rates: $84 to $180, double, EPB. Two-night minimum stay on weekends preferred.

Open: All year.

Facilities and activities: Dinner available, with seventy-two-hour advance reservation, Wednesday through Saturday, $18 per person. Outdoor hot tub, sauna, gazebo, gift shop, picnic table, fire pit in old brick silo for marshmallow roasts, thirty-five acres of woods to roam, toboggan hill. Nearby: restaurants, mountain towns, shopping, hiking, fishing, golf, cross-country skiing, one hour to downhill skiing.

Recommended Country Inns® Travel Club Benefit: 10% discount, Monday–Thursday.

The Blackwell House Bed & Breakfast
COEUR D' ALENE, IDAHO 83814

People passing by with no intention of spending the night cannot resist ringing the doorbell and asking if they can see the interior of this stately mansion. From the attractively appointed parlor to the music room with its antique grand piano, from the sweeping staircase to the upper floors of absolutely picture-perfect guest rooms, this inn is a designer's showcase— the perfect place for a wedding. And wouldn't you just know—there's a minister on call to perform the ceremony!

Built by F. A. Blackwell in 1904 as a wedding gift for his son, this magnificent, three-story structure was allowed to deteriorate over the years to the point that, when Kathleen bought it in 1982, it took nine months, one hundred gallons of paint remover, 282 rolls of wallpaper, nineteen tons of sod, and unmeasured amounts of laughter and tears to help bring it around to the masterpiece it is today.

The morning repast is served in the Breakfast Room, where French doors open out onto the patio and spacious lawns. A fire in the fireplace removes the early-morning chill, fresh-ground Irish cream coffee warms the tummy, large bowls of fruit center the round, cloth-covered tables, and baskets of huckleberry muffins soon appear hot from the oven.

The second-floor Blackwell Suite is a pink-and-white dream with oak-spool bed; white wicker settee, table, and chairs; white ruffled curtains with pink tiebacks; white eyelet-trimmed comforter and bed ruffle; pink floral wallpaper; dusty rose carpet; and claw-footed bathtub sequestered in its own little alcove.

But, before you decide on this one, you must also see the former servants' quarters and children's playroom on the third floor. Smaller but ever so cozy, the three rooms share a sitting area with love seat, and they, like the others, are exquisitely decorated.

The hospitality here even extends to your friends, who are welcome to join you for late-afternoon tea and cookies or wine and munchies. If you haven't yet tried staying at country inns, The Blackwell House would be a great place to start.

How to get there: From city center, go east on Sherman Avenue (main street) for approximately 5 blocks. Inn is on the right.

Innkeepers: Kathleen Sims and Margaret Hoy
Address/Telephone: 820 Sherman Avenue; (208) 664–0656
Rooms: 8, including 3 suites; 6 with private bath.
Rates: $70 to $114, double, EPB and late-afternoon refreshments; champagne in room for special occasions.
Open: All year.
Facilities and activities: Catered luncheons and dinners for six or more guests; weddings, and receptions. Minister on staff. Music room with grand piano, large yard with gazebo and barbecue, within walking distance to downtown. Nearby: Lake Coeur d'Alene, "World's Longest Floating Boardwalk," Tubb's Hill nature trails, shopping, restaurants, hiking, fishing, boating, bicycling, downhill and cross-country skiing, snowmobiling.

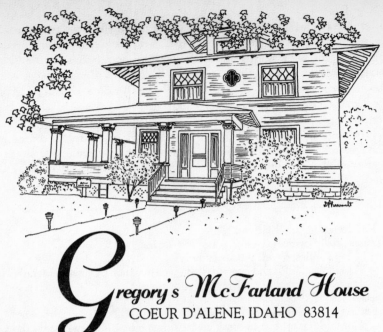

Gregory's McFarland House
COEUR D'ALENE, IDAHO 83814

This inn hosts many weddings and receptions, due to its lovely facilities and attentive innkeepers. Warm and hospitable, Win and Stephen clearly enjoy seeing to it that brides and grooms have a memorable wedding day. And, year after year, many couples return to celebrate their anniversaries.

The McFarland House just keeps getting better and better, with the addition of more and more quality antiques. Guests have the use of all the common areas, including the more casual family room with its regulation oak-wood pool table, television, VCR, and stereo.

And then there's the pretty-as-a-wedding-cake conservatory. Looking out onto the beauti-fully landscaped backyard, it features pink wicker chairs padded with pink floral cushions, pink tablecloths, place mats, and napkins; and pots and pots of pink geraniums. I am convinced that, even on a cloudy day, this room must glow with cheerfulness.

The conservatory is where I had breakfast, and it was gourmet to the last crumb. A frothy fruit drink made of blended fresh fruits and skim milk and served in stemmed glassware began the affair. Next came a fresh fruit cup, muffin, and Irish cream coffee. A light and fluffy egg dish garnished with spears of fresh asparagus and slices of wheat toast completed this extraordinarily delicious meal.

Many of the antiques throughout the inn are from Win's family. My room had a circa-1860 bed with a pink-on-white bed cover, ecru eyelet ruffled skirt, and piles of eyelet-trimmed pillows. Later, when I returned from dinner, Win had left a mint surprise, Stephen brought ice water to my room, the ceiling fan circulated the cool evening air filtering through the imported lace curtains, and the floral-upholstered love seat beckoned me to read awhile. It feels very good here.

I have another reason for especially liking this inn. The Gregorys' three kitty cats, Sweet Boy, Valentino, and Lil Darlin', gave me my "cat fix" for the day. It surely helped for the moment, but, three days later, I was happy as usual to get home to my own cream Persian, Murphy, and my calico, Garfy.

How to get there: From midtown, go east on Sherman (Coeur d'Alene's main street) to 6th Street. Go north on 6th Street to Foster. Inn is on the northeast corner.

Innkeepers: Winifred and Stephen Gregory
Address/Telephone: 601 Foster Avenue; (208) 667–1232
Rooms: 5; all with private bath. No smoking inn.
Rates: $75 to $150, single or double, EPB, afternoon wine, tea, soft drinks, and cookies. Reduced off-season rates available. Special packages available for skiers and wedding parties.
Open: All year.
Facilities and activities: Picnic lunches available if arranged in advance. Private entrance and area for weddings; minister and photographer on staff. Landscaped grounds, piano. Nearby: Lake Coeur d'Alene, "World's Longest Floating Boardwalk," Tubb's Hill nature trails, restaurants, shopping, hiking, fishing, horseback riding, swimming, waterskiing, sailing, snowmobiling, downhill and cross-country skiing.

The Cary House Bed & Breakfast

HAGERMAN, IDAHO 83332

The love seats on The Cary House's front porch, on the redwood deck, and in the Moonlight Garden give even the shyest romantics a gentle nudge. Add to this an acre of landscaped lawn and gardens to roam, exquisite guest rooms, and elegant candlelit breakfasts, and romance soon becomes full-blown.

Built in 1908, this Victorian farmhouse was one of the most elegant of its day. Natural springs provided water for the farm, which supplied strawberries, eggs, and milk to miners in Sun Valley. The builder's daughter, Ruth Cary, occupied the house until 1988, when it was purchased by the innkeepers, Darrell and Linda Heinemann, and Linda's parents, owners of the horse farm just across the highway.

A painstaking two-year restoration turned the rather dilapidated structure into a stunning inn filled with turn-of-the-century antiques. A red velvet settee and matching armchairs with carved wooden backs, an ornate coffee table, a rocking chair, and bay window enhance the parlor.

Upstairs, honeymooners luxuriate in the Victorian Room. A white quilted spread covers the queen-sized brass bed, while a mirrored armoire, lace curtains, skirted table, and dried flower arrangements further adorn these spacious quarters. Here, windows on three sides look out onto horse pastures and the canyon rim.

The Garden Room draws its name from an

arch-shaped wall hanging featuring a basket of flowers quilt-stitched by Darrell's grandmother. Wallpaper with pink, blue, and yellow blossoms on a white background enlivens this corner room. A bird cage filled with artificial buds and tiny artificial birds overlooks the claw-footed tub in the private bathroom.

Breakfast here is country gourmet, highlighted, in season, by raspberries and red potatoes fresh from the garden out back. Both Darrell and Linda love to cook, and guests are the fortunate recipients of such delights as souffléed apple pancakes, Grand Marnier French toast, or sausage and cheese strata. Fruit, homemade coffee cakes, and pastries add to the morning meal. The kitchen, blessed by a circa-1900 Majestic wood-burning stove, has a homey, country feel.

How to get there: From I–80N, turn south onto Highway 30 at Bliss and proceed for 7²⁄₁₀ miles. After crossing the Malad River and Riley Creek, look for a long row of poplar trees on the left. The Cary House is on the right.

Innkeepers: Darrell and Linda Heinemann
Address/Telephone: 17895 U.S. Highway 30; (208) 837–4848
Rooms: 4; all with private bath. Central air conditioning and ceiling fans. No smoking inn.
Rates: $55 to $75, single or double, EPB, turndown service, and homemade truffles. No credit cards.
Open: All year, except for Christmas holidays.
Facilities and activities: Horses. Nearby: scenic byway, Craters of the Moon National Monument, Sawtooth National Forest, Rose Creek Winery, fossil beds, hot springs, river rafting, fishing, hiking, bicycling, bird watching, golfing, arts and crafts shops.

The Voss Inn
BOZEMAN, MONTANA 59715

Often referred to as one of Montana's most romantic bed and breakfasts, The Voss Inn is located in Bozeman's historic district. Many a couple, bent on a blissful weekend, walks hand in hand through this inn's English cottage perennial garden, up the steps, past Victorian wicker furniture on a porch ablaze with geraniums, and into the lovely parlor. And it only gets better from here.

As meticulously scrubbed, starched, pressed, and polished as an Easter-morning Sunday School class, The Voss Inn exudes perfection. Antique beds, private sitting areas, breakfast nooks, and bay windows all add to the charm of this stalwart, red-brick Victorian. Every room I

peeked into was captivating. The Sartain Room on the main floor features a provocative tub and bathing alcove; the front parlor is graced with an ornate, etched-glass chandelier; the Chisholm Room, a favorite with honeymooners, boasts a magnificent 9-foot brass headboard with an antique brass lamp hanging from it, a claw-footed bathtub, and an antique gas fireplace.

Flowered wallpaper banks the staircase leading to the immaculate upstairs guest rooms. I entered my favorite, Robert's Roost, by descending three steps into a bright and cheerful garden of white wicker, deep green walls sprinkled with tiny white blossoms, white ruffled curtains, and a private balcony. The bed, brass and iron, has a white eyelet spread and is embellished with dark green, rose-flowered pillows. A miniature bottle of liqueur and two small glasses waited on the bedside table.

Frankee tiptoes upstairs and leaves early morning coffee and tea in the hallway. Then, a little later, she brings fresh fruit, orange juice, homemade cinnamon rolls and muffins, and wonderful egg-soufflé dishes to the hall buffet. She has twelve different breakfast entrees that she chooses from, and, even if you stay a week, you will not get a repeat performance. Breakfast is taken to tiny tables in the guest rooms, and that's a definite plus because you'll want to spend as much time as possible in your newfound hide-away.

Privacy is carefully protected at this inn. According to Frankee, "We endeavor to provide personal and attentive service without disturbing our guests' privacy. They may join us and other guests for tea and conversation if they like, or they can choose to have no interaction at all. The choice is entirely theirs." If you are celebrating a honeymoon or anniversary, let her know in advance so she can have champagne or wine in your room awaiting your arrival.

How to get there: From I–90, take exit 306 into Bozeman. Turn south onto North 7th Avenue, left onto Main Street, and proceed to South Willson. Go south on Willson for approximately 3½ blocks to the inn.

Innkeepers: Bruce and Frankee Muller
Address/Telephone: 319 South Willson; (406) 587–0982
Rooms: 6; all with private bath, some with air conditioning, fans available for others.
Rates: $80 to $90, double, EPB, afternoon tea, and nightcap.
Open: All year.
Facilities and activities: Airport pick-up if requested in advance. During winter, transportation to ski slopes for nominal charge. Nearby: Lewis and Clark Caverns, Museum of the Rockies, Bridger Bowl and Big Sky ski areas, restaurants, shopping, hiking, fishing in blue-ribbon trout stream, downhill and cross-country skiing; personalized daytrips into Yellowstone National Park and other points of interest, including gourmet breakfast and picnic lunch.

Copper King Mansion Bed & Breakfast

BUTTE, MONTANA 59701

"A mile high, a mile deep, and always on the level," was the motto in Butte, Montana (elevation 5,280 feet) when its nineteenth-century copper mines burrowed an equal depth underground. The man most noted for the extraction of ore from the region was William Andrews Clark, better known as the "Copper King," who later became a U.S. senator.

Clark built this mansion in 1884 at a cost of $250,000—a mere half day's wages at the height of his earnings (estimated at $17 million a month). He spared no expense to procure the best craftsmanship and quality. German wood-carvers chiseled ornate figures in the Philippine mahogany fireplace. Rosewood, cherry, and oak are among the nine different woods that adorn the house, including the hand-carved central staircase and parquet floors. Frescoed ceilings and jeweled Tiffany stained-glass windows are part of the opulent decor.

While the building attests to Clark's wealth and taste, the preservation and renovation of the home reflect the resourcefulness of two women, the great-grandmother and grandmother of the current innkeeper, Maria Wagner. They acquired the building, stripped of its appointments, in 1953, and filled it with period pieces dating from 1880 to 1930, the era when the copper magnate and U.S. senator called Butte home. Today, twenty original items from the Clark family are among the priceless furnishings.

Guests seeking a romantic interlude can pamper themselves regally with a stay in the Master Suite, with adjoining sitting room and private bath. A carved headboard stands sentinel over the satin and hand-crocheted bed covers. Overhead, a fresco of nudes has been restored—a group of nuns, former occupants, had discreetly painted over it. Perfume bottles and an ivory manicure-and-comb set leave the impression that Clark and his wife still use this room.

No matter which quarters one chooses, there's no need to fear missing anything at this inn. Overnight lodging includes a tour of the mansion as well as a delicious breakfast of French toast, quiche, or omelet served on Limoges china with silver service. Tasteful elegance reigns in the dining room under a gold-embossed leather ceiling hung with a crystal chandelier.

How to get there: From I–90, exit onto Montana Street and follow it north to Granite Street. Turn left onto West Granite and proceed for several blocks to the inn.

Innkeeper: Maria Wagner
Address/Telephone: 219 West Granite Street; (406) 782–7580
Rooms: 4; 2 with private bath, 1 with TV. Pets allowed with prior approval. No air conditioning (elevation 5,280 feet).
Rates: $55 to $95, single or double, EPB, wine or beer, and tour of the mansion.
Open: All year. Mansion tours for public occur between 9:00 A.M. and 5:00 P.M., May through October. During this season, bed and breakfast guests check in between 5:00 and 9:00 P.M. and must check out by 9:00 A.M.
Facilities and activities: Robes for shared bath, bottled water. Nearby: World Museum of Mining, Arts Chateau Gallery, historic walking tour, ghost towns, hiking, fishing, horseback riding, snowmobiling, downhill and cross-country skiing.

Izaak Walton Inn
ESSEX, MONTANA 59916

For couples seeking seclusion and total privacy, a stay in one of this inn's cozy "little red cabooses" would be a great choice. Genuine Great Northern cabooses, now resting on the hillside overlooking the inn, have been totally remodeled with pine interior and accented with blue-and-white pinstripe bedding and red pillows and include a mini-kitchen, private bath, and deck. If you prefer complete isolation, you can forego the meals offered in the inn's dining room by requesting, in advance and for an additional fee, that your tiny cupboard and fridge be stocked in anticipation of your arrival.

I recommend that you, on at least one of your nights here, first pamper yourselves in the Finnish-style sauna and, later indulge in a moonlit dinner on your caboose's private deck. As Larry and Lynda proclaim, "At our inn, time stands still and lets you catch up." Allow a couple extra days here, and there even will be time to "catch up" on a little old-fashioned courting.

Built in 1939 to accommodate service crews for the Great Northern Railway, whose enormous task it was to keep the mountain track open during winter, the inn is still very much involved in the railroad business. It is here that "helper" engines hook onto lengthy freight trains and help push them over the Continental Divide. The inn is also a designated flag stop, with Amtrak passing through daily. If you decide to arrive via Amtrak, inn personnel will meet you at the platform to help with luggage.

Fifteen to twenty freight trains pass by the front door of the inn each day; and, whether resting in one of the charming guest rooms, playing volleyball in the playfield, or downing a few in the Flag Stop Bar, one is hard-pressed to keep from running outdoors like a kid to watch as the massive trains chug by.

The Izaak Walton is packed with signal lanterns, vintage photographs, and all sorts of train memorabilia. In the Dining Car Restaurant, you may be seated next to a striped-capped engineer from the train waiting out on the tracks or sharing a meal and spirited conversation with members of an international rail fan club.

Highlights of our stay at the Izaak Walton: lovely accommodations, light and fluffy breakfast crepes filled to overflowing with huckleberries; a dinner of honey-glazed chicken sautéed with orange slices and onions; the sighting of whole families of shaggy, beautiful mountain goats zigzagging their way down the hillside to a salt lick; and spotting a yearling bear cub peacefully munching his way along the side of the road.

Wildlife photographers can have the time of their lives here: black bears, mountain lions, mountain goats, spawning salmon, and, from early October to early November, a sometimes large migration of bald eagles.

How to get there: Inn is ½ mile off of Highway 2, on southern rim of Glacier National Park between East and West Glacier. Watch for sign for Essex turnoff.

Innkeepers: Larry and Lynda Vielleux

Address/Telephone: Off Highway 2 (mailing address: P.O. Box 653); (406) 888–5700

Rooms: 31; 11 with private bath, 20 share several baths. Four private cabooses with private bath, 1 with gas fireplace. No air conditioning (elevation 3,860 feet).

Rates: $72 to $92, double, EP. Caboose: $350 for 3 nights; $600 for 7 nights, based on 4-person occupancy; EP. Five- and 7-day packages, including meals, available. Personal checks preferred.

Open: All year.

Facilities and activities: Full-service dining room, bar, sauna, laundromat, ski shop, gift shop with Montana-made items; Amtrak flag stop # E.S.M., train activity, train memorabilia; cross-country ski rentals, snowshoe rentals, guided cross-country ski tours into Glacier National Park, guided snowshoe treks. Nearby: Glacier National Park and Bob Marshall Wilderness Area, constituting more than a million acres of wilderness; fishing, hiking, horseback riding, rafting, wildlife viewing, photography, cross-country skiing.

The Sanders - Helena's Bed & Breakfast

HELENA, MONTANA 59601

Montana Senator Wilbur Sanders and his wife, Harriet, built this Queen Anne home in 1875, at the beginning of his political career. An important figure in Helena, Sanders also founded the Montana Historical Society and was its president for twenty-six years.

Innkeepers Bobbi Uecker and Rock Ringling realized the importance of preserving as much of this landmark structure as possible when they undertook the restoration of the mansion. A museum in its own right, the inn still houses most of the original furnishings belonging to its first family. Today, as then, rich wooden paneling, gleaming oak floors, and priceless antiques add elegance throughout the inn.

The luxurious Colonel's Room features the Sanderses' 8-foot-high headboard of bird's-eye maple, matching dressers (one with a marble top), and a bay window. Modern amenities are tastefully hidden away in armoires and dressers.

The sleep chamber called Teddy's Buckaroo, named in honor of Bobbi's cattleman father, appeals to honeymooners. A four-poster brass bed, draped with a canopy of mosquito netting, dominates this room. The adjoining bathroom, however, is the drawing card. A 5x5-foot tile enclosure with dual shower heads invites guests to linger amid lush potted plants.

Lest the inn showcase only the Sanderses' past, some items modestly pay homage to Rock's family. A portrait of his great-grandfather Alf T. Ringling, one of the five brothers who began the famed Ringling Bros. Circus, hangs prominently in the Colonel's Room. Above the upper stairway is a bust of "Chili Bean," a roping steer who performed at Madison Square Garden and spent his old age at the Ringling Ranch.

Come morning, both Bobbi and Rock appear in chef's hats. Bobbi's concoction of orange soufflé and the Sanderses' recipe for cream cheese–filled French toast delight guests.

The huckleberry pancakes, mushroom crepes, and Grand Marnier French toast also receive raves from visitors.

How to get there: From I–90, take the Capitol Area exit and follow Prospect Street west to Montana Street. Turn left onto Montana Street and proceed to 6th Avenue. Turn right onto 6th Avenue and right again onto North Ewing. Inn is on the left.

Innkeepers: Bobbi Uecker and Rock Ringling
Address/Telephone: 328 North Ewing; (406) 442–3309
Rooms: 7; all with private bath, phone, TV, and air conditioning. No smoking inn.
Rates: $70 to $90, double; EPB, snacks, and beverages.
Open: All year.
Facilities and activities: On National Register of Historic Places, flower gardens. Nearby: St. Helena's Cathedral, Holter Museum, Myrna Loy Theater, historic governor's mansion, state capitol building, Historical Museum, cultural center, fishing, down hill and cross-country skiing.

$\mathcal{G}$old $\mathcal{H}$ill $\mathcal{H}$otel
GOLD HILL, NEVADA 89440

Not many years ago, this luxurious country inn was nothing more than a decaying six-room, one-bath hotel and bar. Built during the gold rush to the Comstock Lode in 1859, the hotel served a bustling community that received as many as fifty scheduled trains a day, hauling commodities in and ore out. The stone section of the building still stands, and a new wooden addition has been added to replace that which disappeared sometime before 1890. It is the oldest operating hotel in Nevada.

A walk through this comfortably elegant hotel reveals quality antiques and a genteel ambience unexpected in this rather remote section of Nevada.

The guest rooms boast period furnishings and lovely decor, but our choice, and often that of newlyweds, was Room 6, with a private balcony; stone fireplace; a beautiful circa-1850 half-tester bed; marble-topped dresser and bedside tables; wet bar; fine-print blue wallpaper; and an extra-large bath. The pink-draped corner windows look out to the Sierra Nevada mountain range.

In the hotel's Crown Point Restaurant, the tables are clad with white linen and set with crystal stemware and fine china. Soft rose drapes and upholstered chairs, sea green carpet, and an antique sideboard contribute to the elegance of this room. There is an extensive wine list featuring wines from France, Germany, California, and Washington state.

How to get there: From Reno, take Highway 395 south to Highway 341 turnoff to Virginia City. At Virginia City, continue south for 1 mile to Gold Hill. Hotel is on the right.

Innkeepers: Doug and Carol McQuide

Address/Telephone: Highway 342 (mailing address: P.O. Box 710, Virginia City, NV 89440); (702) 847–0111

Rooms: 11, plus 2 guest houses; 9 rooms and guest houses with private bath. Second-floor guest rooms with wheelchair access.

Rates: $45 to $125, double, continental breakfast.

Open: All year except January.

Facilities and activities: Full-service dining room with wheelchair access, closed Mondays and Tuesdays; Great Room lounge; Tavern Bar, weekly lectures by local historians. Nearby: restaurants, saloons, gambling casinos, excursion train, mine tours, hiking, fishing, exploring; downhill and cross-country skiing at Lake Tahoe, approximately 35 miles away.

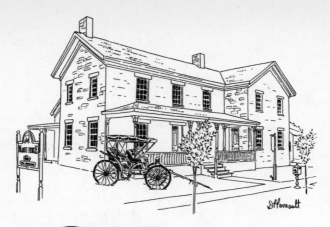

Manti House Inn
MANTI, UTAH 84642

This inn is one of our favorites, and we can't decide if it's the country charm of hand-stitched quilts (two on every bed!), hand-crafted furniture (a superbly executed pie safe stands in the upstairs hallway), the inn's culinary creativity, or perhaps the warm welcome we received at this English vernacular masterpiece, built of limestone in 1868.

All the rooms are exquisitely done: tiny-printed wallpapers, gigantic four-posters, and claw-footed bathtubs.

We stayed in the bridal suite, and we heartily recommend that you reserve ahead for this one with its raspberry-sherbet carpet, white-railinged stairway leading down to the hot tub, private balcony, tiny window seat, and massive four-poster, so high it takes a two-step platform to climb into bed.

Lace-covered French doors partition off the built-for-two, rose-colored tub and Jacuzzi with wraparound mirrors and ruffled burgundy drapes.

Breakfast here is wonderful. If it hadn't been for the aroma of bacon and oven pancakes, made with lemon and nutmeg from an old family recipe, we'd probably still be in that lovely room.

Delicious ice cream concoctions ranging from the usual shakes and sundaes to the "John D. T. McAllister," named after a prominent

Mormon church member and Utah citizen are served in the Ice Cream Parlor (summers only) amid white wrought-iron tables and chairs. This extravaganza consists of two and a half pounds of ice cream, three sauces, bananas, whipped cream, nuts, and cherries. As the menu says,

"Enough for a family of five."

How to get there: From I–15 at Provo, take Highway 89 southeast to Manti. From I–70 at Salina, take Highway 89 north to Manti. Inn is on the main street of town.

Innkeepers: Beverly and Charles Futrell
Address/Telephone: 401 North Main Street; (801) 835–0161
Rooms: 7, including 2 suites; all with private bath. No smoking inn.
Rates: $50 to $100, double, EPB.
Open: All year.
Facilities and activities: Ice cream parlor, gazebo, hot tub. Nearby: horse-drawn carriage rides, hiking, fishing, hot-air ballooning, golf, tennis, swimming, museum; Mormon Miracle Pageant, largest outdoor pageant in the U.S., performed each July.

Washington School Inn
PARK CITY, UTAH 84060

Although the perfect hideaway for grown up childhood sweethearts, there's no more "readin'," 'ritin', and 'rithmetic" at the old Washington School. The three Rs now more accurately stand for "romance," "rendezvous," and "resplendent." Built in 1889, the structure served as a public school for forty-two years, became a social hall during the '30s, and lay vacant from the '50s until 1984. The hammered-limestone exterior, bell tower, dormer and classroom windows, and curved entry porticos have been retained, thus qualifying the inn for the National Register of Historic Places.

The entry hall still has the feeling of an old-fashioned schoolhouse, with exposed original timbers supporting the three-story bell tower. A library/mezzanine overlooks the elegant living room, where complimentary beverages await your arrival and refreshments are served during the afternoons.

Each morning an antique sideboard in the formal dining room is lavishly spread with breakfast items such as eggs Florentine or cheese strata served with bacon, ham, or sausage; fresh fruit and lemon-nut bread; homestead pumpkin bread; Grandma Anderson's brown bread; or, perhaps, Utah beer bread.

All guest rooms are elaborately custom-decorated and bear the names of former school teachers. "Miss Thatcher" has a brick fireplace, king-sized bed, rose carpet, and, heavens to mercy!, a pink-flowered love seat and a wet bar. "Miss Thompson" has a green iron-and-brass bed, fireplace with round windows on either side, and, also, a love seat and wet bar. Our favorite room was "Miss Urie." Bright and sunny, it has pink and blue flowers sprinkled on yellow wallpaper, a chatting corner, and a writing alcove. A pine chest sits at the foot of a pine four-poster with burgundy pillows plumped on the lemon yellow bedspread. An antique book acts as doorstop.

Couples especially enjoy the lower level of the inn, which features a wine cellar and a luxurious whirlpool spa with stone floor, bent-willow furniture, dry sauna, and steam showers. Wouldn't the Misses Thatcher, Thompson, and Urie have loved this as their "Teacher's Room"?

Some comments I gleaned from the guest book that I would like to share with you: "Long live our marriage, thanks to our first night at the Washington School Inn." "A wonderful honeymoon retreat." "Just like another honeymoon." "Great place for newlyweds." "Beautiful, charming place to spend a romantic weekend."

How to get there: From I–80, take Highway 224 south to Park City; 224 turns into Park Avenue at Park City. Inn is on the right side of street.

Innkeepers: Nancy Beaufait and Delphine Covington

Address/Telephone: 543 Park Avenue (mailing address: P.O. Box 536); (801) 649–3800 or (800) 824–1672

Rooms: 15, including 3 suites; all with private bath. Wheelchair access. No air conditioning (elevation 7,000 feet).

Rates: $100 to $300, single or double, EPB and afternoon refreshments. Rates vary with season.

Open: All year.

Facilities and activities: Lunch for groups of ten or more. Hot tub, Jacuzzi, sauna, steam showers, concierge services. Nearby: restaurants, golf, tennis, hiking, fishing, horseback riding, sailboarding, sailing, waterskiing, Park City Ski Area, Park West Ski Area, Deer Valley Ski Resort, downhill and cross-country skiing.

Recommended Country Inns® Travel Club Benefit: 10% discount, Monday–Thursday, subject to availability.

Rainsford Inn
CHEYENNE, WYOMING 82001

The hospitality here is first class, with a friendly greeting upon arrival and, quite possibly, a bear hug when you leave.

This outstanding, turn-of-the-century inn sits in a quiet, tree-shaded neighborhood within walking distance of downtown Cheyenne. A gracious ambience greets guests as they enter the antiques-filled parlor. Here lace curtains filter the afternoon sunlight, wood floors gleam, a player piano awaits would-be musicians, and a vintage rocking chair begs travelers to come sit by the fire.

From the entryway, an oak staircase leads to four guest rooms on the second and third floors. The School Room is particularly enticing with

its red, navy, and cream-colored patchwork quilt displaying old-fashioned school houses. Here, tiny classroom chairs, rag dolls on an antique bench, a framed "Teacher's Rules," and a braided rug present a nostalgic glimpse of long-ago school days.

While any one of the lovely, individually decorated rooms is sure to invite special moments, perhaps the most romantic of all is the Moonlight and Roses Suite. Blessed with lace-covered bow windows, an ornate, antique bed with matching armoire and marble-topped dresser, oak floors, ceiling fans, whirlpool tub, sitting corner, and gas fireplace, this chamber is just as popular with not-so-newlyweds as it is with newlyweds. By special arrangement, innkeepers John and Nancy will cater a romantic candlelight dinner, set before the fireplace.

The first-floor guest room is designed for those with special needs. Light and airy with a bay window, it features a heart motif quilt on the queen-size antique bed, a matching dresser, and roll-in shower with bench, handrails, and hand-held shower head.

In addition to homemade breads, jams, and granola, breakfast might include sausage and cheese casserole or waffles and bacon.

One more thing: Be sure to ask John and Nancy to show you the hidden staircase they discovered during the renovation of the house.

How to get there: Located in Cheyenne on the corner of 18th and House streets in the Rainsford Historic District, east of downtown area.

Innkeepers: John and Nancy Drege
Address/Telephone: 219 East 18th Street; (307) 638–2337
Rooms: 5; all with private bath, cable TV, and phone jack, 4 with whirlpool tub.
   Wheelchair accessible; 1 room with roll-in shower designed for handicapped. No smoking inn.
Rates: $75 to $100, single or double, EPB, snacks and beverages. Seniors and military, 10 percent discount.
Open: All year.
Facilities and activities: Player piano, sunporch, candlelight dinner with advance notice.
   Nearby: state museum, Old West Museum, Vedauwoo Park, Curt Gowdy State Park, Cheyenne Frontier Days, Wyoming–Colorado Railroad excursions (45 miles, at Laramie), rock climbing, fishing.

The Wildflower Inn
JACKSON, WYOMING 83001

Sherrie confided to us that she and Ken dream of one day saving an evening just for themselves. They plan to choose their favorite guest room, pack the well-used champagne bucket with ice, take along the crystal glasses etched with wildflowers, gaze at the stars from the private deck, and hear nothing but the melancholy vocalizing of happy frogs. Now how could you go wrong with romantic innkeepers like these?

Made of glowing lodgepole pine inside and out, with balconies, gables, and, everywhere, wildflowers, this inn is at once both elegant and country. In the expansive sitting room, Native American rugs hang on log walls, a freestanding wood stove stands before a massive river-rock wall, and the polished wood floor is centered with a colorful braided rug. This room, along with the solarium and dining room, looks out onto a wooded three acres of aspen and cottonwood trees, a creek-fed pond, and a meadow where horses graze. Just the day before we visited, a mama duck and her baby ducklings had paddled into the pond, lingered a while, and then ventured on downstream.

The guest rooms have a secluded feeling, and all five are beautifully decorated. Indian Paint Brush has a cathedral ceiling and private deck. The queen-sized hand-hewn pine-log bed, made by Ken, sports a bed ruffle made of blue-and-white ticking and a red print down comforter. Red-and-white checked curtains flank the windows, and red plaid Ralph Lauren towels brighten the private bath.

Sherrie is a master of spontaneous, creative cooking and serves a full outdoorsman's breakfast, including homemade granola, fresh fruit, oatmeal muffins, and either buttermilk pancakes, French toast, or an egg dish. She will see to it that you don't leave hungry.

Besides appealing to romantics, this inn is popular with outdoor enthusiasts. Ken is a ski instructor and climbing guide, and both he and Sherrie are authorities on the many interesting things to do in the Jackson Hole area.

After a day of hiking or skiing, put your sports gear in the separate storage area, pile into the hot tub, relax, and watch the day fade to twilight over misty fields and distant mountains.

How to get there: From Jackson, go west on Highway 22 toward Wilson. Before the town of Wilson, turn right onto Teton Village Road. Turn left onto first road past Jackson Hole Racquet Club (also called The Aspens). Inn is at end of roadway.

Innkeepers: Sherrie, Ken, and Jessica Jern

Address/Telephone: Off Teton Village Road (mailing address: P.O. Box 3724); (307) 733–4710

Rooms: 5; all with private bath and TV. No air conditioning (elevation 6,200 feet). No smoking inn.

Rates: $120 to $130, double, EPB. Inquire about off-season rates.

Open: All year.

Facilities and activities: Solarium, hot tub, deck. Nearby: Yellowstone National Park, Grand Teton National Park, National Elk Refuge, restaurants, art galleries, artist studios, museums, Old West Days, Mountain Man Rendezvous, Jackson Hole Arts Festival, Grand Teton Music Festival, Dancers Workshop, summer theater, acting workshops, rodeo, chuckwagon dinner shows, stagecoach rides, covered wagon trips, photography, wildlife viewing, hiking, fishing, biking, golf, tennis, climbing, horseback riding, llama treks, rafting, ice skating, sleigh rides, snowmobiling, dog sledding; downhill, helicopter, snowcat, and cross-country skiing.

The Historic Virginian Hotel
MEDICINE BOW, WYOMING 82329

If Medicine Bow, Wyoming, is not on your route, you might consider adding it to your itinerary, because you may never have a better chance to experience a truer example of an elegant Old West hotel.

As we sat on a red velvet settee in the Virginian's upstairs parlor, I wished for a long skirt, ruffled blouse, and high-top shoes to replace my jeans and Nikes. A visiting gentleman paused to ask incredulously, "Can you really *stay* here? Do they actually take in *guests*?" That's how authentic the furnishings and decor are in this 1911, National Historic Landmark hotel. It's like a "hands-on" museum where you can not only touch but actually sleep in the beautiful, many-pillowed beds, bathe in one of the oversized claw-footed tubs, sip a cup of tea in a plush parlor, and feel like wealthy turn-of-the-century honeymooners.

The three-story building is named after Owen Wister's 1902 novel *The Virginian*, of "When you call me that—smile" fame. The walls of the Shiloh Saloon are covered with memorabilia from the novel and the movie of the same name; and signed photographs of Wister and his best friend, Theodore Roosevelt, who encouraged the author to write such a story, are in several rooms.

The Owen Wister Suite features a lace-canopied bed and a sitting room, enhanced by a matching, ornately carved, red velvet settee, rocker, and chair set, all in mint condition. This is a chamber meant for fantasizing, where it's easy to imagine that you are the heroine of a romance novel, an adored bride recently wed to a cattle baron or to the owner of a rich gold-producing mine. Such a room must have witnessed many a scene like this; these walls, could they talk, would have wonderful stories to tell.

An abundance of doilies, pillows, quilts, and comforters contributes to the inn's cozy feeling, and an original sign in Room 30 advertises OATS FOR HORSE 1 CENT A GALLON. HORSES STABLED FREE. LIQUOR 6¼ CENTS A GLASS, WINE 25 CENTS A GALLON.

The Eating House serves light lunches, and The Owen Wister Dining Room offers plentiful fare, such as 16-ounce steaks. Less hearty meals of chops and seafood are also available.

This hotel sits out on the "lone prairie" where, indeed, the antelope still roam, and it is a must for anyone wanting a true glimpse of Old West elegance.

How to get there: From I–80 at Laramie, take Highway 30 north. Or, from I–25 at Casper, take Highway 220 south to Highway 487, then drive south on 487 to Medicine Bow. Hotel is on the main street.

Innkeepers: Vernon and Vickie Scott
Address/Telephone: Main Street of Medicine Bow (mailing address: P.O. Box 127); (307) 379–2377
Rooms: 21; 4 suites with private bath, 17 rooms share baths. Pets permitted with prior arrangements. No air conditioning (elevation 6,563 feet).
Rates: $22 to $35, double; $65 to $70, suite; EP.
Open: All year.
Facilities and activities: Full-service restaurant, saloon, ice water brought to rooms in antique pitchers. Nearby: museum, tours of world's largest wind generator, world's largest dinosaur find; Fossil Cabin, said to be the oldest building on earth; ghost town; hiking, fishing, downhill and cross-country skiing.

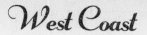

West Coast

by Julianne Belote

I once facetiously told a friend that the secret of my forty-two-plus years of marriage to the same man was never to have a meaningful conversation. I now concede there *is* another factor: frequent visits to romantic country inns.

Who can deny the spell cast by precisely the right ambience? For some couples, a Jacuzzi tub and champagne breakfast in bed rates a ten on their romance scale. Other equally romantic couples want to walk beside windswept surf or dine by candlelight in an intimate, beautifully appointed dining room.

This collection reflects a range of lodgings from simple to splendid, all of them for true romantics. The old Rodgers and Hart song says, "My romance doesn't need a castle rising in Spain." Right. But it is also worth noting that these West Coast inns are undoubtedly a lot more comfortable than most castles.

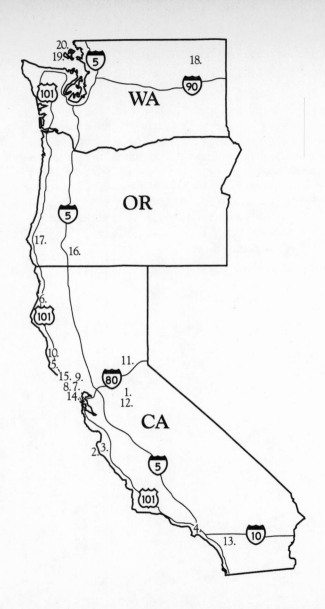

West Coast

Numbers on map refer to towns numbered below.

Olive Metcalf

Imperial Hotel
AMADOR CITY, CALIFORNIA 95601

I am smitten with this new addition to gold-country lodgings. The 1879 red-brick building with a painted white balcony stretching across the top story sits at the end of the main street running through tiny Amador City, population about 179 citizens. The entire scene reeks of Western nostalgia—it's old, authentic, and romantic.

The outside of this venerable hotel is thoroughly old-fashioned, but inside you'll find it has been stylishly renovated with all the modern amenities and a first-class restaurant. First stop should be the beautiful, old full bar, not a reproduction but the real McCoy. In addition to the usual spirits, they stock a large selection of beers and California wines. The friendly service you

find here is indicative of the atmosphere throughout the hotel.

The dining room has a certain touch of elegance with high ceilings, white tablecloths, and fresh flowers, yet it is welcoming and casual. The intimate room (seats fifty-five) has a changing display of local artwork that stands out beautifully against white walls. Dine in your traveling clothes, by all means, but you won't feel out of place if you want to dress for a special occasion, either.

The dinner chefs offer a menu that is both continental and California fresh. The appetizers are so good that it takes careful planning to save room for the entree. Roasted garlic with Brie and polenta crostini topped with prosciutto were the two we chose. The main event was a roast pork loin in prune sauce followed by an excellent salad with a house dressing I wish I could duplicate. The pastry chef had several hard-to-pass offerings and after all her work, how could we skip a poppy-seed butter-cream tart with fresh raspberries? Eating it seemed the only kind thing to do.

Six bedrooms upstairs are not large, but unexpectedly comfortable and whimsically decorated. One has an Art Deco feeling with Maxfield Parrish prints and a ceiling fan. One has a vivid hand-painted headboard over the king bed and bright folk art on the walls. Rooms One and Two are slightly larger than the others and open onto the front balcony. (The traffic going by does fade away by 10:30 or 11:00.)

Each room has a radio and a sparkling white-tiled bathroom that sports a hair dryer and heated towel bar.

Two balconies are upstairs, one at the back and one at the front of the hotel. A small library is at one end of the hall, with a desk, telephone, and door opening out to the balcony.

In the morning the innkeepers place coffee and newspapers in the hallway outside the guest rooms for early risers. Breakfast is a full, fresh meal prepared with the same skill as the dinner menu. Guests have the option of eating in their rooms, the second floor balcony, or downstairs in the dining room.

How to get there: Amador City is 2½ hours from San Francisco on Highway 49.

Innkeepers: Bruce Sherrill and Dale Martin
Address/Telephone: Highway 49 (mailing address: P.O. Box 195); (209) 267–9172
Rooms: 6, all with private bath, air conditioning. No smoking in rooms.
Rates: $65 to $95, double occupancy, continental breakfast. Two-night minimum when Saturday is involved.
Open: All year.
Facilities and activities: Full bar, restaurant; Sunday brunch and dinner every night. Wheelchair access to dining room. Nearby: antiques and specialty shops in town; attractive opportunities for photographers in town and nearby mines; many wineries; seasonal events include fall Miwok Big Time Days at Indian Grinding Rock State Park, Daffodil Hill's spring blooms, Amador City's Calico Christmas.
Recommended Country Inns® Travel Club Benefit: 25% discount, Monday–Thursday, subject to availability.

Olive Metcalf

Ventana Inn
BIG SUR, CALIFORNIA 93920

The Big Sur Coast has always welcomed the offbeat, and even this sybaritic paradise was designed as a "different" kind of place: no tennis, no golf, no conventions, no Muzak, no disco delights.

What it does offer is a window (*ventana* means "window" in Spanish) toward both the Santa Lucia Mountains and the Pacific Ocean from a redwood and cedar lodge on a magnificent slope. This is the ultimate hideaway, a tasteful, expensive world of its own harmonizing with the wilderness surrounding it. For activity there are two 75-foot pools (heated all year) and two separate bathhouses with luxurious Japanese hot tubs, one of them with saunas. And there are

walks over grassy slopes, through the woods, or on the beach. From every point your eyes go to the spectacular Big Sur Coast, where boulders send white foam spraying into the air.

Some rooms in the cottages clustered around the lodge look down into a canyon of trees; others face the ocean. Their uncluttered blend of natural fabric and design makes each room seem to be the best one. Every detail—folk baskets holding kindling, window seats, quilts handmade in Nova Scotia, private terraces—has been carefully conceived.

A gravel path leads to the Mobil four-star restaurant, with the opportunity of seeing native wildflowers and an occasional deer or bobcat on the way. The food is colorful California cuisine: fresh fish, veal, chicken, creative pastas, and a good wine list. The place to be at lunch is the expansive terrace with its 50-mile view of the coast. Dinner inside is a candlelight-and-linen affair. If you've walked the hills enough, indulge in one of the many desserts from the in-house bakery.

A continental breakfast buffet, accompanied by baroque music, is spread in the lodge lobby by the rock fireplace: platters of melons, papayas, strawberries—whatever is fresh—pastries and breads baked in the Ventana kitchen, honey and preserves, yogurt and homemade granola. An afternoon wine-and-cheese buffet has an incredi-ble array of domestic and imported cheeses.

The Ventana Store near the restaurant (books, baskets, original designed clothing, handmade knives, bird whistles) is as intriguing as its staff—all of whom seemed to be bilingual and have fascinating histories.

If "trickle-down economics" has dropped a little gold your way, this is the place to liberate your plastic for a romantic splash.

How to get there: On State Highway One, Ventana is 311 miles (about a six-and-a-half-hour drive) north of Los Angeles. The inn's sign is on the right. From San Francisco, the inn is 152 miles, 28 miles south of Carmel.

Innkeeper: Robert E. Bussinger
Address/Telephone: Big Sur; (408) 667–2331 or (800) 628–6500
Rooms: 60; all with private bath and TV, most with fireplace, some with private hot tub on deck.
Rates: $175 to $890, double occupancy, continental breakfast and afternoon wine-and-cheese buffet.
Open: All year.
Facilities and activities: Restaurant serves lunch, dinner; cocktail lounge; The Ventana Store; hot tubs, saunas, swimming pool; guided nature walks, massages, and facials available. Nearby: hiking, picnicking.

Olive Metcalf

Robles Del Rio Lodge
CARMEL VALLEY, CALIFORNIA 93924

How does a hilltop hideaway sound, one that is just outside one of the West Coast's most romantic towns?

Driving the twisting road up to Robles Del Rio gives you a feeling that you're deep in the heart of California countryside, though it's only a ten-minute drive from Carmel. The lodge looks just right for its rustic setting. Surrounded by live oak trees and perched on the mountaintop (well, high hill) surveying the valley below, this is true country-inn feeling. A tree-shaded flagstone terrace extends from the lodge with flowers in profusion and a pool, Jacuzzi, and an outdoor fireplace to be enjoyed night and day.

It was built in the 1920s, the oldest resort still operating in the Carmel Valley. The lodge is now owned by the Ron Gurries family, with son Glen and his wife Adreena as resident managers. Former longtime owner Bill Wood lives just across the road. He ran the place for more than forty years and approvingly watches the renovations and improvements going on. He can reminisce about the early days of the lodge, when Arthur Murray would check in for a month or so, when Alistair Cooke visited after the war, and how the swimming pool was dug with horse and plow because they couldn't get a tractor up the crooked road.

Six rooms are in the main lodge; the others are in separate buildings scattered over nine acres. These rooms are unpretentious but entirely comfortable, and the views are wonderful. Some have a rustic board-and-batten decor, and others have a more contemporary country look, using Laura Ashley fabrics. The cottages with outfitted kitchens and fireplaces are convenient for longer stays.

Beginning with a bountiful breakfast buffet set in the main lodge living room, good food is a big part of the Lodge's appeal. With a crackling fire going to chase away the morning chill, much of the original 1920s furniture still in place, and wide views of the valley, this room has a good feeling.

Lunch or dinner in The Ridge restaurant, also in the main lodge building, is a dining experience equal to the best available in Carmel or Monterey. Chef Andre relies on Monterey agriculture for daily deliveries of whatever is freshest and best.

His wine list, too, has a deliberate regional focus. (Did you know more grapes are grown in the Monterey region now than in Napa?) Notice the hand-painted china, the fresh flowers, the broad deck overlooking the valley. What a seat to watch a fog bank form over Carmel and quietly roll in. A fresh rockfish soup and a chicken breast stir-fry with ginger, bell pepper, and tomatoes were pretty impressive, too.

How to get there: From Highway One at Carmel, drive east on Carmel Valley Road about 13 miles to Esquiline Road. Turn right and follow the signs up the hill to the lodge, about 1 mile.

Innkeeper: Glen Gurries
Address/Telephone: 200 Punta Del Monte; (408) 659–3705
Rooms: 33, including some cottages; all with private bath and cable TV, some with fireplace and kitchenette. Wheelchair access.
Rates: $89 to $250, double occupancy, generous continental breakfast.
Open: All year.
Facilities and activities: Exceptional restaurant, The Ridge, serves lunch and dinner; Cantina serves wine and beer. Swimming pool, tile hot tub with Jacuzzi, sauna, tennis. Nearby: golf, horseback riding, 12 miles to ocean beaches, surrounding woodlands to hike, ten minutes to Carmel attractions.
Recommended Country Inns® Travel Club Benefit: 25% discount, Sunday–Thursday.

Blue Lantern Inn
DANA POINT, CALIFORNIA 92629

Dana Point is one of those picturesque little beach towns that epitomize the glamour of southern California's coast—except that it's even better than most of them. Not as crowded as Newport and Balboa, not as rowdy as Santa Monica and Venice, not as nose-in-the-air exclusive as Malibu.

Blue Lantern Inn has a prime location atop Dana Point bluffs. When he stopped along this coast in 1834, Richard Henry Dana wrote in his journal, which was to become *Two Years Before the Mast*, "High table-land running boldly to the shore, and breaking off in a steep hill, at the foot of which the waters of the Pacific are constantly dashing."

Sound romantic? You bet it is—and gorgeous too. Ask for a balcony room so that in the morning you can look down on a sparkling harbor, a 121-foot replica of Dana's brigantine *Pilgrim*, and, beyond the harbor breakwall, on a clear day, a view of the curve of Catalina Island.

For an inn so splendidly situated, the Blue Lantern more than lives up to its promise of comfort. Looking rather Cape Cod in style, the ambience inside is serene, understated, and luxurious. The lobby/sitting room has overstuffed couches and a massive stone fireplace that blazes a welcome at the slightest hint of a chill. A lavish and beautiful breakfast buffet is served at one end of this area, where you help yourself and sit at tables for two or four. On our visit breakfast included juices, melon slices, strawberries, blueberries, granola, cheese quiche, and muffins. The friendly help kept coffee cups filled and tables cleared.

An adjacent library features bleached oak paneling and more comfortable, cushy chairs. Afternoon tea and wine, with fresh fruit, cheese, and raw vegetable platter, are served here.

Our room had a fireplace, a small balcony large enough to sit on, and a huge bathroom featuring a separate shower and Jacuzzi tub-for-two, with a shutter door to fold back and watch the living room fire while you soak.

Every guest room is spacious, and some, like the Tower Suite, are downright lavish. Soft, muted colors like seafoam, lavender, periwinkle blue, and beige; traditional furniture; original art, and printed wall coverings combine for a romantic setting. Refrigerators and terry robes are just part of the scene.

The most unexpected aspect of your stay may be the warmth of your welcome and the genuine hospitality of the staff. It may sound cynical, but at an upscale Orange County beach inn, I almost expected a certain amount of slickness. How pleasant to be surprised.

How to get there: From Los Angeles, take 405 Freeway south to the 5 Freeway south. Exit at Pacific Coast Highway and veer to the right. Continue on PCH for 2½ miles to Street of the Blue Lantern. Turn left; inn is on the right.

Innkeeper: Tom Taylor
Address/Telephone: 34343 Street of the Blue Lantern; (714) 661–1304
Rooms: 29; all with private bath, Jacuzzi tub, wet bar, color TV, and fireplace, most with panoramic ocean views. Handicapped facilities.
Rates: $135 to $350, double occupancy, buffet breakfast and afternoon tea, wine, and hors d'oeuvres. Special celebration packages.
Open: All year.
Facilities and activities: Library, exercise room, facilities for weddings and private events. Nearby: Dana Point Yacht Harbor; shops, galleries, and cafes of Dana Point and neighboring Laguna Beach.

Olive Metcalf

Harbor House

ELK, CALIFORNIA 95432

The windswept solitude of this stretch of Northern California's shore is one of nature's tens. And for an inn on the bluffs above the rocky coast, Harbor House has it all: a dramatic location, unique architecture, fresh decor, and fine food.

The house was built in 1916 entirely of virgin redwood by the Goodyear Redwood Lumber Company as a place to lodge and entertain its executives and guests. In the 1930s the house was converted to an inn, and it then variously faded and flourished over the years. The inn's newest owners are warm hosts who understand exactly what a spell this inn can cast.

The large living room, completely paneled in redwood with a high-beamed open ceiling, sets the tone: quiet and unpretentious. Comfortable sofas and a piano are grouped on a rich Persian rug before a huge fireplace, with books and a stereo nearby. (Christmas here sounds wonderful—the redwood room glowing in firelight, a giant tree, roasting chestnuts, festive dinners, and music by local musicians.) Bedrooms and cottages are freshly decorated, many with pastel watercolor prints by a local artist of flowers and birds indigenous to the area.

Ocean views from the dining room are breathtaking. On blustery North Coast days, some guests choose to spend the day in this redwood-paneled room watching the churning surf.

It's comforting to know that you don't have to leave this warm atmosphere to find a restaurant. Wonderful food is in store for you here; you should plan on long romantic dinners.

The Turners subscribe to that old verity of California cooking: Use only the freshest, best ingredients possible, and keep it simple. Many ingredients are plucked right from the inn's own garden. What they don't grow, they purchase from the finest local sources, like baby potatoes and the locally raised lamb. Fresh fish is often featured, prepared with Harbor House nuances. All the breads and breakfast pastries are home-made. Desserts also tend to reflect whatever is fresh. Typical are poached pears with raspberry sauce, or a sweet flaky pastry stuffed with apricots and cream. A fine California wine list and a good selection of beers are offered. Dinner is a fixed menu, changing every night, but with advance notice, they'll try to accommodate any special dietary needs.

Mendocino's attractions are only twenty minutes farther north, but I'm all for staying right here. Walking the beach, discovering the seclud-ed patios and paths—one leads to a waterfall and grotto—these are the quiet seductions of the inn. If you're in during the day, a bottle of local wine and a cheese platter from the kitchen are available to hold body and soul together until dinner.

How to get there: From the Bay area, take Highway 101 to Cloverdale, then Highway 128 west to Highway One. The inn is 6 miles south on the ocean side of Highway One.

Innkeepers: Helen and Dean Turner
Address/Telephone: 5600 South Highway One (mailing address: Box 369); (707) 877–3203
Rooms: 10, including 4 cottages; all with private bath, 5 with private deck, 9 with fireplace.
Rates: $165 to $250, double occupancy, MAP. Midweek winter rates. No credit cards.
Open: All year.
Facilities and activities: Dinner by reservation. Private beach, fishing, ocean kayaking with guide. Nearby: Mendocino shops, galleries, restaurants, forest walks, local wineries; golf, tennis, horseback riding.

Olive Metcalf

Hotel Carter
EUREKA, CALIFORNIA 95501

Ever since first hearing Rodgers and Hart's "There's a Small Hotel," I've thought the song—and small hotels—were the quintessence of sophisticated romance. In Eureka's charmingly restored Old Town district, the Hotel Carter brings the essence of that lovely song to mind. It is a perfect rendezvous—intimate, glamorous, and serving some of the best food and wines available north of San Francisco.

Most first-time visitors assume that Mark Carter restored the yellow Victorian-style building, but it is newly constructed, modeled after a nineteenth-century Eureka hotel. It blends the exterior look and ambience of the past era with today's luxurious conveniences, all done with Carter's impeccable taste in detailings and furnishings. (He also built from scratch the magnificent Victorian-style B&B across the street.)

You may very well fall in love with the hotel the minute you step into the lobby. Despite the Old World elegance of 14-foot-high ceilings here and in the adjoining dining room, even the casually dressed traveler will feel at home in an atmosphere both chic and inviting with plump sofas and chairs. The work of local Humboldt County potters and painters is showcased brilliantly against the salmon-colored walls. The Carters set out fine regional wines and hors d'oeuvres before a marble fireplace here each evening.

But your outstanding taste treats will come at breakfast and dinner in the intimate dining room. Since the days when Christi Carter, while also managing two babies, cooked at their B&B what came to be known as the famous Carter Breakfast, she has always taken the lead in searching for the best chefs, the finest ingredients, and true cutting-edge cuisine. The Hotel Carter has become the right place to see that concern for excellent cooking come to fruition.

Our dinner one night began with baby greens dressed with a strawberry vinaigrette, fresh grilled swordfish with lemon butter, three perfect vegetables grown in the Carters' garden, a new small grain (something akin to couscous), and crusty baguettes. A local chardonnay and a pinot noir *had* to be sampled. A scrumptious apple walnut tart served with homemade ice cream and coffee saw us off to our room impressed with the quiet service and fine food.

The guest rooms are decorated in pale earth colors, with peach and white linen, and are furnished with handsome antique pine furniture combined with appointments we appreciate— telephones, remote-controlled televisions hiding in wardrobes, and whirlpool tubs. Our suite on the second floor, with a fireplace, window seat, and view of Humboldt Bay, was a spot we would love to return to often.

If it weren't that the Carters are such nice people, I'd say, "Keep this delightful hideaway a secret."

How to get there: From Highway 101 in downtown Eureka, proceed west on L Street through Old Town to the hotel.

Innkeepers: Mark and Christi Carter
Address/Telephone: 301 L Street; (707) 444–8062
Rooms: 19 rooms, 4 suites; all with private bath, TV, and telephone, 8 with whirlpool baths, suites with fireplace. Smoking in lobby only.
Rates: $89 to $300, EPB, evening wine and hors d'oeuvres, cookies and tea at turndown.
Open: All year.
Facilities and activities: Restaurant serves dinner Thursday through Sunday. Lobby and dining-room showcase of contemporary art, tours of kitchen gardens available.
Nearby: walk along brick pathway bordering marina, through restored Old Town with specialty shops, restaurants; hundreds of restored Victorian homes, many art galleries in town.

olive Metcalf

Gaige House
GLEN ELLEN, CALIFORNIA 95442

The name *Rouas* is well known around Northern California for fabulous lodgings and California cutting-edge cuisine. You've heard of Auberge du Soleil? One of the designers and partners of that highly acclaimed inn, Ardath Rouas has now turned her skills to a more intimate country inn, this 1890 Italianate Queen Anne called Gaige House.

The immense Victorian has been completely restored with the finest modern conveniences while keeping its romantic ambience. First and foremost, the guest rooms are of unsurpassed comfort: down comforters and bed linens of Egyptian cotton (one full-time person is employed to do nothing but iron them); huge tiled bathrooms and first-class lighting; fresh floral bouquets; and inviting, cushy furniture.

The entire mansion is filled with fine furniture and riveting art that Ardath has collected from around the world. She displays it not just in the common rooms but throughout the house. Just one of the pieces that caught my eye is an enormous armoire from Bali that dominates the drawing room. Despite the elegance of polished oak floors, Persian rugs, and red velour sofas, this is an inviting room.

Each of the nine guest rooms is uniquely decorated. The largest (the Gaige Suite) could be called the "oh, wow!" room, since that's a frequent reaction on first seeing it. A huge four-poster canopy bed, puffy sofa in the sitting area, private deck overlooking the lawn, pool, and wooded hills, and a gorgeous tiled bath with a large Jacuzzi tub make it a favorite honeymoon suite. For a less expensive choice, consider one of the garden rooms facing the pool. They're smaller but still stylish, with queen-sized beds and private entrances.

Breakfast is a hearty meal here, served in the dining room or on the deck at tables for four. It includes fresh-squeezed juices and local seasonal produce (some of which is grown at the inn), and perhaps ham and eggs or oatmeal waffles. I realize you don't go to country inns with kitchens on your mind. Nevertheless, take a look at this one. Sensational!

When you've had enough sporting in the 40-foot pool, lounging on the great deck built over Calabezas Creek, strolling around the beautiful grounds, and exploring this elegant house, there is much more in the surrounding countryside to discover. The little hamlet of Glen Ellen that Jack London made famous is one of the most beguiling settings in the Sonoma wine region. Not smothered with tourists, abundantly picturesque, the Sonoma Valley is at the heart of Northern California's history. Historic landmarks and museums are nearby as well as dozens of premium wineries, fine restaurants, and local galleries. Not to be missed is the museum of London memorabilia and the remains of Wolf House, his private residence claimed by a fire before it was completed.

But it is the quiet beauty of this area that you will remember . . . and who you were with when you paused here.

How to get there: From Highway 101, take the Napa/Vallejo exit (Highway 37) for 7½ miles. Turn left on Highway 121 for 6½ miles, to Highway 116, going to Glen Ellen/Petaluma for 1½ miles. Continue for 8¼ miles straight to Arnold Drive through Glen Ellen to inn on the left.

Innkeeper: Ardath Rouas
Address/Telephone: 13540 Arnold Drive; (707) 935–0237
Rooms: 9, including 2 suites; all with private bath and air conditioning, 2 with fireplace. TV, radio, phone available on request. No smoking inn.
Rates: $100 to $185, double occupancy, EPB and afternoon wine and cheese.
Open: All year.
Facilities and activities: Swimming pool, beautiful grounds and decks. Accommodates weddings and special events. Nearby: Jack London State Historic Park; wineries in Glen Ellen, Kenwood.

Olive Metcalf

Applewood, An Estate Inn
GUERNEVILLE, CALIFORNIA 95446

Applewood, formerly called The Estate, is an unexpected taste of glamour in the forested hills hugging the Russian River. As it twists through the Guerneville area, the river's beautiful natural setting has long been a popular choice for "resorts," cabins, cottages, and campgrounds. But . . . this is something quite different.

It's not always easy to relax in handsome surroundings, but that's not the case in this Mission Revival–style house. It was built as a private residence in 1922 by a financier, Ralph Belden, and you know what grandiose ideas the wealthy in those days had when it came to building even their vacation homes. This one is imposing, but it remains an inviting country home. On the main floor a large rock fireplace divides the living room from a many-windowed solarium. On the lower level, bedrooms open to another comfortable sitting room. At this writing, four new, even more deluxe accommodations are near completion on a rise behind the main house.

I call the decor *Architectural Digest*—with warmth. Darryl studied design in San Francisco, and the house shows it. There's no one "look" but, rather, an individual, personal style. He's designed stylish slipcovers for some of the chairs and smart duvet covers for the beds. There are fine antiques among some just-comfortable furniture. Both he and Jim are always looking for interesting pieces, but they admit that as much as they've bought, it seems to disappear in the large house.

Bedrooms are wonderfully romantic, and there's not a Laura Ashley in the lot. Billowing cotton draperies at an expansive bow of casement windows graced Number 4, my room. But every room, from smallest to grandest, has style, comfortable seating, and good reading lights. The luxury you'll find isn't in ostentation, it's in quality, such as down pillows and comforters, fine linen, and fresh bouquets.

And it's not just ambience that you're buying at Applewood. The food is quite special. On the sunny morning of my visit, breakfast was served on a terrace by the pool, at a table set with heavy silverware, linen napkins, and a silver coffee pot. A beautifully arranged fruit plate, fresh juice, hot muffins, and a bacon-avocado-tomato omelet were perfection.

The outstanding food and surroundings make this a fine choice for entertaining . . . a small party or just for one special someone. I can't imagine a more romantic place for an intimate dinner than here in the Solarium in front of the fireplace. Some recent winter menus included interesting starters like bruschetta with roasted peppers, caramelized onions and fennel, succulent entrees like chicken gallantine stuffed with chèvre, sun-dried tomatoes, and roasted garlic, locally grown salad greens and vegetables, and beautiful desserts. Everything is freshly made.

The innkeepers have succeeded in making this classic house a class-act inn by applying a simple philosophy: only the best of everything.

How to get there: From 101 north, take River Road/Guerneville exit just past Santa Rosa; go west 14 miles to Guerneville. At the stop sign at Highway 116 and River Road, turn left, cross the bridge over River Road. The inn is ½ mile further on the left. Local airport pickup.

Innkeepers: Darryl Notter and Jim Caron
Address/Telephone: 13555 Highway 116; (707) 869–9093
Rooms: 10; all with private bath, television, telephone. No smoking inn.
Rates: $125 to $225, single or double occupancy, EPB; two-night minimum on weekends.
Open: All year.
Facilities and activities: Fixed-price dinner Tuesday through Saturday; reservations required. Swimming pool, spa; facilities for private parties, small business seminars. Nearby: restaurants, golf, tennis, horseback riding; canoeing and other river activities; Guerneville shops; many local wineries; Sonoma Coast beaches. Armstrong Redwood State Reserve.
Recommended Country Inns® Travel Club Benefit: Stay two nights, get third night free, November–March, except holidays.

olive Metcalf

Madrona Manor
HEALDSBURG, CALIFORNIA 95448

Country inns continue to spring up in Northern California faster than yuppies are going out of style, but Madrona Manor stands alone. First, it is a truly dramatic Victorian mansion sitting in the midst of landscaped grounds and eight wooded acres. But even more notable is its outstanding California restaurant, the only one in Sonoma County rated three stars by *Chronicle* food critic Patricia Unterman.

Approaching the Italianate mansion up the long driveway brings feelings of pleasant anticipation. Elegant accommodations await inside: antique furnishings, period wallpapers and rugs, and rooms with original plumbing and lighting fixtures. The third floor has renovated rooms

with fireplaces, queen-sized beds, and antique reproduction furniture from Portugal. Less opulent but more modern rooms are in two other outbuildings and the Carriage House. The newest suite is in the Carriage House, where you can relax in a Jacuzzi tub or before the fireplace in the sitting room.

The fine cooking is served in two high-ceilinged, attractive dining rooms. Former Chez Panisse cook Todd Muir runs the kitchen. He and his staff work in a modern kitchen (contrasting with the rest of the 1881 setting) complete with a mesquite grill and a smokehouse in back that produces smoked trout, chickens, and meats. The gardens produce all the flowers for the dining room and guest rooms as well as herbs and specialty produce for the kitchen.

You shouldn't miss dining here during your stay ... it's always a culinary treat. The menu lists four- and five-course prix-fixe dinners, priced, respectively, at $40 and $50 at this writing. But smaller appetites are also taken into account. Both of the prix-fixe menus list prices for each course so that one can order à la carte.

My first course of individual goat-cheese soufflé was perfectly crusty on top, with a softly oozing middle. Every element of the meal, down to dessert of amaretto-soaked cake with chocolate-ricotta filling, was meticulously prepared.

The wine list is both extensive and reasonably priced, which, even though this is the heart of the wine country, is not always true up here. Some selections from small local wineries are at near-retail prices.

Breakfast for guests is as carefully done as dinner. It includes the wonderful house bread, toasted; a perfectly timed soft-boiled egg; loads of seasonal fruit; oatmeal and granola; ripe, room-temperature cheeses; and house-smoked meats. When the weather allows, take this meal outside on the palm terrace.

What a beautiful place for a special celebration.

How to get there: From San Francisco, drive north on Highway 101, 12 miles north of Santa Rosa; take the Central Healdsburg exit; follow Healdsburg Avenue north to Mill Street, turn left, and it becomes Westside Road. Inn is ¾ mile on the right. From the north, take Westside Road exit from Highway 101; turn right. Inn is ½ mile on the right.

Innkeepers: John and Carol Muir

Address/Telephone: 1001 Westside Road (mailing address: Box 818); (707) 433–4231 or (800) 258–4003, fax (707) 433–0703

Rooms: 18 and 3 suites; all with private bath, telephone, and air conditioning, 18 with fireplace. Wheelchair access.

Rates: $135 to $225, double occupancy, EPB.

Open: All year.

Facilities and activities: Dinner nightly, Sunday brunch. Swimming pool. Nearby: golf, tennis, hiking, canoeing, fishing, winery tours, picnics, bicycling, Redwood State Park.

Recommended Country Inns® Travel Club Benefit: Stay two nights, get third night free, Monday–Thursday, subject to availability.

Olive Metcalf

Agate Cove Inn
MENDOCINO, CALIFORNIA 95460

A friend of mine who pursues a lively romantic life insisted that she had discovered a jewel in Mendocino that I had missed. "Fabulous views," she raved. "Best breakfast I ever had at an inn," she went on. "It was so low-key . . . so fresh." Naturally, I had to check it out immediately—besides, traveling the Northern California coast is hardly a tough assignment. As it was an election year, I was ready to forgive a little exaggeration from a friend, but I was also prepared to be underwhelmed. Score one for my friend.

Agate Cove Inn is indeed a jewel. Sitting above and behind Mendocino Village on a bluff above the ocean, it appears to be an old farmhouse. That is just what the main house is, built

in the 1860s by Mathias Brinzing, who established the first Mendocino brewery. Some of the original candlestick fence still runs through the beautiful old-fashioned garden.

Scattered through the grounds are the cozy cottages, each (except for one room where you have to make do with only a lovely garden view) with views of the ocean, a fireplace, a decanter of sherry, and a private deck for watching the sea.

The rooms have king- or queen-sized four-poster or canopied beds, handmade quilts, and country decor that goes for comfort rather than excessive cuteness. The luxury cottages have a large double shower or oversize tub, and considering California's water problems, it would be a crime to use one of them alone.

The main house has a spacious living room for guests to enjoy. A red-brick fireplace, colorful wing chairs, love seats, quilts, antiques, and books all bring a country warmth. The room opens onto the breakfast room, with stunning ocean vistas. For some of us, breakfast really begins with the morning San Francisco newspaper on the doorstep—and that's the way they do it at Agate Cove, too—then a short walk through the garden to the main house. Select your juice and fresh fruit and choose a table, already set with fresh, home-baked bread and jams. You must divide your view between your entree being cooked on an antique woodstove nearby and the drama out the window of crashing waves on the rocks.

Mendocino is an enchanting seaside village, but it is not undiscovered. Agate Cove puts you close to all the village attractions but just enough removed to feel that you're in a very special, romantic hideaway. For quiet, uncrowded—some say the most beautiful times—come during the winter season.

How to get there: About a three-hour drive from San Francisco via highways 101 and 128. When you reach Mendocino, take Lansing Street exit after the traffic light. The inn is ½ mile north of the village.

Innkeepers: Sallie McConnell and Jake Zahavi

Address/Telephone: 11201 North Lansing Street (mailing address: P.O. Box 1150); (707) 937–0551; in Northern California, (800) 527–3111

Rooms: 10; all with private bath, ocean view, and cable TV, 9 with fireplace. No smoking in rooms.

Rates: $85 to $185, double occupancy, EPB. Ask about cash discount rates, midweek rates.

Open: All year.

Facilities and activities: Accommodations for weddings and special-occasion parties. Nearby: short walk to Mendocino Village galleries, Art Center, restaurants, specialty shops; hiking, canoeing, horseback riding, tennis, golf accessible.

Recommended Country Inns® Travel Club Benefit: Stay two nights, get third night free, Sunday–Thursday, December–March, except holidays, subject to availability.

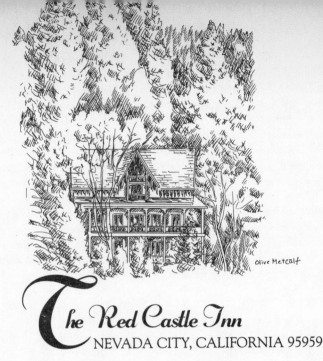

Olive Metcalf

The Red Castle Inn
NEVADA CITY, CALIFORNIA 95959

It's little wonder its current owners fell in love with this brick Victorian mansion when they first visited back in the seventies. Looking for all the world like the cover background for a Victorian romance novel, The Red Castle has an undeniably romantic appeal.

Hanging on a hillside nestled among dense trees, The Red Castle is an impressive sight from many places around Nevada City. The Gothic Revival mansion is wrapped in rows of white, painted verandas and lavished with gingerbread trim at roofline and gables. From the private parking area, you can walk around a veranda, with stylish canvas draperies tied back at each pillar, to the front of the house, where you can survey the historic mining town's rooftops and church steeples.

Since it was built in 1857, the castle has had a succession of caring owners who have maintained it without compromising its elegant period character. The Weavers have brought not only their respective professional skills in architecture and design but also some impressive art, including several Bufano sculpture pieces, and fine furniture. Seven guest rooms and suites range over the four floors, each one of them a vibrantly decorated, tasteful delight. Most furnishings are Victorian, but not fragile or frilly. An explosion of color from wallpapers, fabrics, and rugs has an engaging effect in combination with the dramatic architecture. The two-bedroom Garret Suite, on the fourth floor, has a sitting room, bath, and balcony. It was from here that the original owner's son used to serenade the town with impromptu trumpet concerts.

A cozy sitting room/parlor off the entry hall has cushy upholstered sofas, wing chairs, and an inviting collection of gold rush history and art books. We helped ourselves to an elegant tea spread here and took it outside. Three small terraced gardens, one with a fountain and pond, are idyllic sitting and strolling areas. A path through cascading vines leads down to Nevada City's main street.

The Weavers are proud of their vintage inn and are enthusiastic about Nevada City. They'll arrange a horse-drawn carriage tour through the town's historic district. They always have good suggestions for restaurants and local events. Their own Victorian Christmas celebration sounds like a truly memorable feast.

The lavish breakfast buffet is a splendid sight—all of it homemade. Ours was typical, but the menu varies every day: juice, poached pears, glazed fresh strawberries, a baked egg curry with pear chutney, cheese croissants, banana bread, jams, Mary Louise's grandmother's bread pudding (what a treat!) with a pitcher of cream, and, of course, great coffee.

How to get there: From Highway 49 at Nevada City, take Sacramento Street exit to the Chevron station; turn right and immediately left onto Prospect Street. The driveway takes you to the back of the house. Walk around the veranda to the front door.

Innkeepers: Mary Louise and Conley Weaver

Address/Telephone: 109 Prospect; (916) 265–5135

Rooms: 7, including 3 suites; all with private bath. Third- and fourth-floor rooms air conditioned. No smoking inn.

Rates: $70 to $140, double occupancy, EPB and afternoon tea. Two-night minimum Saturdays April 1–December 31.

Open: All year.

Facilities and activities: Saturday morning carriage rides, historical narratives and poetry readings, Victorian Christmas dinner and entertainment, picnic baskets by advance request. Nearby: walking path to downtown shops, restaurants, antiques; local theater, musical events; swimming in mountain creek; cross-country skiing twenty minutes away.

©live Metcalf

The Estate by the Elderberries
OAKHURST, CALIFORNIA 93644

A nine-room castle/hotel called Chateau du Sureau (translates to "Chateau by the Elderberry") and an extraordinary restaurant called Erna's Elderberry House comprise this remarkable inn. There is simply nothing else like it on the West Coast inn scene.

Both of the white-stucco, turreted, and red-tile-roofed buildings are the result of Erna Kubin-Clanin's dream to create an outstanding restaurant and then a small, very personal auberge in the California mountains. The astounding thing is that this uncommonly elegant lodging and sophisticated restaurant are in Oakhurst, a nondescript little town nestling in the rocky foothills of the Sierra Nevada, 20 miles from the south entrance of Yosemite National Park.

Plenty of people (especially her bankers) called her mad, but Erna opened her restaurant, Elderberry House, in 1984. Remote it may be, but Craig Claiborne of the *New York Times* found it, was captivated with the food, and stayed three days—sometimes helping Erna in the kitchen. Rave reviews in *Gourmet* and other publications followed, and Elderberry House was on the map.

Erna turned her sights next to building an accommodation as splendid as was required by guests who made their way to Oakhurst for her food. Chateau du Sureau opened in 1991, a $2 million, nine-guest-room inn reminiscent of Erna's native Austria or a luxurious hillside estate in Provence. Don't give a thought to perhaps feeling ill at ease in an atmosphere this elegant. Just the opposite is true. I've rarely seen service of this caliber combined with such genuine warmth and hospitality.

Kathryn Kincannon, the "directrice," is on the steps waiting to greet you on arrival and tour you through the castle, from the tiny chapel to the kitchen. Everything you see speaks of luxury and comfort: antique tiles, oriental rugs, tapestries, magnificent furniture, fresh flowers, and sumptuous bathrooms. The Grand Salon soars to an 18-foot beamed ceiling, with an 1870 piano from Paris the focus of attention two steps up in the circular Music Tower. We were still trying to absorb the splendor of our guest room surroundings when a chambermaid tapped at our door with tea and gourmet snacks.

That evening we walked through the lighted garden to Elderberry House for a leisurely paced, magnificent six-course dinner. We went with the restaurant's selection of three wines for the dinner, though you can choose from a large list. Back to the Chateau to lounge before the fire with some fine port, and so to bed.

I hope you won't just look at the rates and turn the page. Long after you've forgotten how much it cost, you'll remember dining and staying at this castle by the elderberries.

How to get there: Drive north on Highway 5 toward Sacramento. Take Highway 99 to Fresno. Exit at Highway 41 through Fresno and continue on another 40 minutes to Corsical, 7 miles south of the Chateau. At inn's sign, turn left at the second lane, through the gates on the right.

Innkeepers: Erna Kubin-Clanin, owner; Kathryn Kincannon, directrice
Address/Telephone: 48688 Victoria Lane (mailing address: P.O. Box 577);
(209) 683–6860, fax (209) 683–0800; restaurant reservations (209) 683–6800
Rooms: 9; all with private bath, wood-burning fireplace, balcony, CD stereo system, 1 with handicapped access. TV and phone available upon request.
Rates: $250 to $350, double occupancy, European-style breakfast and afternoon tea. $3,500 for Chateau exclusive (up to 18 persons).
Open: All year.
Facilities and activities: Swimming pool, walking paths, small chapel; restaurant serves a six-course prix fixe menu ($38.50 to $40 without wine) Wednesday through Monday, and Sunday brunch; will arrange weddings and other special celebrations. Nearby: Yosemite National Park, Badger Pass ski area, boating and skiing on Bass Lake.

Olive Metcalf

Villa Royale
PALM SPRINGS, CALIFORNIA 92264

Only a few blocks from slick downtown Palm Springs with glamorous big hotels lining the main drag, a heartwarming alternative lies low on the desert plain just waiting to beguile you. Everything conspires at Villa Royale to make you think you're in an old European resort. Winding brick paths connect a series of courtyards with ancient-looking pillars under the redtile roofs of surrounding rooms. Shade trees and pots of flowers are everywhere, as are exotic vines and palms, small gardens and fountains. And on a March day visit, the cascading bougainvillea was dazzling.

From the blazing Palm Springs sun, you step into a lobby/sitting room with a cool brick floor and squishy sofa and chairs. Just outside the door in the courtyard are bicycles ready for guests to borrow for sightseeing around the quiet residential streets or touring the shopping plazas. The kitchen will pack you a picnic basket to take along on request. Owner/innkeeper Bob Lee, along with a well-trained staff, is always ready to help. I like the generous attitude here. There aren't just *two* bikes; there are lots of them. You don't get just *one* extra towel for the pool; you get big thick ones, as many as you need.

The variety of accommodations at Villa Royale is only one of its attractions. Whether you take a standard guest room or splurge on a deluxe studio with kitchenette, private patio, and spa, all the colorful ambience of flowers, fountains, and dramatic views of the San Jacinto Mountains is available to everyone. Every room, large or small, is decorated in an individual international style, the result of Bob's frequent buying trips to Europe. Each one has interesting treasures: woven hangings and table covers, wall carvings, bright pottery, sculpture, pillows, and antique furniture.

Across the first courtyard is the dining room, with a glass-enclosed casual area where breakfast is served looking out at the pool. The brick floor extends into a more formal interior room with a wonderful feeling. Armchairs with rush seats and cushions surround tables skirted with dark floral cloths to the floor and topped with lighter-color linen. The walls are a rosy adobe, and the soft lighting, beautiful china, and glassware create an atmosphere I would like to get used to. Our dinner in the restaurant was an attractively presented, relaxing experience: tortellini soup, green salad, scampi, and a marvelous fresh mango sherbet with fresh peaches and raspberries.

Visually rich as days are here relaxing in the sunshine surrounded with colorful flowers, wait 'til you see it at night! Dozens of small ornate brass lanterns hanging from trees and vines gleam with tiny lights and cast light and shadows throughout the courtyards. If you aren't enchanted, check your pulse.

How to get there: Proceed through downtown Palm Springs on its main street, North Palm Canyon. When it becomes East Palm Canyon, look for Indian Trail and turn left. Inn is straight ahead.

Innkeeper: Robert Lee

Address/Telephone: 1620 Indian Trail; (619) 327–2314, fax (619) 322–3794

Rooms: 31 suites and rooms; all with private bath, TV, phone, and some with fireplace, kitchenette, and private spa. Limited wheelchair access.

Rates: $75 to $300, double occupancy, continental breakfast. Lower summer rates and for longer stays.

Open: All year.

Facilities and activities: Restaurant serves lunch and dinner; full bar. Two swimming pools, bicycles, spas, courtyards with fountains, outdoor fireplaces. Nearby: golf, tennis, horseback riding, Palm Springs shops, restaurants, aerial tramway ride up Mt. San Jacinto.

Casa Madrona Hotel
SAUSALITO, CALIFORNIA 94965

John Mays knows how to create an atmosphere. He's turned this luxurious old mansion perched on a hill above Sausalito into one of the most romantic inns you'll find. Of course, he has a lot going for him with a town almost too winning for words and spectacular views of the yacht harbor.

Casa Madrona is more than a century old. Time had taken its toll on the former residence, hotel, bordello, and boardinghouse when John Mays rescued it in 1978. It nearly slid off the hill during the rains of '82, but renovations already begun saved it from gliding away.

Since then Mays has added an elegant tumble of cottages that cascade down the hill to Sausalito's main street. Each one is different, with dormers, gables, peaked roofs, and hidden decks. Amazingly, the whole gray-blue jumble lives perfectly with the old mansion.

You've seen "individually decorated" rooms before, but these beat all. Mays gave each one of his hillside cottages over to a different Bay Area decorator. The range of their individual styles resulted in rooms with themes from nautical, to equestrian (The Ascot Suite), to a Parisian Artist's Loft. Most have private decks and superb views. And since it is fabled, sybaritic Marin, there are luxurious tubs for two (sometimes elevated and open to the room), refrigerators stocked with fruit juice and mineral water, and fresh flowers.

(But you won't find any peacock feathers.)

If you're indifferent to unique rooms surrounded by lush gardens, exotic bougainvillea and trumpet vine spilling over decks and walkways, perhaps elegant food will ring your bell. A beautiful wine bar and uncluttered dining room in the old house on top of the hill are lighted and decorated to enchant. Only white linen on round tables and fresh flowers compete with the view from the deck of the bay and Sausalito Yacht Harbor . . . that is, until the food is served.

We began with what I thought was a California standard but which has become a part of American cuisine: radicchio and Belgian endive salad with baked chèvre (goat cheese).

Perfection. Our waiter was agreeable when I ordered another first course (Asian crab cakes and lobster mayonnaise) instead of an entree. (I love places that encourage you to order by *your* appetite instead of *their* rules.) Others at our table raved about a grilled rare Ahi tuna and a guava-and-macadamia-crusted rack of lamb. The meal could not have been lovelier.

If this inn can't rekindle a dying ember, no place can.

How to get there: Cross the Golden Gate Bridge; take Alexander Street exit to center of town. San Francisco Airport pickup available. Ferry service from San Francisco.

Innkeeper: John Mays

Address/Telephone: 801 Bridgeway; (415) 332–0502 or (800) 288–0502

Rooms: 34; all with private bath, some with fireplace, private deck, water view.

Rates: $105 to $245, double occupancy; cottages, $165 to $185; 3-room suite, $415; continental breakfast and wine-and-cheese social hour.

Open: All year.

Facilities and activities: Dinner, wine and beer bar nightly; lunch Monday through Friday; Sunday brunch. Outdoor Jacuzzi. Nearby: Sausalito's shops and galleries, ferryboat rides across the bay, fine dining, hiking, bicycling.

olive Metcalf

Timberhill Ranch
TIMBERCOVE, CALIFORNIA 95421

When your stress level hits an octave above high C and you can't bear making one more earth-shaking decision . . . when you want to seclude yourself with nature (and a close, close friend) for some spiritual renewal . . . when you demand the best in fine food, service, and amenities . . . then head for Timberhill Ranch.

This classy resort on a very intimate scale is off the beaten track, perched high in the hills above the Sonoma coast. Once you've checked in at the reception and dining area, you're shuttled to your cottage in a golf cart, and not a telephone or a discouraging word will ruffle your brow until you grudgingly conclude it's time to go home.

That Sonoma has fabulous climate, rugged beauty, unspoiled high meadows, and redwoods is undisputed. What *is* surprising is to find an inn with such luxury blending into these surroundings. All credit must be given to the two innkeeping couples who planned and built 80 percent of the resort themselves. Their vision accounts for keeping the ranch an underdeveloped oasis of tranquility; for only ten cottages, despite eighty acres of land; for building their world-class tennis courts far from the swimming pool, because "when you're lounging quietly by the water you don't want to hear tennis chatter."

The spacious, cedar-scented cottages are situated for maximum privacy. Each has a stocked minibar, a fire laid, a well-appointed tile bath, handmade quilt on the queen-sized bed, comfortable chairs, good lights, and a radio. In the morning breakfast is delivered to your door to enjoy on your private deck as you look out at a stunning view.

What more? Superb food served beautifully in an intimate dining room with windows overlooking hills and forest—but without reservations, hurry, hassle, or check to interrupt. (Breakfast and dinner are included in the rate.) The six-course dinners (now open to the public by reservation) are what you might expect in one of San Francisco's finest restaurants. Here's a sample of one recent night: chilled artichoke with lemon mayonnaise, beef barley soup, salad with hearts of palm, raspberry sorbet, loin of lamb with red-pepper butter (among five other entree choices), and a dessert selection including puff pastry blackberry torte.

The four owners are hands-on innkeepers, always giving a level of personal attention far removed from a slick resort atmosphere. One told me, "We really like taking care of people and giving them the kind of service and privacy we looked for when we used to get away." As I watched the reluctant farewell of one couple, the hugs and promises to be back soon, I decided that Timberhill has all the right stuff, including a warm heart.

How to get there: From Highway One north of Fort Ross, turn east on Timber Cove Road. Follow to Sea View Ridge Road. Turn left, follow to Hauser Bridge Road and inn sign on the right.

Innkeepers: Barbara Farrell, Frank Watson, Tarran McDaid, Michael Riordan
Address/Telephone: 35755 Hauser Bridge Road, Cazadero 95421; (707) 847–3258
Rooms: 15 secluded cottages; all with private bath, fireplace, minibar. Handicap access.
　　Smoking restricted to designated areas.
Rates: $350, double occupancy, Friday, Saturday, Sunday; $296, double occupancy,
　　weekdays; MAP.
Open: All year.
Facilities and activities: Lunch. World-class tennis courts, swimming pool, outdoor Jacuzzi,
　　hiking. Nearby: 4 miles to ocean beach; Salt Point State Park, Fort Ross,
　　The Sea Ranch public golf course.

Olive Metcalf

Mt. Ashland Inn
ASHLAND, OREGON 97520

A late April snow was falling as I drove up the road to Mt. Ashland Inn, making the passing scenery all the more breathtaking. At 5,500 feet, just 3 miles from the summit, the beautiful inn sits nestled in the Siskiyou Mountains 16 miles south of Ashland, a snug haven of outstanding craftsmanship and hospitality.

The cedar-log structure was handcrafted by the Shanafelts from lumber cut and milled on the surrounding property. But don't picture a cottage in the woods improvised by a couple with some land and a chain saw. Jerry's remarkable design and woodworking skills are apparent everywhere your eyes rest—in hand-carved mountain scenes on the doors, the decorative

deck railing, log archways, stained-glass windows, and a unique log-slab circular staircase. Most amazing to me were the twelve Windsor chairs he made one winter, each one a smooth, perfect piece of art.

The peeled-log walls of a common room draw you in with the warmth of cushy furniture, brilliant oriental rugs, mellowed antiques, and a stone fireplace. Can you imagine how the fire, music playing softly, and hot spiced cider hit me on this cold afternoon? Right. It was sleepy time in the mountains.

Each of the guest rooms upstairs has a view toward Mt. Shasta, Mt. McLoughlin, or some part of the Cascades. Probably the most romantic room is the Sky Lakes Suite on the ground floor, with a Jacuzzi for two, a rock wall with trickling waterfall (operated by the guests), a rock patio, a wet bar, and a view of Mt. McLoughlin. The rooms have queen- or king-sized beds.

When I looked out the window in the morning, the fir trees were thickly frosted with snow, and I felt like Heidi in Oregon. But pretending I was roughing it in the wilderness just wouldn't fly in the face of all the comforts: big chairs with reading lights by the windows, a queen-sized bed topped with a handmade quilt, and the woodsy aroma of cedar filling the air.

Breakfast in the dining room was fresh juice and fruit and a tasty entree of puffy orange French toast. Daffodils on the table were picked that morning as they popped through the snow.

If you must stir from this comforting cocoon,

a cross-country skiing path that ties into old logging roads is out the back door. Three miles up the road, Mt. Ashland offers fairly demanding downhill skiing. For hikers, the Pacific Crest trail passes right through the property. The premier attractions in the area are the Ashland theaters, about a twenty-minute drive (to good restaurants, also) from here.

One bonus of being up the mountain is that when Ashland is covered in clouds and fog, you're often in a pocket of sunshine here.

How to get there: North on Highway 5, take Mt. Ashland exit 6; turn right under the highway. At stop sign turn left, parallel highway ½ mile. Turn right on Mt. Ashland Road to ski area. Inn is 6 miles from the highway.

Innkeepers: Jerry and Elaine Shanafelt

Address/Telephone: 550 Mt. Ashland Road; (503) 482–8707

Rooms: 5, including 1 suite with Jacuzzi for two; all with private bath and individual thermostat; VCR available. No smoking inn.

Rates: $80 to $130, double occupancy, EPB and beverages. Special rates November through April, excluding holidays and weekends.

Open: All year.

Facilities and activities: Light suppers available in winter by prior arrangement for additional charge. Hiking, sledding, cross-country and downhill skiing. Nearby: river rafting, Ashland Shakespeare Festival February through October, Britt Music Festival June to September in Jacksonville.

olive Metcalf

Tu Tú Tun Lodge
GOLD BEACH, OREGON 97444

Here is a hideout for couples whose romance never glows more brightly than when they're fishing together, but dims when faced with the gritty realities of camping. Consider the motto of the Tu Tú Tun Lodge: "Casual elegance in the wilderness on the famous Rogue River."

That's summing it up modestly, for this is a very special blend of sophistication and out-doors-lover's paradise. Top-notch accommodations and superb food are those of a classy resort, but the young owners create a friendly atmosphere that's more like that of a country inn.

Guest rooms are situated in a two-story building adjacent to the lodge. Each has comfortable easy chairs, extra-long beds, a dressing area, and a bath with tub and shower. Special touches that make wilderness life civilized aren't forgotten—fresh flowers, good reading lamps, and up-to-date magazines. Two recently redecorated rooms now have Japanese-style soaking tubs in their outdoor area. The suites can accommodate up to six persons each. No telephone or television intrudes as you watch the changing colors of the Rogue's waters at sunset from your private balcony or patio.

A bell at 6:30 P.M. calls guests to the lodge for cocktails and hors d'oeuvres. Dirk and Laurie introduce everyone, and by the time they seat you for dinner at round tables set for eight, you'll feel you're dining with friends. The set entree dinner they serve is outstanding. It always features regional specialties, frequently grilled over mesquite. Fresh chinook salmon, soup, crisp salad made from locally grown greens, freshly baked bread or rolls, and raspberry sorbet are a typical dinner.

After dinner, guests usually gather around the two fire pits on the terrace overlooking the river to enjoy a drink, inhale the scent of jasmine, and take in the beauty all around. There's much to talk about as you share ideas for the next day's plans. If those plans call for an early-morning rising for fishing, a river trip, or hiking, breakfast and lunch baskets will be ready for you.

One adventure almost every visitor to the lodge tries is the exciting 104-mile white-water round trip up (and down) the river. Jet boats stop at the lodge's dock to pick up passengers in the morning.

The inn's name comes from the Tu Tú Tun Indians, who lived in a village on the very site of the Lodge. *Tunne* meant "people"; *Tu Tú Tunne* were "people close to the river."

This is my idea of romantic-style roughing it. Is that the cocktail bell I hear?

How to get there: Driving north on Highway 101, pass through Gold Beach, cross bridge, and watch for signs on right to Rogue River Tavern. Turn right and drive 4 miles to tavern; follow signs another 3 miles to lodge on the right.

Innkeepers: Dirk and Laurie Van Zante
Address/Telephone: 96550 North Bank Rogue; (503) 247–6664
Rooms: 16, including 2 suites each accommodating 6; all with private bath.
　　Wheelchair access.
Rates: $115 to $155 for river-view rooms; $159 to $169 for suites; $189 for garden
　　cottage; double occupancy, meals extra. MAP daily rate for two including hors
　　d'oeuvres: $190 to $200.
Open: April 27 to October 27. Two suites with kitchens available all year.
Facilities and activities: Breakfast, lunch, dinner for guests or by reservation, full bar.
　　Swimming pool, 4-hole putting green; jet-boat white-water Rogue River trips;
　　salmon and steelhead fishing, seasoned guides available. Nearby: scenic flights over
　　Siskiyou Mountains, hiking, beachcombing, scenic drives, gambling in Gold Beach.

Olive Metcalf

Run of the River
LEAVENWORTH, WASHINGTON 98826

It's safe to say that before you leave Run of the River you'll be planning a return visit. Situated on two acres in an alpine meadow in the Cascade Mountains, this log inn is a hidden jewel. For a romantic hideaway, for nature lovers, for the world-weary, this is a beautiful, safe haven with all the comforts you could desire.

The six bedrooms are uniquely private and quiet. While each is distinct, all the rooms have the warmth of log walls, tall cathedral pine ceilings, hand-hewn log furniture, luxurious baths, and private decks.

They differ in their appointments of colorful Northwest Indian objects, excellent-quality bed linens, and handsome furniture pieces.

Three rooms have lofts, snug places to take a snooze or read away a quiet afternoon. But it's the private deck that is each room's most important appointment; it puts you in a front-row seat for one of nature's "tens" on the gorgeous scale.

The inn sits in a meadow sliced through by the Icicle River and surrounded by the magnificent Cascade Mountains. A small island in the river is a wildlife refuge, and if you sit quietly, you'll see the movement and hear the subtle sound of nature all around you—a host of migrating waterfowl, Canada geese, bald eagles, osprey, and the kingfisher, fluttering above the water to dive in and nab a fish. In summer at twilight, deer drink from the river, and there is even an occasional black bear.

Every season has its special rewards here, but innkeepers Monty and Karen say they look forward most to winter. Covered with fresh white snow, meadow and river frozen, Cascades white-tipped, the inn and the entire valley are a spectacular sight. This is when young, enthusiastic innkeepers (like M. and K.) go into action. They know a dozen great cross-country ski trails, which ones are worth buying a pass for, which are free. They'll book you on an old-fashioned sleigh ride or a snowmobile safari. They'll provide the carrots and charcoal if you want to build a snowman in the meadow, and they'll have a fire, the hot tub, and hot coffee ready when you come inside.

A large common room with an attractive kitchen in one corner is the heart of the inn. A big, full breakfast is served here at a long pine table. Windows across the front of the room look out at the meadow and river. You could very cozily spend the day right here.

I haven't told you the delights of spring, summer, and fall at the inn or detailed the Bavarian Village of Leavenworth's attractions, but here's the main lesson: Run of the River is quite special, with two especially caring—and fun—innkeepers.

Slow down . . . listen . . . watch . . . breathe in and out . . . feel the air. This just might be heaven on earth.

How to get there: Traveling south on Highway 2 through Stevens Pass or driving north from Wenatchee, exit at East Leavenworth Road. Drive exactly 1 mile and turn down gravel driveway to the inn.

Innkeepers: Monty and Karen Turner
Address/Telephone: 9308 East Leavenworth Road (mailing address: P. O. Box 285); (509) 548–7171 or (800) 288–6491
Rooms: 6, including 2 suites; all with private bath, spacious deck, and cable TV, 3 with Jacuzzi tub, some with loft. No smoking in inn or on grounds.
Rates: $90 to $140, double occupancy, EPB and afternoon refreshments. Two-night minimum stay on weekends and holidays.
Open: All year.
Facilities and activities: Hot tub; mountain bikes available March through November; magnificent views of river and wildlife from decks; will arrange horse-drawn sleigh rides, horseback rides, cross-country ski lessons, rafting, day hikes. Nearby: bird refuge; hiking or cycling along river; cross-country and downhill skiing; snowshoeing; Bavarian Village with Leavenworth's restaurants, unique shops.

Clive Metcalf

Edenwild Inn
LOPEZ ISLAND, WASHINGTON 98261

When your request for a reservation is answered with a map of an island, a ferry schedule, and the assurance that ferry landing, sea-plane, and airport pickup is available, I say you're on your way to an adventure. The Edenwild Inn on Lopez Island is such a place. Just getting there is a romantic adventure.

The island slopes gently up from the ferry landing to reveal rural nature at its most picturesque. Pasture, fields, and farms are interspersed with dense woodland, and the shoreline is notched with bays and coves.

The recently built inn is about 4½ miles from the ferry landing. A broad porch dotted with chairs wraps around three sides of the large

house, giving it an inviting, traditional look. Dozens of antique rose bushes and a green lawn brighten a brick patio and pergola to the parking area. Inside is a spacious, casually elegant country house with pale oak floors and fresh bouquets. Bright fabrics cover sofas and chairs grouped before the fireplace. An old upright piano sits here, and the work of some wonderful local artists is displayed here and all through the inn. Breakfast and other meals are served in the adjoining dining room.

Each one of the seven bedrooms appeals to me. It could be because they are new and fresh, or perhaps it is the comfortable built-in beds, or the terrific looking black-and-white tile bathrooms, or the views—Fisherman's Bay, garden, or San Juan Channel. From Room 5 we thought our view of the main garden and the channel the best in the house . . . until we watched a magnificent sunset that beat them both.

In addition to a full, family-style breakfast for house guests, Susan offers wintertime island visitors (November through April) her version of a soup kitchen. Her collection of great soup recipes is the source for lunches of a bowl or cup of homemade soup, freshly baked bread from an island bakery, and desserts. Susan is also having fun during the winter months with Saturday-night ethnic dinners—anything from Chinese to Cajun. The only thing certain is that you'll need a reservation. This energetic innkeeper and her staff will see that you eat very well and have a wonderful time here.

An unexpected bit of excitement occurred as we were packing the car to leave. An awfully attractive man helped put our bags in the trunk and then blushed modestly when we recognized his well-known face. When he's at the inn, this first-rate actor is strictly Susan's husband.

If you're young and have more energy than money, you should consider buying a "walk-on" ferry ticket (much cheaper than with a car), bring just your bicycle and backpack, and arrange for an inn pick-up. This is a wonderful island for bicycling.

How to get there: From the Lopez Island Ferry Landing, proceed 4½ miles to Lopez Village Road. Turn right.

Innkeeper: Susan Aran
Address/Telephone: Lopez Road (mailing address: P. O. Box 271); (206) 468–3238
Rooms: 8; all with private bath, some with fireplace. Handicapped facilities. No smoking inn.
Rates: $90 to $140, double occupancy, EPB and afternoon aperitif. Winter rates November through April.
Open: All year.
Facilities and activities: Facilities for small weddings and small conferences. During the summer, gourmet takeout food to eat on outdoor patio or in dining room; during the winter, lunch and Saturday-night ethnic dinners by reservation. Nearby: Lopez Village shops, hiking, bicycling.
Recommended Country Inns® Travel Club Benefit: 10% discount.

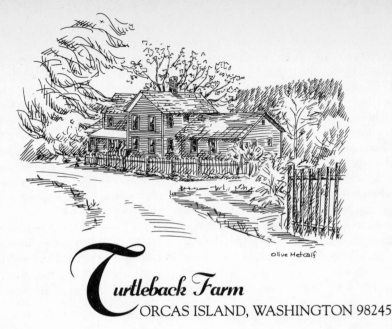

Olive Metcalf

Turtleback Farm
ORCAS ISLAND, WASHINGTON 98245

When an escape from the fast track is high on your list of romantic priorities, a picturesque inn on one of the San Juan Islands is an ideal choice.

Set back from a country road, Turtleback Farm looks like an attractive, well-kept old farmhouse, a big green two-story clapboard building. Featured in numerous articles, and despite a remote location, it is usually booked months in advance. This may well be the gem lodging of Orcas Island.

The reasons are clear once you settle in. This is a first-rate, impeccably maintained inn. It delivers the quiet country charm but with all the comforts you could ask for.

The inn, once an abandoned farmhouse that was used to store hay, is now restored from the ground up. There are seven guest rooms, a parlor, dining room, and a tree-shaded deck that runs the length of the house. This is a wonderful place to sit on a warm day and enjoy looking out at acres of meadow with mountains beyond. We're talking idyllic, tranquil setting.

Even if the weather turns dismal, the comforts of this house will keep you charmed. The decor is tasteful and nonfussy, with muted colors and mellow wood trim and floors, and open-beam ceilings. Each guest room has a modern bath appointed with antique fixtures, claw-footed tub, pull-chain toilet, and wall shower. The pedestal sinks came from the Empress Hotel in Victoria. There's a cozy parlor where you can curl up and read before a fire. (The custom here is, "If you find a book you can't put down, take it with you and just return it when you finish.")

The dining room is still another place to enjoy the view and have a cup of tea or a glass of sherry. An outstanding breakfast is served here, course by course at individual tables on bone china. The menus change, but a typical morning would see juices, local berries, granola, an omelet with ham, and English muffin. Seconds are always offered.

What do you do on an eighty-acre farm if you're fresh from the city? If you're smart, you settle yourself on the deck with a blade of grass between your teeth, a big hat tipped down over your nose, and think things over—very, very

slowly. Then there are the exhausting demands of critter watchin'. There are ducks and blue heron, sheep, chickens, a rambunctious brown ram named Oscar, and visiting Canada geese. You're welcome to fish the large pond by the main house—it's stocked with trout. If you're a picnic fan, the paths leading to private little spots will be irresistible. The Fletchers make every effort to acquaint you with all that the island offers. They'll make arrangements for you to charter a boat, rent a moped, play golf, or whatever sounds good to you.

How to get there: From Orcas Island ferry landing, proceed straight ahead on Horseshoe Highway to first left turn; follow to Crow Valley Road. Turn right and continue to the inn, 6 miles from ferry landing. Fly-in: Eastsound Airport.

Innkeepers: Bill and Susan Fletcher
Address/Telephone: Crow Valley Road (mailing address: Route 1, Box 650, Eastsound);
(206) 376–4914
Rooms: 7; all with private bath and individual heat control. Wheelchair access. No smoking inn.
Rates: $70 to $110, winter; $70 to $150, April 1 to November 1; double occupancy, EPB and afternoon beverage.
Open: All year.
Facilities and activities: Farm; pond stocked with trout. Nearby: hiking trails in Moran State Park; bicycle and moped rentals; swim, picnic at Lake Cascade; fishing, kayaking, sailing; good restaurants.

Indexes

Alphabetical Index to Inns

Inns on or near Lakes or Rivers

Inns at or near the Seashore

Inns with, or with Access to, a Swimming Pool

Inns with Downhill or Cross-Country Skiing Nearby

Inns with, or with Access to, Golf or Tennis Facilities